LOOKING FOR THE NEW DEAL

Women's Diaries and Letters of the South

Carol Bleser, Series Editor

LOOKING FOR THE NEW DEAL

Florida Women's Letters during the Great Depression

EDITED BY ELNA C. GREEN

The University of South Carolina Press

Published by the University of South Carolina Press
Columbia, South Carolina 29208

www.sc.edu/uscpress

Manufactured in the United States of America

15 14 13 12 11 10 09 08 07   10 9 8 7 6 5 4 3 2 1

Library of Congress Cataloging-in-Publication Data

Looking for the New Deal : Florida women's letters during the Great Depression
/ edited by Elna C. Green.
    p. cm. — (Women's diaries and letters of the South)
  Includes bibliographical references and index.
  ISBN-13: 978-1-57003-658-3 (cloth : alk. paper)
  ISBN-10: 1-57003-658-6 (cloth : alk. paper)
  1. New Deal, 1933–1939—Florida—Sources. 2. Depressions—1929—Florida—
Sources. 3. Women—Florida—Correspondence. 4. Women—Florida—Social
conditions—20th century—Sources. 5. Sholtz, David, 1891–1953—Correspondence.
6. Roosevelt, Franklin D. (Franklin Delano), 1882–1945—Correspondence. 7. Florida
—Social conditions—20th century—Sources. 8. Florida—Economic conditions—20th
century—Sources. 9. Florida—Biography. 10. American letters—Florida.
I. Green, Elna C.
  F316.L66 2007
  973.917—dc22

                                                          2006026405

This book is dedicated to my mother, Carolyn F. Green, herself a daughter of the Depression, who has supported this work in innumerable ways.

Thank you, Mom

CONTENTS

ILLUSTRATIONS

List of Illustrations

Franklin Roosevelt, Claude Pepper, and Miami mayor
   Robert Williams

Migrant worker family, Belle Glade

CCC camp in Sebring

Townsend roadside sign, Frostproof

Migrant family shelter, Belle Glade

Beautician training, Ocala

Francis Townsend in Miami

Townsend roadside sign in north central Florida

SERIES EDITOR'S PREFACE

Looking for the New Deal: Florida Women's Letters during the Great Depression is the twenty-third volume in what had been the Women's Diaries and Letters of the Nineteenth-Century South series. This series has been redefined and is now titled Women's Diaries and Letters of the South, enabling us to include some remarkably fine works from the twentieth century. This series includes a number of never-before-published diaries, some collections of unpublished correspondence, and a few reprints of published diaries—a potpourri of nineteenth-century and, now, twentieth-century Southern women's writings.

The series enables women to speak for themselves, providing readers with a rarely opened window into Southern society before, during, and after the American Civil War and into the twentieth century. The significance of these letters and journals lies not only in the personal revelations and the writing talent of these women authors but also in the range and versatility of the documents' contents. Taken together, these publications will tell us much about the heyday and the fall of the Cotton Kingdom, the mature years of the "peculiar institution," the war years, the adjustment of the South to a new social order following the defeat of the Confederacy, and the New South of the twentieth century. Through these writings, the reader will also be presented with firsthand accounts of everyday life and social events, courtships and marriages, family life and travels, religion and education, and the life-and-death matters that made up the ordinary and extraordinary world of the American South.

Carol Bleser

Other Books in the Series

A Woman Doctor's Civil War: Esther Hill Hawks' Diary
Edited by Gerald Schwartz

A Rebel Came Home: The Diary and Letters of Floride Clemson, 1863–1866
Edited by Ernest McPherson Lander, Jr., and Charles M. McGee, Jr.

*The Shattered Dream: The Day Book of
Margaret Sloan, 1900–1902*
Edited by Harold Woodell

The Letters of a Victorian Madwoman
Edited by John S. Hughes

*A Confederate Nurse: The Diary of
Ada W. Bacot, 1860–1863*
Edited by Jean V. Berlin

*A Plantation Mistress on the Eve of the
Civil War: The Diary of Keziah
Goodwyn Hopkins Brevard, 1860–1861*
Edited by John Hammond Moore

*Lucy Breckinridge of Grove Hill: The
Journal of a Virginia Girl, 1862–1864*
Edited by Mary D. Robertson

*George Washington's Beautiful Nelly:
The Letters of Eleanor Parke Curtis
Lewis to Elizabeth Bordley Gibson,
1794–1851*
Edited by Patricia Brady

*A Confederate Lady Comes of Age:
The Journal of Pauline DeCaradeuc
Heyward, 1863–1888*
Edited by Mary D. Robertson

*A Northern Woman in the Plantation
South: Letters of Tryphena Blanche
Holder Fox, 1856–1876*
Edited by Wilma King

*Best Companions: Letters of Eliza
Middleton Fisher and Her Mother,
Mary Hering Middleton, from
Charleston, Philadelphia, and
Newport, 1839–1846*
Edited by Eliza Cope Harrison

*Stateside Soldier: Life in the Women's
Army Corps, 1944–1945*
Aileen Kilgore Henderson

*From the Pen of a She-Rebel: The Civil
War Diary of Emilie Riley McKinley*
Edited by Gordon A. Cotton

*Between North and South: The Letters of
Emily Wharton Sinkler, 1842–1865*
Edited by Anne Sinkler Whaley
LeClercq

*A Southern Woman of Letters:
The Correspondence of Augusta Jane
Evans Wilson*
Edited by Rebecca Grant Sexton

*Southern Women at Vassar: The
Poppenheim Family Letters, 1882–1916*
Edited by Joan Marie Johnson

*Live Your Own Life: The Family Papers
of Mary Bayard Clarke, 1854–1886*
Edited by Terrell Armistead Crow and
Mary Moulton Barden

*The Roman Years of a South Carolina
Artist: Caroline Carson's Letters Home,
1872–1892*
Edited with an Introduction by
William H. Pease and Jane H. Pease

*Walking by Faith: The Diary of
Angelina Grimké, 1828–1835*
Edited by Charles Wilbanks

*Country Women Cope with Hard
Times: A Collection of Oral Histories*
Edited by Melissa Walker

*Echoes from a Distant Frontier:
The Brown Sisters' Correspondence
from Antebellum Florida*
Edited by James M. Denham and
Keith L. Huneycutt

*A Faithful Heart: The Journals of
Emmala Reed, 1865 and 1866*
Edited by Robert T. Oliver

ACKNOWLEDGMENTS

I would like to thank several students who helped with the preparation of this manuscript. Seth Weitz and Christopher Wilhelm conducted background research. Robert Ryals and David Nelson worked to identify illustrations in the Florida State Archives Photographic Collection. George Raboni and Antoinette Miller spent long hours transcribing the handwritten letters. India Van Brunt helped to translate shorthand notations.

Financial support for this project was provided by the Allen Morris Endowment of the Florida State University Foundation.

Encouragement and good cheer came from my colleagues in the History Department at Florida State University.

The archivists, as always, were the foundation of the project. Thanks are owed to the helpful professionals at the National Archives (especially Gene Morris), the Roosevelt Library, and the Florida State Archives.

ABBREVIATIONS

Carlton   Governor Doyle Carlton
CCC   Civilian Conservation Corps
Cone   Gov. Fred P. Cone
ER   Eleanor Roosevelt
FDR   Franklin D. Roosevelt
FERA   Federal Emergency Relief Administration
FSA   Florida State Archives
PWA   Public Works Administration
Sholtz   Gov. David Sholtz
WPA   Works Progress Administration

LOOKING FOR THE NEW DEAL

INTRODUCTION

Although the Great Depression was a national (and in fact a global) event, it nevertheless had its regional, state, and local variations. In Florida, many people found themselves living in depression conditions as early as the mid-1920s. The famous Florida "land boom" of the 1920s was followed by the infamous land bust, which caused tremendous financial troubles during the second half of the decade. Two major hurricanes and the arrival of the Mediterranean fruit fly added to the economic woes of other residents of the Sunshine State during the 1920s.[1] Sharecropping, tenancy, and racism trapped still more Floridians in chronic rural poverty.[2] By the time of the stock market crash of 1929, despair and upheaval were already all-too-familiar parts of daily life. The dramatic economic downturn that followed Black Tuesday merely spread the misery more broadly.

Every state was overwhelmed by the crisis, but Florida was especially ill prepared to handle an event of this magnitude. The state's constitution limited governmental responses: the constitution forbade bonded indebtedness, which meant that the state could not borrow money to ease itself through the emergency. Cities and counties were permitted to borrow money by issuing municipal bonds, but they had already done so aggressively during the 1920s and were generally in default on those loans by the time of the Depression. By 1929, Florida already had the highest per capita public debt in the country. Local governments had little credit left with which to raise new funds. The hands of government, both local and state, were effectively tied.[3]

Neither public nor private charities were prepared for such an unprecedented burden either. Although the state had seen dramatic population growth in the first decades of the twentieth century, its social welfare institutions had lagged behind. Charities, orphanages, homeless shelters, and other forms of private philanthropy existed in a few cities; the Red Cross, Travelers' Aid, YMCAs, and other such facilities were sprinkled through some of the larger communities like Jacksonville and Tampa. They helped as many people as they could, but it resembled a drop in a very large bucket. Nor was public welfare any better. Even compared to other states in the South,

1

Florida's public welfare system was underdeveloped. The State Board of Public Welfare had been created by the legislature in 1927 but was given only supervisory functions and had no "relief" funds of its own to distribute.[4] Many counties, especially rural ones, had no public welfare offices at all. The small number of counties with functioning systems seldom had adequate staffing or funding to handle the huge numbers of people needing assistance[5] —the average grant was less than five dollars per month per family.[6] The social work community lamented that "Florida has been slower than any other state to conceive its responsibilities as a State. The inability of cities and counties to cope with the problems during the worst years of the depression did not result in State assistance as it did in many other states."[7]

And the needs were indeed great. Although Florida's was not a "smoke-stack economy," nevertheless by 1930, it had the highest unemployment rate in the southeastern region.[8] In Jacksonville the county welfare board reported that it was giving aid to more than 3,900 families and individuals in 1931, a 31 percent increase from the year before.[9] Poor houses throughout the state were flooded: Dade County's poor house held 130 people in 1930, including forty-one children.[10] The state's problems were compounded by the continuous stream of newcomers pouring into the state, perceiving "the sunshine state" to be an easier place to weather out the winter months if unemployed or homeless. "Hobos" appeared at the northern borders every year in the fall at the rate of about one hundred a day.[11] The state suddenly realized that it had no law on the books that permitted the deportation of nonresident dependents, and transients became "one of the major social problems of the state."[12]

Like the rest of America, desperate Floridians turned to Franklin D. Roosevelt in 1932, electing him to the presidency based on his promise of a vaguely worded "new deal." Closer to home, they selected a governor who promised to follow Roosevelt's lead. David Sholtz, a native New Yorker like FDR, allied himself closely with the New Deal, hoping to capture as much federal funding for the state as possible. A flurry of new federal programs followed, providing jobs to the unemployed and reforming many of the country's basic economic structures. "Relief" checks sustained many families through the crisis; businesses and banks slowly reopened; and the federal government began to appear for the first time as an important and immediate presence in the lives of common people.[13]

The New Deal permeated life in Florida. The Civilian Conservation Corps, which put young men to work on parks and land reclamation projects, hired forty thousand workers across the state.[14] The Works Progress Administration (WPA), utilizing the labor of tens of thousands of Floridians, built schools, roads, bridges, courthouses, and airports. Farmers gained benefits through the price supports of the Agricultural Adjustment Act; industrial workers got higher wages through the National Recovery Act. The Federal Writers' Project interviewed and recorded oral histories of surviving ex-slaves. The Federal Theater Project staged productions in Miami, Jacksonville, and Tampa.[15] The National Youth Administration pumped nearly two million dollars into the state's economy in three years' time.[16] The size and scope of the relief effort was enormous.[17]

Despite the vast bureaucracy run from a distant city, the New Deal nevertheless seemed immediate and personal to many Floridians. Franklin and Eleanor Roosevelt were the human, personal, faces of the federal government. People far from the center of power in Washington nevertheless perceived the president and the first lady as close, accessible, and approachable. Franklin's radio "fire-side chats" and Eleanor's newspaper columns brought the Roosevelts into their homes on a daily basis. The Roosevelts carefully cultivated public relations through an efficient White House staff that answered tons of mail promptly, wrote warm and personal encouragements to nearly all correspondents, forwarded job requests and other letters to the proper federal agency, and followed up on the enormous volume of requests that reached the White House.

To a lesser degree, Floridians also saw their state executive as an immediate and personal contact. Governors regularly traveled the state, especially during election seasons, and many local residents heard them speak and were often able to meet them in person. Even "transplanted" governors such as Dave Sholtz had contacts with many people through family, business, and other connections. Residents across the state felt free to write their governor and to correspond in very personal terms. Some wrote the governor's wife, feeling that was a more certain route to the governor's attention.

Not surprisingly, the letters to these officials poured in by the thousands. Some were typed and formal, others handwritten and barely legible. They asked for jobs and for advice. Many offered their endorsements of New Deal programs; more than a few sent their criticisms. They offered suggestions for new programs; they complained of political chicanery. Their letters were full of both desperation and dignity. They presented themselves as humble supplicants, honorable citizens, grateful beneficiaries, and reproachful constituents.

Although many of the letters were forwarded on to other agencies for some action, still the presidential and gubernatorial files were filled with them and hundreds of boxes of them now rest at the Roosevelt Library in Hyde Park, New York, and the Florida State Archives in Tallahassee. From the papers in the Roosevelt Library, I have selected correspondence from more than one hundred women from Florida to reproduce here. From the Executive Papers in the Florida State Archives, I have selected nearly two hundred more. Another, smaller, group of letters comes from the files of the WPA in the National Archives in College Park, Maryland. I chose letters for inclusion for their breadth and their depth. There are letters from both blacks and whites, from rural areas and from urban centers. North, central, and south Florida are all represented; the writers were both newcomers and native-born Floridians. I tried to eliminate too much repetition in the requests, but part of the point of this collection is in fact the repetition: these were extremely widespread problems, even if the writers did not realize it. Read by the boxful, the impact of the Depression is made clear by the sheer repetition of the requests for help.

Several themes emerge from this correspondence. First was the great faith and trust that people placed in their elected leaders. Perfect strangers shared intimate details of their lives, without fear that the information might be shared. They frequently expressed their confidence that the president and the governor had their interests at heart. Writers sometimes wrote more than once, certain that the Roosevelts or Sholtz remembered them and their problems.

Another theme of these letters was the assumption of a governmental contract with its citizens. Numerous writers pointed out how long they had paid taxes to the government, and made explicit that this fact should make them worthy of assistance. They frequently emphasized how long they had lived in the state, or how many family members had served in the military. In other words, they believed that they had earned their benefits. They did not see government assistance as undeserved charity. Just as clearly, however, these correspondents saw their requests to government authorities as a last resort. Letter after letter emphasized their previous efforts to help themselves. They often noted impending deadlines for foreclosures, indicating that this was a last, desperate effort on their parts.

Correspondents frequently tried to personalize their stories, giving details about themselves and their families, and occasionally included photographs, poems, manuscripts, or other materials that might capture the attention of someone reading their letters. When possible, they mentioned any personal contacts that they had ever had with anyone in the Roosevelt administration or in state government. Many mentioned their loyalty to the Democratic Party. A few drew attention to their affliction with polio, trying to connect with this personal aspect of the president's life.

Women especially drew parallels with their own lives and that of Eleanor Roosevelt.[18] They drew sympathetic attention to their own roles as mothers and wives. They praised her efforts at marriage and motherhood. Women frequently expressed their admiration for her unusually public life, and felt closer to her than nearly any other female figure of the day. Remarkably large numbers of correspondents viewed Eleanor as the conduit to Franklin. They pleaded for her to intercede on their behalf. They asked her to slip their letters to him at breakfast, during prayers, or before bed. Many asked her to hand their letters to him personally. (We cannot know if they felt disappointment to learn that *her* secretary had forwarded the letter to *his* secretary, effectively voiding all the personal contact along the way.) Although more women than men took this approach, there were also men who approached her hoping to gain her influence over her husband.

Franklin Roosevelt's campaign speech in 1932 had called for help for the "forgotten man."[19] Several letters reproduced here directly referred to that speech but called for help for the forgotten women and the forgotten mothers. The letters also illuminate the extent to which women's experiences of poverty and dislocation were different from those of men. Women felt more vulnerable than men since they had fewer opportunities for employment. Jobs, when they could be obtained, paid less than what men could earn. Often dependent upon someone else for their support, women felt keenly that dependence and the limitations it imposed.

Responsible for the care of children and frequently elderly relatives as well, women nevertheless could never earn the same income as men when they worked. Their status as economic dependents meant that women often worked to protect their husbands' role as provider. If a husband was in jail or in the hospital, a wife might write to secure his release. If a husband refused to support his family, by abandonment or other means, a wife might write to try to force his financial support. Women faced challenges that were uniquely female.

At the same time, women were often more experienced in dealing with welfare and charitable organizations. For generations, women had been the ones who served as the contact point between their families and the providers of relief. Women were the ones who went to the mission houses or who had to deal with the district visitors or the caseworkers. Women (and their children) were the overwhelming majority of those using orphanages, poorhouses, free clinics, free kindergartens, day nurseries, and settlement houses. Hence women were often well versed in the procedures for getting assistance, and they appeared to feel less shame than did men who asked for relief. As historian

Linda Gordon has written, there were a variety of reasons why women felt less threatened by asking for help.[20] Even women who worked for wages still felt dependent on a male breadwinner for support. Dependency was a normal state for most women of this generation, and dependency on relief seemed little different from dependency on a husband or father.

By far, the most common reason that people wrote to the Roosevelts was to ask for help in finding a job. Although the White House never did anything to encourage this directly, nevertheless many people throughout in the country concluded that the surest route to a federal job was to write the president or the First Lady directly. Some started with their congressional representatives, but far more just started right at the top, with a letter to one of the Roosevelts. Even though a state congressman might be a well-known figure in the community, many people identified more closely with FDR and ER than with their congressman or senator.

Even where their goal was not necessarily a federal job, many writers believed that they had a better chance of obtaining other types of work by writing to the Roosevelts. People wrote in hopes of getting private sector jobs like teaching, working in the local phone company, or writing for magazines. Many thousands of Americans wrote Eleanor Roosevelt, asking her to write letters of recommendation for them as they applied for jobs. (Those who were personally unknown to the First Lady, which constituted the majority of the correspondents, received standardized replies explaining that she was unable to provide such letters of reference to strangers.)

Still others hoped that either the president or the First Lady would help them by purchasing goods from them. They wrote to offer a wide variety of items for sale. The offers were always gently declined: "Mrs. Roosevelt regrets that she is unable to comply with your wishes, but owing to the great number of articles offered to her, she has made it her rule not to purchase anything in this way. However, she suggests you get in touch with an antique shop in some nearby city as they may be able to aid you."[21]

Although it might be tempting to read some of the letters as greatly naive, it is important to recognize that they also stand as testimony to the great trust that individuals placed in the Roosevelts. The writers shared personal details, sometimes quite intimate, about their lives. Although some expressed cynicism about local politicians or local bureaucrats, they seldom seemed to view the governor, the president, or the First Lady in those terms. The correspondents trusted their leaders and had great faith in their abilities to get things done.

Unfortunately, we cannot always know what their leaders did in response to the requests. The governor's files do not usually include a copy of the response sent to the letter writer. The Roosevelts' papers frequently include copies of the response, most of which were standardized replies such as this:

> Mrs. Roosevelt has asked me to reply to your letter in which you request assistance in obtaining employment on a WPA project. I know you will realize that Mrs. Roosevelt cannot answer personally all the many letters she receives. She is, however, deeply concerned with the problems of the people of the country and gives a great deal of attention to them. I am sorry to learn of the difficulties you are having. . . . I am, therefore, referring your letter to the Florida WPA for consideration.

Hundreds of others received a brief but comforting note: "Mrs. Roosevelt has asked me to refer your letter to an official in one of the Government departments who may be able to assist you in some way. She is extremely sorry to hear of the difficult time you are having and sincerely hopes that some plan can be worked out that will be of help."[22] (Since the replies were generally form letters, I have not reproduced them all here. In a few cases, where the reply was personal or notable for some reason, I have included it.)

Although this collection of letters does not tell us all we would like to know about Florida women in the 1930s, they expressed a generation's complex responses to the calamity of the Great Depression. They looked for help, for answers, for scapegoats. The letters permit us one angle from which to peek into the private world of everyday people during what were hardly everyday circumstances. As such, they are a priceless historical source. They also are simply fascinating reading.

Notes on Methodology

I have transcribed the letters in their entirety, except in a handful of cases (noted by ellipses) where repetition seemed especially unnecessary. Spelling and punctuation have remained as originally written, except in a few instances where I felt readers might need some assistance with the text. For the sake of brevity, I have omitted standard salutations such as "Dear Mr. Sholtz" or formulaic closings such as "Sincerely yours."

Where possible, I have included information on the correspondent derived from the federal census for 1930. I was not able to locate all the writers on the census, but when I could, the details seem helpful in understanding the individual's situation. Readers will note that information from the census is sometimes inconsistent with details in the letters (this is particularly true with ages). Being entirely self-reported and not confirmed by outside sources, the census can be problematic. Nevertheless, the details can be valuable, and I thought it worth the effort to include them.

Letters to FDR and ER, unless otherwise identified, come from the Roosevelt Presidential Library in Hyde Park, New York. Letters to Carlton Doyle, David Sholtz, and Fred Cone come from the Florida State Archives in Tallahassee. Letters identified as "WPA" come from the National Archives and Records Administration, College Park, Maryland.

Chapter 1

BEFORE THE NEW DEAL

B efore the New Deal was launched in 1933, there were no federal programs for individuals to turn to for assistance. Hence the letters in this chapter all come from the governors' papers. Doyle Carlton, a lawyer from Tampa, had the misfortune to be elected governor on the eve of the stock market crash. His administration then had to deal with an economic depression of unprecedented scale, in a state with few tools at its disposal. The governor cut state jobs in order to save money, which reduced the state budget but also had the effect of adding to the state's unemployment problem. He suggested a sales tax to raise revenue but vetoed an inheritance tax that would have served the same purpose. Carlton did extract some banking reforms out of the state legislature, but bank failures—some of them quite spectacular—continued.[1]

In the absence of a positive program for dealing with the Depression, the state had little to offer needy individuals. The letter writers suggest that someone, somewhere might do something to help them, but they do not know what. Not having specific programs to rely upon or clear solutions to ask for, the letters in this section often took on more a tone of confusion and despair rather than hope.

Many of these early letters concern the few public welfare sources available before the New Deal, the most important of which was county welfare assistance (or "relief.") Writers often complain of the difficulty of getting assistance from the county welfare offices (sometimes referred to as the county commissioners since this was the body that administered county welfare) or of the inadequacy of the assistance given. County welfare programs usually gave a woman a small monthly sum, which varied according to the number of children she had. Occasionally, a family might also receive goods in kind from the county "relief" office. Funded by property taxes at the county level, most counties had extremely limited funds and tried to minimize the amount distributed to each needy family. The result was monthly grants that were pitifully small. The primary recipients of county relief were the elderly, including elderly African Americans.[2] (County relief was the only public welfare available to African Americans in any meaningful amounts, as will be seen below.)

County relief also took the form of "indoor relief," a nineteenth-century term for residence in the poor house. Although poor houses, or almshouses, had been declining in popular support in the early twentieth century, Florida still had at least fifteen such facilities. In 1930 they housed a total of 513 people.[3] The care they provided was minimal, with the exception of the largest homes, which had resident staffs and could provide nursing care and other needs. Hillsborough County's home included a complete hospital, to help care for its 167 residents.

A second source of public assistance before the New Deal was the state's mothers' aid program. Often called "mothers' pensions" or "widows' pensions," these programs emerged in the Progressive era and spread rapidly throughout the country.[4] Intended to allow widowed mothers to care for their children at home without having to go out to work, mothers' aid was granted to widows with school-age children or younger. Married women were not eligible, nor were women who kept "unsuitable" homes—meaning, in most cases, a man living in the house without benefit of marriage. This provision also meant that recipients could not take in boarders, which, for women in this era, was a common means of earning money while caring for children at home. Mothers' aid served as the foundation for the later federal program, Aid to Dependent Children.

Florida's first mothers' pension law passed in 1919 but was made entirely optional at the county level.[5] As late as 1933, twenty-two of the state's sixty-seven counties still offered no mothers' aid.[6] Those counties were concentrated in the northern portion of the state, where plantation agriculture and large African American populations distinguished the region from the southern half of Florida. As a result, less than 1 percent of children receiving mothers' aid in the state were African American.[7] Indeed, in 1931 only one black family in the entire state was paid a mothers' pension.[8] The amounts expended were small: in nine counties the average amount given per child each month was less than two dollars. Such dismal figures ranked Florida forty-first out of forty-three states offering mothers' pensions in 1931.[9]

A third major source of public assistance that predated the New Deal was Confederate pensions. Like other former Confederate states in the late nineteenth century, Florida launched a state-funded welfare program for Confederate veterans and their widows. Beginning as a small program in 1885 and expanding rapidly at the turn of the century, Florida granted pensions to veterans or widows who could prove both honorable service and financial need. The Confederate pension program gobbled up vast amounts of state revenue. Every year from 1903 to 1917, the state spent between 17 and 36 percent of its annual budget on Confederate welfare. By the 1930s the numbers had dropped considerably, given the rapid passing of the Confederate generation. But still, in the first part of the decade, Florida continued to spend more than $1,000,000 per year on Confederate veterans and (increasingly) their widows.[10] (Contrast this figure with the total amount spent on mothers' aid in 1933: $222,286.)[11] Even more than mothers' pensions, the Confederate pension program excluded African Americans from assistance.

Finally, a good deal of correspondence from these years concerns "old age pensions."[12] Another Progressive era reform that had gained widespread support, old age pensions had been adopted by twenty-eight states by 1934.[13] Florida, despite the gentle prodding by its state board of welfare, was not one of them.[14] Many writers lobbied their governor hoping to get the state to adopt old age pensions.

The letters in this section make it clear that Floridians experienced aspects of the Depression that were universal, such as bank failures that wiped out life savings or the foreclosures on their homes. But there were also some Depression events that were unique to the state. Correspondents mention hurricanes and "med flies." In September 1928 a massive hurricane hit Florida. The catastrophic flooding caused by Lake Okeechobee caused tremendous damage and loss of life. Casualty figures were never confirmable, but estimates ranged from eighteen hundred to twenty-one hundred deaths. Many people lost homes and farms as a result of the storm. After the discovery of the Mediterranean fruit fly in Florida groves in 1929, the state began an aggressive eradication program. Tens of thousands of trees were destroyed. Nearly the entire citrus crop for that season was lost. It took years for the citrus industry in Florida to recover.

Lorena Hickok, a journalist hired by Harry Hopkins to investigate conditions throughout the country and report back to him, made some pointed observations about the Depression in Florida. Summarizing conditions in various industries in the state, Hickok wrote:

> Cigar manufacturing: Bad. Little demand except for cheap cigars.
> Machinery taking place of hand work. Lots of unemployment in
> Tampa, cigar headquarters, and little prospect of its being much
> decreased. Miami has a funny unemployment problem. Mostly in the
> South, the labor surplus seems to be agricultural. But 40 per cent of
> the unemployed in Miami are workers in the building trades. . . . The

carpenters and bricklayers and so on came down, of course, during the boom. For two or three years they made lots of money. Many of them bought—and paid for—homes. Now there's no building going on down there, and they're stranded.[15]

So Floridians confronted a catastrophic economic crisis that was simultaneously universal and locally specific. They did so with very little assistance from any public or private quarter. Their pleas for help could be especially poignant in these early years of the Depression.

———

Mrs. Collier (Lake Wales) to Carlton, 7 August 1927

1930 census: She is a 50-year-old widow, white, and living in Starr Lake. She is a citrus farmer, and her two adult sons live with her and work on her farm.

As I have an old confederate $100.00 dollar bill dated 1864—And I wanted to ask is it redeemable and what is its value. if I mail it in. if so, please advise me where and how shall I mail it. and what is its value.[16]

Although clearly written "1927," the date for this letter probably should have been "1929." Carlton was not inaugurated until 1929.

Mrs. A. J. Weissinger (Orlando) to Carlton, 10 January 1929

Replying to your letter of Nov 2nd in regard to the pension applied for in the autumn of 1927 (Mrs. M. M. Bingham, beneficiary), in which you asked me to call your attention to the matter after your inauguration, I wish to state that my Mother, Mrs. Bingham, was denied a pension on some sort of ridiculous technicality, the state actually being in debt to her for more than a year's pension.

Mrs. Bingham has celebrated her eighty-sixth birthday, has not been out of the state of Florida in more than nine years, will never leave the state, and what, is of greater consideration, is the widow of a brave defender of southern ideals, she is much in need of funds, otherwise, you may be assured, a pension never would have been asked by one of my family.

I surely hope you can adjust the matter, as Mother has only a short time to live at best, and it is a sad reflection on any southern state when one of the servants of the sixties must spend their last days without the common comforts of life.

Your [inaugural] address was all and even more than expected, in splendor of constructive promise, and state politics is so favorable toward a lack of handicaps for you, that you stand challenged, Mr. Carlton, as few Florida Governors have been challenged, to write great things in the state's progress.

With every good wish for your being divinely guided in steering our good ship of state.[17]

Mrs. Mattie Parker (Bristol) to Carlton, 8 February 1929

1930 census, misindexed as "Mathie": She is 50 years old, a widow with five children at home. She is listed as a farmer, and the oldest son works as a laborer on her farm.

I am writing this to you for some information concerning the Mothers Aid Pension for widows as I am a widow myself and there is several more in this co[unty] with children of school age[.] our commissioners has failed to give us the Mothers Aid for this term of school and the Clerk of the Court Mr. W.H. Wakes told me that the commissioners didnt make any levy for us and said they were not going to. Will you please inform me as to what can be done about it as there is many of us can hardly make it to send our children to school[.] will appreciate any information you give me[.] I didn't have a chance of an Education my self but I am trying to give my children A chance and as I have 4 children now School age I find it a tough Proposition and there is other widows here realy in worse shape than I. Hopeing an early Reply.[18]

Mrs. J. W. Spence (Seville) to Carlton, 7 March 1929

I am writing you to state my case to you[.] I am a woman with a husband and 4 children but my husband has been down sick for two years and my oldest boy is 16 years old and I had to take him out of school the 20th of November to help me make a living and have not been able to get any help and I have taken in washing to help make a living untill my health is a wreck now. You can get futhur information about my husband sickness from Dr Warren of Palatka Fla. also Dr W.J. Williams of Seville Fla.

And Governor Carlton any kind of help will be greatly appreciated toward making a living or paying a Dr Bill or house rent and especially sending my boy back to school[.] he had just finished the sixth grad[e] and entered the seventh grade[.] we have lived in the State of Fla. for 7 years[.] I lived in Quincy and Greensborough 5 years and Governor Carlton I certainly did all I could for you in the June primary and the very county commission I voted for in Volusia county pays no attention to the condition I am in now. For I sure do need help and that now for there is not much work around here for the Boy and I.

P.S. Please let me know at once if you could do anything for us.[19]

Miss Ethel James (Raiford State Prison) to Carlton, 29 March 1929

1930 census: She is 22 years old, African American, and still in prison.

I am a poor girl and has no one to help me in any way. Therefore I am beging you if it is possible in one of your spair moments, to look over my case. Hon. Gov. and present it too the board. Beging for a pardon, paroll or reduced sentence. I have been here 7 years and 5 month. I have Lifetime. Thanking you and may God help me.

I only have a aged mother and she has my 3 children, which she is not able much longer too suport. . . .[20]

Mrs. Bessie Lee Caster (Pensacola) to Carlton, 5 April 1929

I feel like you can help me out of my wearing and trouble I have been in for the last 2 or 3 years.

My mother sent four of my little sisters and the only Brother that Ive had over to the receiving home for them to take care of untill she could take a treatment at the City Hospitle.

Thay promised her to return them as soon as she came from the Hospitle. But instead thay carried them to Jacksonville Fl. The 2 oldest girls we have been able to get. I understand a offering [orphan] home was for poor children who has not got no folks to take care of them. I am able to care for these 2 girls and little Boy. if I am not I have folks to help do it.

I have tryed every way I know how to get them and postively will not give them up. Will you please help me? Please do? I love my darling Motherless and fatherless sister's and Brother.

May god help you to help me to get them.

If not to get them put closter by Me so I can see them once and a while any way.

I know you are a good man you have power[.] May God help to make them understand the pain and sorrow it is cousing me to go throw with. God help us.[21]

Mrs. J. C. Foard (Mrs. Wallace) (De Land) to Mr. and Mrs. Carlton, 22 April 1929

1930 census: Wallace is 59 years old and the manager of a ladies clothing store. His wife, Jimmie C., is 52 and does not work. Their son, Wallace Jr., is 20 years old and does not work. The family is white.

I am writing you to ask if you can possibly help us to get a position for Wallace Jr. This summer. He needs to work this summer to earn his college tuition for next year. I have written Mr. Bentley of the Road Dept. and said

I was writing you also. Between you two surely you can help out. Wallace is Delta Sigma Phi, President of College Glee Club and a fine Christian boy. He is a good mixer and always has friends. We have had such bitter reverses due to the boom reaction—can not collect one penny on what we sold—and must foreclose on the property if we can not sell the mortgage. And Mr. Foard's health has been bad for six years so we are just where we would appreciate good work for Wallace Jr. Please let us hear soon.

It is a comfort to know our wonderful state is being guided by Christian hands and a clear, unruffled mind.

God bless you both in your wonderful work.

I am inclosing nutbread recipe for you Mrs. Carlton—hope you'll like it as well as the gingerbread.

Love to the children.[22]

Mrs. C. O'Brien (Sarasota) to Carlton, 9 May 1929

I hope you will pardon me for taking this liberty of writing to you.

I see they have just passed a law to give all Widows who are poor a pension but they must have one child. That may be alright but would not help a Widow who is old and poor and to sick to work. One that has no children[,] no relatives to go to. I have lived in Florida 15 years have gone through a Pioneering stage have had all kinds of set backs with crops & grove. Then the Boom came and ruined me altogether. I have paid out Hospital Bills[,] State & County taxes and now have nothing left to live on[,] nobody to turn to for help[.] can't sell a Piece of Property to help out.

I would appreciate a reply and a Remedy for my trouble. Can give References.[23]

Although she believes the mothers' pension law has just been passed, in fact it was a revision of the original law that was passed in 1919. This revision was intended to encourage counties to offer more assistance by clarifying that the program was not limited to the months of the school year.

Mrs. W. L. Sheffield (Ft. Myers) to Carlton, 18 May 1929

1930 census: Willis is 57 years old and a laborer in a sawmill. Lulu is 42 and works as a laundress. Her 19-year-old daughter, also a laundress, and a 4-year-old granddaughter live with them. They are African American.

They have my husband here in the County Jail on charges of Bad checks[.] The checks was post dated checks and they have had him in Jail near three months and they have fine him 25 days and $15 dollars[.] Mr. Carlton he has been through the Worlds War and he fought in the front line trenches & was

15

also wounded[.] he has been examined by the D.R. here and the D.R. says his skull is fractured and the[re] is times that I think Mr. Sheffield is not responsible for these little things he does[.] he is a very nice man to every boddy and is good worker and he is a good provider for his family and Mr. Carlton when they taken him a way from me and the children they taken everything in the world I had for my susport. I have no way to make a living for my children[.] I have had to take them out of school an the a acount of not having bread to give them to eat. And I don't thank that it is rite for them to take all in the world I have and [illegible] not help me to take care of my children[.] so I am going to leave the matter up to you[.] I hope you will find it neassary to have him turned loose for I no you will studdie the case over and see where I need him and need his help to take care of my little children for I cant get one days work to try to take care of them[.] so I am leaving this case up to you and hope you will make it so that I can have him out for my children to be provided for.[24]

Mrs. Rosa Jones (Ft. Lauderdale) to Carlton, 23 May 1929

1930 census: She is 47 years old, white, and living with her daughter and son-in-law. The daughter is a waitress with two young children; her husband is a laborer in concrete construction.

I rec'd a letter from your secretary telling me to make my application through the county commissioners. Well I saw them, and told them my business and they said that Broward County has no widow's pension except for widows with school age children. No[w] listen hasn't the state of Florida got a pension for needy widows regardless of whether they have children or not. I believe they have but I haven't the education to know just how to go about it. I do need this so much. And Governor Carlton if you can assist me in getting it, I will certainly appreciate it, and I know God will bless you for aiding a helpless old widow. Will you please make me an early reply.

The county commissioners said they could see where I needed a pension but that they were unable to help me. Please help me if you possibly can.[25]

Mrs. F. E. Sikes (Miami) to Carlton, 3 June 1929

1930 census: Frances is a 60-year-old white widow. She has two children, one grandchild, and three roomers.

Just a few lines to ask you if the laws of this state provide exemption from taxes for a widow 61 years of age with an almost totally blind daughter who attended the State Institute for the Deaf and Blind at St. Augustine and one Granddaughter 11 years of age who are wholly dependent upon me.

I have been a widow for twenty-five years during which time I have found life's battles & struggles almost undescribable. At times, I could not see how I could stand it any longer, but with the help of the "Almighty" through the hardest of hardships and by denying ourselves of even the common everyday necessities of life, I have managed to clear up the loan placed on our home by my husband and keep up the taxes and improvements (streets, sewers etc) up until 1928, since which time I find it impossible to do at my age. I hardly am able to make a scant living, little medicine etc. necessary to mankind which is very little in my case. I have worked hard at anything I could get in order to have a home when my hair was gray and my feet slow and now I am of that age but can see nothing but high taxes taking all I have worked so hard for and what I have denied my mouth as well as my body for to have in my last days[,] for I understand that 3 years after the first tax certificate is sold, I will be dispossessed and put out of my home (all I have in the whole world). My State and County taxes for 1928 are $620.02 which is higher then they have ever been for during the boom (1925) the year property was most valuable they were $285.00. Some differences and so surprising for property has certainly been on the decline instead of the increase. It is beyond my power of understanding. The city has nearly $700.00 which is a little more than two hundred less then the boom but, my, my how do the officials think I can make that much money? My income is $3.00 (three dollars) a week with selling a chicken once in a while and about three dozen eggs a week which helps me out.

Now "Gov." Carlton, if you wish information or data regarding my reputation and character, I can refer you to many of the leading men of this city such as Judge W. F. Brown (Court of Crimes)[,] Judge T. E. Price[,] W. H. Combs[,] Mitchel D. Price (undertaker)[,] Dr. J. C. Turner M.D.[,] John Sewel[,] Dr. E. K. Jandon Md.[,] E. B. Douglas[,] Dr. J. D. Stuart[,] Rev. W. O. Garrett Pastor of 1st Presbyterian Church, Dr. Tallman Md. and many more. I have lived in Miami for 31 years and have worked in many of these families.

Trusting you will acknowledge my plea for Mercy and consider my case as it is (for you may make investigation if you like) and grant me exemption from these awfully high taxes which I cannot meet, which will mean a sigh of relief to an old lady.[26]

Mrs. David Walker (Sanford, Seminole Co.) to Carlton, 5 July 1929

I am making an appeal to you for financial aid for my six children and myself.

My Husband David E. Walker was appointed Constable of District no. 1 of Volusia Co. by Gov. Martin[,] and was killed by Ed Pell[,] a boot legger[,] while on duty the 8th of July 1927. Leaving me with 6 children to care for with no means of support for them. My children's ages are from 13 yrs. to 3 yrs. old. My husband was a brother of Walter E. Walker of Palatka[.] Also a bro. of Ed Walker of Sanford[.] I get $40.00 a mth. from the Co[unty] but when rent and water bills are paid out of that it only leaves $23.80 for groceries and clothes and that is so little for the 7 of us I can't keep out of debt. Rent $15.00. $30.00 for groceries and $10.00 for local expences is what we realy need to live on[.] So if you will please help me in this it will certainly be appreciated. If I could have my house rent of $15.00 paid and have the $40.00 over the rent we would live that way and stay out of debt.

Thanking you for this help in advance[.] I await a reply in return mail. P.S. I live at Sanford Seminole Co. Fla. Am only visiting my parents here[.][27]

Mrs. Dinah Davis (Gainesville) to Carlton, 8 July 1929

Please pardon me for taking up your most valauble time on the following little matter, which I have all most written to every body in the state about. and so far with out gaining any help in the matter. it looks to me simply because I am a poor colored widow woman that there ought to be no notice taken of me. My Deceased Husband, the late Charlie Davis, who Died November the 4th 1928[.] I took out a sick and accident policy on him some ninthteen (19) years ago. Up to six (6) years ago I paid a weekly preium of 25¢ per week. at that time the company was sold out to the Carolina Life. at which time I encrease the preium to 50¢ per week. in turn a bout two (2) years ago Carolina Life Bussiness was sold out to the United American Life Insurance Co. which home office is in Jacksonville Fla. and a bout September 1928 the United American sold all it Bessiness around Gainesville to the American Bankers Insurance Co. of Chicago Ill. I had all my premium paid up in full at the Death of my Husband. There being due me on said policy $one hundred and ninty three dollars ($193.00)[.] this amount the American Bankers Insurance Co. have absolutely refuse to pay me. and have ignored every letter I've written to them. beside paying this on my husband insurance, I paid an additional one dollar & five cent ($1.05)[.] My policy and premium reciept book was sent to Mr. B.T. Avery, the state Mng of Tampa Fla. last November 1928 and since then Mr. Avery has ignored all letters sent to him a bout this claim. I have the honor to be your Excellency Obedint Severant, Dinah Davis, and I know you will see after my Entrest.[28]

Ethel Collins (Jacksonville) to Carlton, 9 July 1929

1930 census: This may be Ethel Collins, who, with her husband, lives with her brother's family. She is 34 years old and white with no children at home. Her husband, Jack, is a fireman.

18

Just a few lines asking you little information[.] Can you please help me to get pardon for my little 13 year old boy who comittid a crim[.] I dont know just how to do are speak out[.] I trust that you will understand what I mean[.] I am a poor women havnt got any money and two more children and a poor mother to provide for and I would Hilly arprechate it if you would speak one word for the child[.] I am not able to Employ a Lawer and I trust you will please think on him[.] I havn't had no steedy work this hole year but I thank god that it aint no worst[.]

Sectroy if you please just have Mercy for Jesus sake[.] I ask god to come down on his Bond one more time[.] I aint been able to go out thear to even see him[.] I send al that I can to him[.] god will bless you and al of your undertaken if you will just think on Mercy of this poor child[.] This is from his Mother.[29]

Mrs. Alice Tounsell (Marianna) to Carlton, 10 July 1929

I will write to please send me a little money to live on during my Baby sickness and also my husban is at the Chattachoochee Hospital[.] he is all ok now and he wants to get out to work for his wife and chrildren. he is all right now. And I want him out of that Place, and they don't want to turn him loose. I need him[.] if he was out of that place, I would not have to ask no one for anything to get me nothing to eat. But as he is there I will be oblige to ask for help, to live on[.] at the present time I have one child of 5 months old. and one 4 years old so please let me here from you by return mail. So please send me some money and see that Dr. Fralman turns my husban loose[.] send him home to me and the kids. I need his work and his help to help me take of the chrildren so please let me here from you by return.[30]

The Chattahoochee hospital referred to here is the Florida State Hospital, which served for decades as the state's institution for the indigent insane.

Mrs. Coker (Winter Haven) to Carlton, 12 July 1929

is it posible for you to in some way to get relief for the poor starving people in Fla. there is people here in Winter Haven actually starving to death. the city gives the Red Cross a good bit but it seems that the Red Cross gets the benifit of it[.] at least the poor starving people dont get it. in the winter people from other states come here and take the work. the fruit is handled by people from other states and the people that lives here dont get but verry little work and in the summer they have nothing to do or live on. I myself am really suffering[.] if I dont get some work in a few more days I wont be able to work if I could get it. I am a widdow[.] no one to care for and no one to take care of me[.] I am entirely dependent on my work[.] I am old and not verry well able to work but do manage to keep going as long as I can get what work I can do.[31]

Mrs. Phoeby Simmons (Falmouth) to Carlton, 6 August 1929

1930 census: "Phoebe" is a 47-year-old white widow living in Nebo. She is listed as a farmer, and her five sons all are listed as workers on her farm.

Kind Sir I am writing you in regards of myself and little children[.] I have three helpless children and myself disable to work and cant get any help[.] I have two cripple boys[,] one with only one leg and one hand and one with only one hand and I am afflicted so I cant work and my husband are dead[.] will you Please help me[.] if you Please it will be hiley appreached[.] will you please help me[.][32]

Mrs. J. R. Kimbrough (Adel, Georgia) to Carlton, 5 August 1929

1930 census: John is a 63-year-old carpenter contractor. Stella, 43, is a seamstress. Both were born in Georgia; they are white.

We have been living in Florida 6 yrs. Have 4 boys ages 14-11-6-4. My husband's health has failed & doctors have said he will never be able to make a living for the family any more. We are completely undone. I see no chance of sending the boys to school. I called on the Red Cross and they said no one thought we needed help because we allways looked so clean and nice. Well there you are! My experience has been so far, people expect you to look like a tramp if in need. Not so. I mean to keep up appearance as long as possible. Now we are simply in a critical condition.

I have been told Florida has a pension for such a[s] I can prove to be. Now will you please give me any information you can at once. I will be here some weeks yet. Hoping for good news.[33]

Mrs. Dicy Reynolds (Linen Room, Seminole Hotel, Jacksonville) to Carlton, 12 August 1929

I am writing you in behalf of the women of Florida who have to work for a living to suport themselves and children. I myself a widow woman with one child 11-yr of age will be in the 6th grade in this term begining in Sept. I am only getting $35.00 a month, having to put in 16 hours pr day—every other day—without any relief during the 16 hours. Cant there be something done to shorten the hours or require a better salary for the women that are forced to work to live.

There is no other state in the union that pays so little a bit of attention to the salary people are forced to work for to earn a living. So please look into the matter—but dont mention my name please.[34]

Miss Ethel Dees (Mayo) to Carlton, 14 September 1929

1930 census: Ethel is 16 years old, white, and living with her mother and stepfather, Thomas Brown, in Lafayette County. She has four siblings, one of whom works as a farm laborer.

I have been informed that you would help those who couldnt help themselves. My mother was left a widow when I was (eight 8) years old[.] also I have 4 other brothers, and sisters, and we have to make our living the best way we can, and now I am Seventeen year old and would like to get me some kind of a job so that I could help make [a] living for my little brothers and sisters. I am oldiest of them all[.] My mother was never able to send me to school, and we need help very much so if you would help me to get a job somewhere, I would certainly appreacate it. I would like to take 16 weeks course in a beauty parlor so if you can help me in any way I wold appreacate very much for I want to try to send my little brothers and sisters to school[.]

Let me know as soon as possible for I have got to find work some place if I can for we are in need.[35]

Mrs. Catherine Peacock (Altha) to Carlton, 21 October 1929

1930 census: Catherine is 58 years old, white, and the wife of a farmer. They have three children at home; the eldest works as a hospital attendant.

· I received your reply and did as you advised. And the county comissioners told me they could not help me in no way for the county is owing too much borrowed money. They told me I deserved a Pension[.] Governor I worked as I told you before for my parents and brothers & sisters 16 years and then my father was blessed with a good home and farm and didn't live long there after my Brothers who hadn't shown no helping hand whatever devoured what my Father left. I maried before my Father dies and they leased the timber for quite awhile and ever child was due to get $10 per year and they wouldn't give me my $10. Not one time and in 1910 or 1911 they [illegible] the farm still not giving anything and then I had to take my Mother and support her again besides my children. Don't you think I deserve my Fathers pension? I can give you my witnesses any time you may call for them. Please lend me a helping hand Governor.[36]

She appears to be asking to receive her father's Confederate pension. Although many people hoped that they could inherit a parent's Confederate pension, the state paid only the veteran or the widow and not any other dependents.

Mrs. Lydia Cartwright (McDavid) to Carlton, 26 October 1929

Am writing you at the request of a friend who advised me to. My husband is in Prison at Raiford for-7-seven years an I am alone as we have no children an I am sick all the time an unable to work to support myself an would like to know if I can get any help from the state as I have no income of any kind. Will you Please advise me if the State will help me in any way or is there a Pension for Widows who are left as I am with out support of any kind.

Hoping to hear from you as soon as convenient.[37]

Mrs. Julia B. Timmons (Ocala) to Carlton, 12 November 1929

1930 census: Julia is 51 years old, white, and married to Elmer, who works as a "helper" in his son-in-law's drugstore. Their daughter and son-in-law live with them.

I deposit some money in the Ocala Metropolitian Saving Bank private for safe keeping, in a private Box, and I and then also my child had some money in that Bank on checking account and the bank is closed and they will not pay me any of the money[.] They say I cant get it.

They kept my statement three month's before they would send it to me. And when they did send it I am three hundred dollars and some over short of the money I had deposit in that Bank. Dear Governor if there's any way in the world for me to get my money please help me.

The President of that Bank said the bank is not <u>Broke</u> but they closed to keep from lending any more money.

I dont realy believe the <u>Governor</u> will allow them to treat us that way.

Please pay this your best attention and do what you can in my favor.[38]

Mrs. John Varn (Georgetown) to Carlton, 12 December 1929

1930 census: John and Mina Varn are living in Miami, where he is a building contractor. She is 29 years old and does not work.

I am going to appeal to you for aid. I owe $70.00 dollars on the church fixtures, I raised donations to build this church[,] the only one here[.] Will you please send me a check to cover same as a donation[.] I will appreciate it so much & will always feel grateful to you thanking you. The Mediterranean fruit fly has affected the financial status of the State, also severel banks closing causes times to be dull. Thanking you for past favors and wishing you a Happy and Prosperous New Year[.][39]

Mrs. H. B. Crawford (Live Oak) to Carlton, 17 December 1929

I am writing you for advice concerning the mother's and orphans pension as I cannot get much information here regarding same. I am a widow with two children age 7½ and 3½ years living with my aged parents and not physically able to work and no means of support[.] I understand every other county in our state pays the pension except this one (Suwannee). Now any advice you may give me will be appreciated. Let me hear from you at an early date and kindly oblige.[40]

Miss Rebecca Leonard (Martin) to Carlton, 18 December 1929

1930 census: She is 12 years old, white, and the daughter of P. S. and Mamie. Her father is a farm laborer.

Excuse me if I am taking the liberty of writing you these few lines and I hope that you will not be annoyed. The circumstances oblige me to do so.

It looks as though there will be no santa for me[,] my brother & sister this year agin. We are not what you may call us poor. We have a farm of our own though it is under margage, Dad has tried it's very best especially this year to raise enough stuff that we might would of got out of debt. This "unlockly" we have failed due to the eatmospheric condition and some commission merchants parasites who have robbed us of our produce malitiously fraudulently and willfully. After which we all had pitched in and helped dad on spare time in the work.

Now we are practically on the verge of collapse. We are not starving as we can raise food twelve months a year in Florida, "you know!" but it requires some money to buy clothes[,] some food that we can not raise here, up keeping of the farm buildings, fencing, emplements ect ect. There we need seeds and fertilizer for somthing we need to grow for the ready cash necessary as staple crops could not keep us afloat due to the fack that we can not produce the quantity and that we can not get a fair price for our staple product such as corn & peanuts ect.

This fertilizers and seed can not be had on time payment or on credit nowhere that we no of. And it is this popuse of this letter to you that partly explains some of the things we are in need of. We appeal to you for some finantial help that we may purchase with, the materials with which to work and produce food and feed for men and beasts.

Now kind sir we do not ask you to give us a christmas present nor make any kind of donation, we only ask you to loan us on interest basis—say of about two hundred and fifty dollars or less, that would be sufficient for this season. This much would enable us to produce several thousand dollars worth of stuff. As for co-operation and economy my dad can prove it's worth[.] therefore wont you please help us in this matter in some manner as the time is at hand for action on the spring culture.

Thanking you for your kind attention you may give in this letter in our behalf and our plight. I beg you to exuse me in writing this letter for the benifit of all of us here as I am only a school age child with my sixth grade education not quiet complete, for this reason I can no do better in writing.

I and all of us in the family wish you and your family a Merry Christmas and a happy New Year.[41]

Mrs. Catherine Peacock (Altha) to Carlton, 26 December 1929

No doubt you will be glad when I quit annoying you with letters[.] have been writeing you concerning Pensioners. But this time Im writing you concerning the Rum men[.] Rum is ruining this country[.] some is getting rich selling rum while the ones that don't make or sell it is going broke[.] for our men folks every time they get a $1.00 they go to the rum man and get their Pints & quarts. There is 2 men right here in Altha that sells rum every day. Mr Joe Hiers the Barber is one[.] some-time he keeps it in his toilet & in Mr Murpheys smoke house one of his clost neighbors and in an old field near his house some-times[.] He lives west of Altha in a new house recently painted I think and Mr Roy Peacock lives clost to the Rail Road south of Turvavilles store in an old white painted house with an open hall. He keeps Rum & sells it[.] thats all he does and it can be proved.

He dosent work at nothing in this world[.] He dosent keep it in his house I don't think. I have been informed he kept it somewhers around the house. George Stone of Altha also handles it frequently[.] He runs a cafe in town for a blind to sell shine. To my honest belief Mr Sheriff Clark knows it[.] He has choices they tell me when he is reported to a still if it's the Big men He will send them word to move the still before he arrives[.] I trust that you will do away with all this rum in Calhoun County anyway.

PS Pleas don't let it be known don't let it be known that I have written you concerning this for they would sneak on me & burn me up in my house[.] I am poor like I've told you before[.] can't provide for my family and if my son hauls a load of wood to town he goes to either one & gets rum with the money[.] he's afflicted has a head trouble bad[.] he's not right in his mind and when he gets whiskey in him theres nothing to be done with him[.] he does very well till he gets rum in him.[42]

See her previous correspondence from 21 October. This is still during the period of legal prohibition, which lasted until 1933.

Mrs. Rosa Richardson (Wildwood) to Carlton, 2 January 1930

1930 census: Rose is a 50-year-old African American and a widow with four children and a son-in-law at home. She works as a laundress, her oldest daughter is a cook, and her son-in-law is a lineman for a railroad.

I am writing you again concerning my cases in Jacksonvill Fla[.] the 12 year old child Virginia Richardson that died for the want off water & the wright kind of medicine & because I was goin too put the law too them, thay was goin too see the Salvasion Army people. If thay taken me out off thire hands till thay got through with me. So thay put me in Jail & helt up all my mail & sent me off too the Sylum on Mrs F. T. Holmes papers.

Thay was trying to reack my life. No Drs signed me up for the Sylum. Now I was nervious tho who woulden be after lieing over the Dead Child and puting me in Jail & Changing my name to Mrs. F. T. Holmes & I was supposed too have a son in New York City. It give me a shock. And as for as my insainty. If I get in the Court house I will show them who needs too be in the sylum. & the prison too.

Governor. As my farther & mother old & my Husband is dead & I have too Childern too lookout for will you have the warents served on the parties in Jacksonvill Fla & Perlimenary hearing in Jacksonville Fla As thay have done me so dirty. I am not going to stand it.

Now the people in Sumter Co have worked hard to get you in as our Governor for we belived you was the wright one too make our State a better State & I thank you for what you have all ready done.

Let me know what you will do for me by return mail.[43]

Lizzie Cobb (West Palm Beach) to Carlton, 10 January 1930

Our government of the Stat of Florida. I am your Humble Servent. I pray that you will Remember me this is my Prayer[.] I Been Storm thrash. I Pray that you will heare my voice[.] this is my Pray.[44]

Mrs. Ada Sorenson (Deleon Springs) to Carlton, 17 February 1930

1930 census: Listed as "Soreonsen," Ada is a 39-year-old widow with eleven children at home. None of them is listed as working.

I am writting you to see if there are any way you can help me to keep my place up and keep my children in school[.] I am a widow left with eleven 11 children to take care of[.] seven of them goes to school. My health is very bad. All so my eye site is bad. My oldest Boy is only in his 9th grade at school and I am trying to keep them all in school if I can but it is a hard task to take care of eleven children and keep my place up to with the expenses I have with them all. Any advice or help you can furnish will certainly be appreciated.[45]

Mrs. L. Stephenson (Panama City) to Carlton, 19 February 1930

I here write you a few lines to let you no a few things I wont you to do for me[.] I am a poor woman have 5 children & am sick all the time most[.] will you do this please governor & I don't let no one no I wrote you this[.] I have a husbon who drinks & all I do doesnt stop him[.] the negros just give him whiskie and gits all my childrens earnings[.] Mr Carlton I will give you the names who I no sells the stuff is Annie Lewis a negro woman in the quarters & a nother is ed Whitors & his two sons runs a filling stashon at the depot[.] their names is Oscar Whitors & Willie Whitias[.] the negro, Annie Lewis all so runs bigest rum house here.

She has just about got all the monie my husbon makes & I cant stop it & all so runs a Disarchilie [disorderly] house to[o][.] so lots more sells it[.] just slip in rite now a officer & let him get Bisie governor.

Do this for me please will you Governor as I am a poor woman & want my own earnings[.] I do not want my home broke up this way[.] were I am going to look for it. Now to be Bursted up[.] Dear Governor[,] mannie thanks to you[.] So I remains a friend.[46]

Mrs. Mollie Jernigan (Munson) to Carlton, 8 March 1930

1930 census: She is 59 years old, white, widowed, and living with her daughter and granddaughter in Santa Rosa County. No one in the household has a job.

I feel drawn in the Spirit to write you, as I want some information as to what I can, that I could obtain some help from the county.

I am a widdow woman and in destitute circumstances[,] havent got any thing at all[,] not even household furnishings to live comfortable; have to make out the Best I can, living about on other Peoples places. Partly disable to work.

I went before the Board of County Commissioners some time ago But they did not Donate me any thing[.] I do not understand how it is, as I see some other widdow women drawing from the County that seem to be in Better circumstances that I am.

I would be very glad if there could be something done, so that I could get some help from the County.

Hoping to hear from you at the earliest posible date.[47]

Mrs. O. C. Whidden (Ft. Pierce) to Carlton, 10 June 1930

1930 census: Nettie is 33 years old, white, and a widow with five children at home.

I am writing you in regards to myself and children. They have cut the check which I get as a mothers pension down to $20 dollars a month and I have 4 children to feed and cloth and am not able to go out to work. And besides, three of the children are to small to be left alone and if I take in a roomer and barder they Sheriff and Judge make me get a rids of him or her and if I even have company to come see me they are always having something to say about it.

They same to think that I can feed and cloth my self and babies on 20 dollars a month and it simply wont buy food and when I go to the well fair bord for help they don't gave me nothing but something that ware out and discarded by others and I don't think its faire[.] I have been a widow for nearly 6 years. and one of the county comittie read the law books and said I was due 41 dollars. But why they wont give it to me are kicks because I try to help my children by renting out a room or two. I cant under stand[.] theire are people who trys to atend to my afiares[.] if they would stop them from talking so mutch I think thy would do the wright thing[.] they even reported I was selling whiskey and the Judge and Sheriff came out and search the place while I was gone[.] They waited and watch me leve before they search. And the Sheriff Brown gave my baby of 5 years money to tell him if I have any thing as liker hid[.] But Dear Sir they did not find any thing for I abolisutly don't handy the stuff[.] they broke my hot Watter Bottole[.] there was nothing in it and why they should treat me so cruel I cant under stand[.] I am writing you this truth to see if you cant help me in ways at making them live me alone[.] They know nothing against me only they love to talk to mutch.

So please do somthing wright away[.] looking for a reply soon and thanking you[.] I am as every yours truly.

I can Prove this.[48]

Mrs. R. L. Mixon (Okeechobee) to Carlton, 27 June 1930

1930 census: Robert L. and Mabel live in Okeechobee with their four children. He is a well driller. The family is white.

I am writing you this letter in regards to my oldest boy. He has alway been a faithful boy to his father and mother[,] was already trusted by others. His repetation here or where ever we have lived will be found the same. He came from Okeechobee to the lake after the storm with you. He was in the Storm. Eleven of us stood on our dinning room table that night and our home was torn to pieces[,] enough left together for us to stay in. The Lord spared us ever one and how it looks empossible to man and was only the handy work of God that we were spared. My son name is Louis and he will soon be Twenty one years old. Up to a week and a half ago[,] He helped his father[.]

He has turned all his earnings to his father or mother and between times has built us a home back here on our place at the lake. We have work so hard to try to have some thing for our children when they become of age. But since the storm we have been seeing so many disapointments and sickness.

That it is impossible for us to do anything to help our boy on to have thing for his self. I have been sick so awful much and have only been back from the hospital about two weeks. He wants to be an air plane pilot[.] it take studing and learning. And I have wondered if you in any way could help him in this. As he stayed and worked so hard after the storm all thoes in distress. He help to find your relations that you came to see about and to find. It made him look so much older[,] the strain he went through during thoes time.

If you can help our son anway or any way you can obtain any help for him I would surley be glad to hear from you. He does not want to join the navy or have to be a goverment man now. I will close hoping to hear from you soon.[49]

Mrs. P. E. Bullard (Jacksonville) to Carlton, 28 June 1930

1930 census: Peter Bullard, 32, lives with his wife and their four children. He is a foreman at the city garage. The family is white.

As a lady in the state where you are governor, I am writing you to see if there is any way you can help me. I am the mother of four (4) children two boy's and two girl's. ages from (4) four to (10) ten. As my husband and I had to separate, the courts here seems to think my husband should have the children as he is making a good salary. I have no employment and am living with my Brother. And I just want to know if there is a law that can give me my children and make my Husband provide for them. I am a good mother. And as all mother's Love my children very dearly. Willing and wanting to do everything I can to make their little lives happy.

We have been having this trouble almost a year now. And I feel I can't bear it much longer.

As a true governor of our State I appeal to you for help, knowing the Love a mother has for her children I am <u>pleading</u> and <u>begging</u> with you to take some interest in my case as no one else seems to want to help me.

I want to live and do the right thing and I cannot do this without somebody's help.

Thanking you in advance for anything you can do for me.

And a heart broken mother.[50]

Mrs. Ella S. Cortis (Zephyrhills) to Carlton, 18 December 1930

1930 census: She is a 68-year-old white widow, born in Massachusetts. She has two elderly women living with her as boarders.

I am enclosing a card which I received from Daddy Flag. In hopes you can help in some way to have the State take hold of this problem of careing for our children. I am a widow of limited means 69 years old, have been a citezan of Fla quite a number of years, & voted here as soon as the women were given the Franchise & I love both the Children & Fla. and it dont seem possible that Fla will see her Children turned out into the streets cold hungry penniless friendless helpless & utterly homeless. You know what the good book says about those who do not provide for their own household & our fair State is full of tourests this winter, and how can we face the fact & explain it to them, so they will have every respect for us. I am a booster for Fla, but I came from a state that takes care of their children till 21 yrs when there is need, & there are lots of state children there. I think it is a great question all over our country. I didn't give us children of our own so we adopted 2. 38 years ago. One 4 yrs and the other was just a nurseing baby. So you see I am greatly interested in these poor children who are not to blame for their plight. Cant the state take hold of this job and help give these little ones a chance in life. Havent we land enough to raise milk & food to feed them, & couldnt convict labor be used to doo the work. I feel sure you will be able to devise some plan to care for our helpless future citizans.[51]

"Daddy Flag" may refer to Henry Flagler, the railroad and hotel entrepreneur responsible for so much of Florida's early-twentieth-century economic development. It is not clear what the card from Daddy Flag represented.

Mrs. Holl Williams (Apalachicola) to Carlton, 21 November 1931

I am writing you again con searned any thing that Mr. Sam husband are holding up from me and my 5 little kids. he are holding my trunk and cloaths and also my children cloaths in it[.] leaves us all neked[.] I saw him on the 19th and he said he was going to keep them[.] I need my cloaths and also my things because I dont owe him any thing at all[.] he claim my husband owe him and is taking my things for it[.] says I cant get my things I payed for my self[.] I went to Sheriff prigeon of that county and he failed to get them for me[.] I am in need[.] my husband has left me and mr. Sam are trying to take my things for it. I am in Apalachicola Fla. trying to work with out my cloaths and please have him to turn my things a loose[.] his address in port St. Joe Fla. Box 164[.] Thanking you for any thing you can do for me in the matter for I dont owe him not anything at all[.] me and my little children are in a suffering condition[.] he told me that he was going to take my things and got my cloaths and trunk and stove and maching and beding all in his house holding them and wont let me have them and that Sherriff want get them is why I applied to you[.] I cant not helped because my husband left and I want

my thing[s] for I need them back bad[.] it is cold[.] my address is apalachicola
Fla. Comerce St. 166

He is telling peoples that he give them to me and have not done so.[52]

Mrs. Annie Esser Bartenfels (Miami) to Carlton, 21 April 1931

1930 census: This may be Anna Bartonsfield, a 40-year-old German immigrant. She lives as a "lodger" and works as a cleaner at the city hospital. She is listed as single.

Pardon the liberty I take in writing you in regard to my personal affair concerning the Bank of Bay Biscayne (a State Bank), which closed its doors June 11, 1930.

This was a terrible blow to me for today I am penniless after such hard struggle for my living.

I have no home, nowhere to go! I am not able to take out insurance that would carry me through illness or death on account of all my money being tied up in the closed bank.

I am a widow. I have worked steady and faithful for a period of twenty years by long hours, small salary and hard work. I saved all I could without spending anything on myself, for the reason I wanted to protect myself in my age. Now my strength is gone and my health is poor—I have no one to depend on.

All that I saved I deposited in this <u>State</u> Bank. I had both a savings and checking account. My Pass Book No. is 8101. The very last amount of $100.00 I deposited on June 3rd, 1930—it was a holiday, the front door was closed, but was advised to go to the side door to enter the bank. My deposit and my statement were marked the "4th of June."

My suffering and distress is very heavy and urgent. I have to depend on domestic work so long as it will last, to support myself and avoid starvation.

Under the circumstances as explained above, I ask you kindly for a widow's right as a citizen. Please will you kindly aid me in this earnest matter to get my hard earned money back in full as I need it so much for my living? I shall appreciate your kindness very much.

Please reply to this matter strictly private as I do not want any publicity.[53]

Mrs. Theo Preiss (Cortez) to Carlton, 23 November 1931

Will you please pardon a poor woman wish [which] have to write to you, as I have nobody wish answer me. I wrote to Chamber of Commerce also Tax Assessor, but get no answer. Will let you know we live one Perico Island by ourself me and Husband[.] we are going on 72 yeare of age. Lost our money in the bank of Bradenton[.] had two big mordgage lost them too as non will pay me a cent[.] no taxes payt one. Now sir we live one this little Homestate [homestead] 38 yeare only 12 acre 60 most swampland.

We have to pay more taxes then the rest our next nieghbor 1 mile closer to Town payt 40 D taxes for 40 acre all Farmt. And we have to pay that same yeare 115 D[.] is this right and since we lost everything we payt no Taxes for two yeare[.] cant loan nothing one the place. Will also let you know me and my Husband worket this rout for 38 yeare and never get a cent for it[.] can we not claim some for the Taxes now[.] my Husband had Rheumatism. And now people told us we go to loose our little homestate[.] wish we worked all by the Hoe as we had no Horse[,] no Auto[.] me and Husband we plandet a mangoe grove[.] had 800 Tree big to get Fruit. Put the Guarantee Fla had we could not sale them[.] we had a man from Tampa wish gets them but wont let hime get [illegible] so they came and spriet [sprayed] our Mangoes twist and now we had no fruit for two yeare[.] had little green one on but all of that spreying must hurt them as they had Mangoes before every yeare.

I wrote that time to Whashington to Fletsher and he wrote us we are to get 2 D for a Tree as that what they go to pay theire and we never get a cent from nobody[.] some get 50 D in Bradenton to cut a bout 3 old guaves trees out. And they not need the money as bad as we too. Now my Dear Governor as we had nobody to go too[.] if you Sir will only help us out and let us know if we can get nothing for our route work or something for our lost in the mangos. I know you surly will be so kind and let me know if we have to loose our little home[.] My Husband sure would not get over if we both worket all our live from sun up to sun down only to pay so mush taxes. . . . and I pray to the Dear Lord to Bless you and Family and Keep you in good Health. Pleas forgive a old nervus women wish in her missery thought you about the only help. Thanking you for kindness.[54]

"Fletsher" likely refers to Duncan U. Fletcher, U.S. senator for Florida from 1909 to 1936.

Mrs. Eleanor Wood (Miami) to Carlton, 25 May 1932

If you will be kind enough to give me some information in this mad rush of campaigning I will greatly appreciate it. To begin with I will introduce my self by saying that I must be a Floridian[.] My people came here in 1813 to Bradford Co. and to the west coast of So. Fla. in 1843[.] I came from the Raulerson & Sloan family of whom you personally know[.] I have also nursed in the Carlton Family when I was located in Arcadia but for the last 13 years my health has been very bad and continues to get worse[.] I have a daughter thirteen years old whose father is dead[.] I married again a man much my senior and not being able to support me[,] he went away[.] I heard from him now and then for a while but I haven't heard in five years and I cant get in touch with any of his people in the west. I am not divorced but never the less regardless to my capablilty I am unable this last year to make any kind a living on account of extreme low blood pressure and weak heart[.] I feel like it would be a relief if I could stop begging charity and I am shure if any body [deserves] a state pension I am one for I have done my share of charity before the days of hospitals starting at the age of twelve[.] I have never advertised my work for that was not the motive that prompted it[.] But Dr. Love of Lakeland could tell any one wanted to know a few things. Dr. Simmons of Arcadia is familiar with every detail of my physical condition up till two years agoe and hospitals records at Jackson Mem. of Miami has a pretty good record since[.] I own one lot worth about [$]25[.]00 if it was salable[.] I have no income and no one to depend on[.] My statement will bear investigation and as the last resort I am writing you because I don't feel like investigating every body down town[.] I thought you could tell me whether or not it would be worth while making an attempt.[55]

Reba Blackwelder (St. Petersburg) to Carlton, 5 July 1932

1930 census: She is 18 years old, white, and a student at the Florida School for the Deaf and Blind.

I received your letter seveal days ago and I was sorry that I did not explain to you at first, but I am going to explain what I want to do. I have been wanting to study Beauty Culture, and also my father and Mother want me to study; but they could not afford to pay. Father is out of work and Mother works as a saleswoman. Perhaps you can help me. Will you please? I do hope you can pay.

I do thank you if you will do something for me.

I hope to hear from you soon.[56]

Mrs. L. A. N. Smith (Brooksville) to Carlton, 18 August 1932

Is there any way you can get through an old age pension while you hold your office. It would make a lot of difference to old people who have always been good citizens but are now without support. I have no faith in David Sholtz, or any other German, and I have known a number. They all loved themselves, and I do not believe he will do anything only what Peter O. Knight wants. I knew enough about him when the strike was on in the phosphate mines some years ago. And as long as he and Perry Wall run Tampa I dont look for any help for common people there. I am sending you a piece printed in the Tribune at Tampa[.] I wouldnt like to write what I think of poor houses, and County Hospitals, I only hope I may never be carried to either one, or any of my friends. Well if you can get an old age pension through pleas do so.[57]

Wall was a businessman and former mayor of Tampa. Knight was an attorney, businessman, and powerful figure in Tampa politics. The strike to which she refers is probably the 1919 strike that involved three thousand phosphate workers in Polk and Hillsborough counties. It eventually spread to other industries across the state, and more than twenty-thousand workers were involved.

At the time of this letter, Sholtz had won the Democratic Party primary and so was generally seen as the governor-elect. However, Carlton would remain in office until the following January.

Mrs. D. L. Scott (Marianna) to Carlton, 27 August 1932

1930 census: D. L. is 58 years old and a laborer at a turpentine still. Katie is 39, has two children, and does not work. The family is white.

I am applying to you for help as I am a poor crippled woman and I am losing my eye sight and am in real need. My oldest child has got to have school books and nothing to buy them with. I need a treatment for my eyes so please assist me any way possible. I have a husband that works for a man that promises him $40 but instead pays him in old stale groceries like the items listed below[:] Salt fish 15¢ lb.[,] Rotten pickled meat 25¢ lb.[,] bug eaten pease 15¢ lb.[,] meal 60¢ pk.[,] sorriest flour $1.00 per 24 lbs.

I know you will not believe it but I wish you could see for your self the mess that we have to eat.

This man which my husband works for is Mr. A. J. McMullian Starr Fla. turpentine man. We haven't had a dollar since last xmas just the rations I have listed above.

Please return and answer[.][58]

Mrs. Bessie Cropper (Bagdad) to Carlton, 9 September 1932

1930 census: Floyd Cropper is 18 years old, white, single, and still living with his parents. He and his father are laborers in a lumber mill.

I want to know if you cant get my Divorce From Floyd Cropper[.] he was sent off for 30 mo[nths] and I have got no one to take care of me and baby.

I want a Divorce from him Just as quick as I can get it[.] Now advise me how to go about it.

Let me hear from you on this.[59]

Mrs. Laura Reed (Crestview) to Sholtz, 30 December 1932

1930 census: She is 55 years old, white, and works as an agent for a dry goods company.

I am writing you this, to let you no my condition; to ask a favor of you as our Governor.

I was borned in 1864; will be 69 years old next April. My father fought in the Civil War; & died when I was 9 years old; Mother; not none of us children has never received a penny of Pension money for his service.

I have been married. I was left a widow 14 years; have neither mother, nor father, sister, nor brother, to care for me.

I have had property in life; but I had mercy on a man that was in trouble; & signed pappers on my property to help him; & that has caused me to be homeless; & pennyless in my old days.

I broke up housekeeping 9 years ago; I am eating with my Christian friends; & trying to sell dry goods from house, to house; to keep myself in clothes; & cant even clothe myself decently.

I was saved in Feb. 1885; & have lived a Christian life.

I Note that several States are Pensioning their needy aged people; the Government as an aid to encourage them, has give $12,000,000 direct relief to indigent aged. The states are to contribute at least as much as the Federal Government.

I Note that the American Federation of labor has took steps to aid against destitution in old age; & that their effects are to be nation wide.

I note that the Governors Hon. Wilbur M. Bucher, Mich.[,] Hon. Charles W. Bryan, Neb.[,] Hon. C. Douglas Buck, Dela.[,] Hon. Wilbur M. Cross, Con.[,] Hon. Joseph B. Ely, Mass.[,] Hon. Frank C. Emerson, Wyo.[,] Hon. George W. P. Hunt, Ari.[,] Hon. Morgan F. Larson, N.J.[,] Hon. Julius L. Meier, Ore.[,] Hon. Fred Olsen, Minn.[,] Hon. Gifford Pinchot, Penn.[,] Hon. Franklin D. Roosevelt, N.Y.[,] Hon. C. Ben Ross, Idaho.[,] Hon. George White, Ohio. have all signed for their States to Pension their needy aged People; & I believe that you are as good a man as these other Governors & that you are as Generous hearted.

So I am asking you, as our Governor; to please sign the leaflet for Fla. to Pension her needy aged People; & help Suffering Humanity.

Please sign and return to me at once.

Thanking you for anything you do to help in this matter; & assuring you of my appreciation.

May the Richest Blessings of God, Rest upon You; in all your undertakings for Him, His Cause.[60]

Chapter 2

1933-1934

T he year 1933 brought Floridians a new governor and a new president—
and a New Deal. Franklin Roosevelt had garnered national attention for
his handling of the Depression as governor of New York. It was widely
expected that he would apply those same skills to the nation as a whole. Dave
Sholtz—a New York–born, Yale-educated lawyer—was a relative novice in
Florida politics when he won election in 1932. Although he had served a
brief stint in the state legislature in the 1920s, his most visible role in public
life had been as president of the Florida State Chamber of Commerce. But
his energy and optimism made him a likely match to the new president.
In a radio broadcast in March 1933, he even sounded Rooseveltian, telling
Floridians to "keep your chin where you have it now—up."[1] Sholtz quickly
identified himself with the Roosevelt administration and worked to extract as
much federal money for the state as possible.[2]

As the New Deal began and the new "ABC" agencies appeared, the public
had to adjust to a new operating system. Suddenly there were new programs,
each with its own fledgling bureaucracy, and much confusion on the local
level about procedures for all these new endeavors. Could two members of
the same family get work relief jobs? Could a mothers' aid recipient also get
money from her son in the CCC? The letters of this chapter are filled with
concerns about these new federal programs.

And, perhaps most important (prior to 1935), the correspondents ques-
tioned what would happen to the elderly. Most could not take work relief
jobs, few would have had school-aged children at home, and most would not
have sons young enough for the CCC camps either. This group would not
likely benefit from wage and hours legislation or any other program of
the first two years of the New Deal. Much of the correspondence discusses
plans for old age pensions, especially the Townsend Plan. First proposed
by California doctor Francis E. Townsend in 1933, the "Old Age Revolving
Pension" plan rapidly attracted a great swell of national enthusiasm. Townsend Clubs sprouted up all across the country, advocating the scheme that
ultimately competed with the Social Security Act for political support.[3]

The Townsend Plan sounded simple. The federal government would provide a monthly pension of two hundred dollars to all citizens over the age of sixty who agreed to two conditions: they had to retire from work, and they had to spend the entire two hundred dollars that month. The scheme was to be funded by a 2 percent tax, assessed at every stage of production and sale. According to the fervent "Townsendites," the plan was flawless. The elderly would live in comfort; the compulsory retirements would open up millions of jobs for the unemployed; the artificially produced expenditures would stimulate the economy.[4]

The popularity of the Townsend plan stemmed from several sources. Old age pensions had been gaining popular support in the decades before the Depression, and several states had passed small scale versions of these pensions during the 1920s. Americans were also increasingly familiar with broader, more comprehensive insurance programs enacted in western countries such as Germany, and several organizations had been agitating for similar efforts in the United States.[5] The Townsend Plan reached the level of a national movement, however, thanks to an aggressive organizational model that tapped the labor and energy of retirees to engage in letter-writing and petition campaigns. The Townsendites entered politics with little hesitation, and launched an intensive lobbying effort that began influencing congressional elections in California as early as 1934. Florida, already a retirement haven by the 1930s, had a large and energetic Townsend movement. The state had a newspaper devoted to the Townsend Plan, the *St. Petersburg Advocate.*

The plan was as controversial as it was popular, however. Most of the debate focused on the cost, which was calculated by some economists as reaching half the national income. It might double the national tax burden. Some predicted the scheme would bankrupt the government. Other critics pointed out that it might encourage the creation of monopolies and other giant conglomerates, as companies merged and integrated in order to avoid the 2 percent taxation on the various transactions.[6]

Roosevelt opposed the Townsend Plan and began pushing for the completion of the administration's social security bill instead. (Observers at the time and historians since have noted that the growing strength of the Townsend movement helped to put pressure on the government to come up with a workable alternative.) But the tremendous popularity of the measure meant that the Roosevelts had to tread very carefully about pension discussions: in the minds of many Americans, to oppose the Townsend Plan was to oppose old age pensions altogether.

In 1934 the question remained unresolved. The elderly population continued to wait, often in desperation.

Mrs. A. N. Ray (Lake Worth) to Sholtz, 11 January 1933

I am writing you for a little information. Will you please help me out? I have one heifer cow for my family. There are six of us so you see that is why I keep a cow. Well, to begin with, I sold two pints of milk to my neighbor and a dairy found it out and reported it to the State Inspector, and he came to all the houses on my street and wanted to know if I was selling milk. They harass me nearly to death.

We can't get enough to eat anyway let alone buy a permit to sell a bottle of milk now and then. You are a lawyer, will you please advise me in regards to the law for a family cow. They tell me I am not allowed to give milk away. Is that true? There was some people I gave milk to, and if I had not the lady would have starved. Has the state man any business in Lake Worth to be telling us what to do? We have our inspector here, so far as I know he is alright.

The dairies is what is causing me so much trouble. Just like I could sell enough milk to ruin them. From one little two gallon cow, and me with six in the family, and none of them working hardly any of the time. I voted for you, and had the pleasure of shaking hands with you when you were here, and you promised us poor people a fair chance, and I think you will do what is the right thing, and let me tell you everybody is invited to my milking house, and we have built a milk house. That is what they made us do with one little cow. And now they want me to pay for a permit to sell milk.

I couldn't sell enough milk to buy a permit. I am sure you can give some light on this, as I am not able to consult a lawyer.[7]

Mrs. Z. Pearl Howell (Nocatee) to Sholtz, 12 January 1933

When I heard you speak in Arcadia during your campaign I said, "surely this is the man who can save Florida from the tangled mess and corruption of unprincipled politics."

My family is one of the few who has steadfastly stood for sane reasonable and fair business principles for all.

We own our little homes; believe that more people should and that non-owners of homes should have less voting power.

My father and mother are aged—unable to do much other than grow a home garden and tend a small flock of chickens.

My husband's mother is in similar condition. They all three must needs look to us in this distressing crisis.

My father could not pay his tax last year. We had hoped to catch it up this year but conditions for us are no better. We do not want our properties to go delinquent.

My husband is an expert box maker by trade but his work this year nor did it last year does not justify a living wage for the dependents even with strictest economy.

I am that practical type of woman who makes pillow cases from worn sheets and aprons from dresses no longer suitable for wear. Professionally, I spent 8 years as a grade teacher in Florida. After taking business training I worked 2 years in Tax Collector's office, De Soto County.

At present I keep a set of books for our Woodmen circle—handle about $50.00 monthly. Politically, I am a Democrat of a very old line and religiously, a Baptist Unity student.

Mr. Sholtz I'm asking for book-keeping or license clerical work in Controller's office preferably, since I feel more familiar with the routine of his department.

I'm writing Mr. Lee and any thing that you can do to help me help others dependent on me will be gratefully appreciated. Thank you and I'm sincerely wishing you a happy and prosperous administration.[8]

Miss Lola Nowling (DeFuniak Springs) to Sholtz, 28 January 1933

1930 census: She is the 11-year-old daughter of Miles, who is a laborer in the turpentine industry.

I am writing you this letter. Not because I won't to but because I need to. I won't to tell you my daddy died last April and left me and my mother and one boy[.] He is eight years old. I am 14 years of age. My daddy left mother a car and three heads of cows. she has sold them to make a living for us. My mother is in bad health can't work and only weighs (91) lbs. She hasn't any relatives but one that helps her and they don't much because they are not able hardly. Me and my brother gets ($2.00) a month each from the country [county]. and we are living on that now part of the time. We don't have much to eat. but we are in a bad shape now. and I want to ask you is they any chance for mother to get a widows pension if you can do anything for her. I surely would be glad and thank you so much. She gave you her vote and mother said if she ever lived till you get this. please give me a quick reply[.] if you don't believe what I have said come and see.[9]

Mrs. M. B. Thomas (N. Miami) to Sholtz, 13 March 1933

I would like a little information regarding the schools in Florida. We don't know who to go to to air our grievience as we were very promptly informed where we did apply that the[y] were running the schools.

We want to know why so many married women are teaching in the public schools when there are several hundred graduates seeking positions as teachers. Over 60% of the teachers in Dade Co. are married whose husbands have good paying position. I will mention just one instance.

The wife is teaching, the husband has a city or county position, the daughter teaches—her husband is a principal. I understand from the maid their monthly income is around $650 all in one house.

Do you think is fair where so many are waiting for teaching position, that all of these married women are holding down the jobs?

I lived in Michigan—and N. Jersey and no married woman was allowed to teach. It is a state law.

I have four girls and two boys, I have been trying to keep in school. Many times they have gone to school hungry and half clothed and me at home have gone with out.

What is the use of slaving your heart and hands out to put children through school when there are no positions. Married women hang on to jobs for years. Single ones get married and leave an opening for others.

Now if you will kindly inform us where or to go where we can go to put a little fight for our rights, we will be very gratefull. There are several hundred who feel the same as I do.[10]

Mrs. C. S. McCarley (Greenacres) to Sholtz, 6 April 1933

In view of the fact that you are trying to cut down expenses in the state and wish to be just in your administration I wish to make a report directly to you of a case of "fraud" which has been going on a long time and of which no investigation has yet been made.

In Greenacres City, Fla (a small subdivision 3 miles west of Lake Worth, Fl.) there is a Spanish War Veteran named George Clifford who receives $75.00 a month pension claiming he has "heart trouble" and he claims that his doctor will swear to it.

Now, this man had been carrying on a big bootlegging business with the $75.00 which he receives each month. And he is known in Greenacres City as "George Clifford, the bootlegger." This man stays drunk continuously and he has been in jail several times. He has no children but he has a wife who helps him in the business. Now, if he had heart trouble he certainly would not be able to drink as much intoxicants as he does.

Therefore in justice to us decent people who live here, I am appealing to you as the highest official in the state to kindly make an investigation of this particular case by using investigators who will be fair as I'm sure you would never hear of this case if I had not reported it to you as the officials here know, but for "reasons" they have kept it quiet.

Now, as I don't care to have any trouble with these people I am asking you to treat this confidentially as I'm sure you will appreciate knowing of things of this kind as there are so many honest men with families who need work so badly and that $75.00 would help a lot towards feeding worthy families.[11]

Mrs. Grace K Mohler (Lake Alfred) to Sholtz, 28 April 1933

Would you kindly inform me if there is a relief fund for the blind in this state? We have been living in Florida since 1920, lived in Lakeland two and a half yrs and from there then moved here to Lake Alfred when my husband N. A. Mohler bought a house and small grove.

We were getting along very nicely until this boom struck us and our story is like hundreds of others—we lost all we had.

Mr. Mohlers eyes began failing one is entirely blind and the other is partially gone. He has been taking treatments for several years but as yet is not able to read or write, and cannot see to work. There was one job at the juice Plant that he did when they were running[.] even that was too much of a strain on the eye, but he tried to do the best he could. As you know these Plants do not run very long and the pay is small. We had an only child, a daughter who graduated from the college at Tallahassee in spring of 1925, she taught school here four years, and in Auburndale three years. She was our main support till last December when she was stricken with the flu and passed away, so now we must get along some how and I feel the burden has shifted upon myself and I want to get something to do. If you care to investigate this matter I can refer you to Dr. W. T. Simpson of Winter Haven, Dr. Dan Galvin, Tampa, Dr. Murphy, Haines City, Mr. T. L. Gardner, Mr. T. O. Goodman, Mr. A. W. Brian, Rev W. D. Harrel all of Lake Alfred.

I regret very much to have to ask this of you but the Plant is closed till next Fall and Mr. Mohler cannot see to work at anything else and I will greatly appreciate if you will give me the desired information.[12]

Mrs. Marandia Adkison (DeFuniak Springs) to Sholtz, 4 May 1933

I am a woman Got one Boy Child 8 years old[.] I own a home in De-funiak[.] I have Been Selling Parched Peanuts on the Streets after trying to Get other work and have managed to live[.] yesterday the Marshal caught me and put me in City Hall Jale Not alowing me to Sell Peanuts on Streets[.] is it against the Law to work for a living in Fla[?] I Can prove By Plents of People I am only a honest woman making for a honest Clean Liveing[.] is it against The law for a woman To work for a honest Liveing in Defuniak Springs Fla[?] if I canot sell why Do others sell[?] write me By Return Mail.[13]

Mrs. Ida E. Tillman (Palatka) to Sholtz, 22 May 1933

I understand there has been a bill introduced to cut the "Civil War" pensions from $40 to $30 per month. I trust you will fight this bill as I can not see how I could get by on less with a daughter wholly dependent on me and this is all we have to live on. I can not see why any one would want to take the Civil War pension away or make them less. There are not many left. My husband, Middleton M. Tillman, who died Feb. 13, 1925, who served in the Civil War in actual service. We all appreciate what you are doing for the people and our state. I believe with you as our Gov. and our good President, we will soon see better times. I want you to be our friend and helper us keep our pension to $40. If can not raise it why cut it with every thing going up in prices. Would make it harder for us who can not work even if had employment. Of course as prices go up labor will. But that cant help such as I am—makes it harder. So heres hoping and trusting we will be raised and not cut to less. With kindest regards to you and all who help us out.[14]

Mrs. Minnie Gay (Lake Butler) to Sholtz, 26 May 1933

I am writing you in regards to the pension that is in Legislature now to grant me a pension for my deseaced husband L. F. Gay, a confederate war veteran who died 1½ years ago, leaving me with a small child and no means of support.

I had to spend the little money I had during his last two years, for he was confined to his bed and was as helpless as a baby.

The doctor and funeral bills are still unpaid, as I can not pay them because my health is bad and I am not able to work. I wonder if it would be possible for me to get his pension from the time of his death untill now. It would help me to straighten up these debts.

Our Rep. Chas. A. Register of Union County has a list of affidavids & requests signed by the County Commisioners and residents of our County, expressing their desire for me to have the pension.

I hope that you see fit after looking into the situation to grant me the pension and if possible the back pension from the time of his death untill now.

I will appreciate the pension more than I can tell you, if I should be fortunate enough to get it and if it is possible to get the [illegible] it would straighten up his debts and leave me his pension each month to help send our daughter to school.

Anything you can do for me will be greatly appreciated.[15]

Mrs. Sarah Harris (Tampa) to Sholtz, 21 June 1933

In addressing you I am taking a liberty that is caused by desperation and I feel that my only hope lies in bringing my case to your notice, so that I may be in a position to know how to act from the advice I seek and earnestly hope will be forthcoming from you.

Your honour. I am a widow, 63 years old without family, relatives or friends to help me along. for 22 years my late husband and I worked hard to accumulate what little I have got. He died suddenly on January 1932, leaving no insurance and no record of monies due him from people he rendered services to in various capacities such as plumbing, painting and paper hanging etc.

The real estate which became mine is unencumbered with the exception of the use I live in, on it there is a $500.00 mortgage which comes due next May. My note for this mortgage amounts to $40.00 a year payable on the 11th of May and the 11th of November.

Your Excellency. I was only able to pay $5.00 last May, leaving a balance of $15.00. I don't know what to do or where to turn to raise money. I am unable to get employment being too old and feeble. I have been unable to sell any of the six places I have got owing to the depression. My taxes have been paid for 1932 and part of 1933. In doing so I have denied myself proper food. I have come to the place where I cannot sleep nights, my mind is dazed. I want advice.

How can I hold on to what I have got until such times as I can sell out. My property consists of 3 lots on the River front in Tampa, my home & garden with neighboring lot and 10 acres in Ruskin, 20 miles from here.

In the event of my not being able to pay my taxes or meet the note on my mortgage am I to lose what I have got? And the work of a lifetime wasted? Is there no way out?

I have got a widow's exemption but that is not sufficient.

If I could sell part, I might be able to hold out but the depression makes that impossible.

Won't you please advise me?

P.S. I may add that I voted for you at last election.[16]

Mrs. Wealtha Prescott (Orlando) to Sholtz, 21 June 1933

1930 census: Written "Weathianne" in the census, she is 72 years old, white, and does not work. Her 16-year-old goddaughter lives with her.

I am going to try and write you a few lines[.] I hope you wont get defender at it because I can not use the pen and ink since I am old[.] I rather talk to you face to face so I could see you and I hope to see you[.] I am writing to you for infermation about old age pensions as I can not find other ways of haven[t] yet[.] is it in circulating yet[?] is it going to be or will it ever be[?] thare is a lot of old fla. crackers we was born and raise here but of them is gone beyond most of us is widow and has been for many years[.] we all ways has been able to paddle our own conoue untell late years ever things has been

42

taken away from us[.] some of them has loss their hom. I have not lost my hom yet but I am expection to loose it at eny tim be cause I have not been able to pay taxes for too years and thay seem dont want to excemp me [illegible][.] I think I ourt to be at my age.

I was born Sep 29 1856[.] now we are at the end of the day we dont no what to do[.] we dont like to ask for help of state of Fla. Fla. should have mircy on it[s] own[.] we are not able to go out to walk eny more[.] we cant be here meny more years at the best[.] we all ways been saven with our means[.] we never spends what we had foolish[ly]. we never belive in lipstick buisness nor bootleger and a lot of other things that is passing through this world[.] we has all ways tried to obay the law of the lands and God['s] law too[.] when men wanted to voted in buisness he knew whare we was but in tim of need he dont no us eny more[.] we need help we need it right now[.] I hope we can have mercy and I hope thay get up old age pension to help out some[.] I think you will do all you can in geting it throught[.] I hop so eny way[.] wel I hope you will remember us old Fla. crackers and remember us in your prayer and I hope you can understand this writing[.] please dont throw this in [trash?] box and for get to answer it[.]

hoping to hear soon[.] we hope thare will be some chance for us.

[P.S.] I been here long be for Orlando was hatch out. [17]

Mrs. Victoria Townsend (Pompano) to Sholtz, 27 June 1933

Just a few lines to ask your ade in my destress. As I know you are able to accist me now listen. Dear Governor, I am a widow with a child depending soly on me for support and I on her. I have two (2) lots one in Haines City, Fla, one in Lake Wales, Fla. I have bargain to sell lot at Lake Wales[.] party's paid some of the money and want pay the balance of the money. But they have built a great large building on the place and the city have got me accessed over a $1000 at Lake Wales, Fla. and I am three (3) years behind with my tax and I have paid out all I could get to lawyers said they could straighten out farme but they haven't did it as yet. So I have did it all I could or all I am able to do. so I am down here and haven't maid my expencesses picking bean at 10 ct. per hamper. I haven't funs enough to get back home. You have maid a way far the mens to live. Please make a way for we poor widows. Please please give me somthing to do for I will loose my home. Please do something about thies tax for I don't see how I'll ever pay them for I have no work to do at all. I am almost in sane. Please advise me at once so my mine can be at ease once more. I know you can tell me something that will consalate me for you are able to do so.[18]

Mrs. Nettie Lightfoot (Daytona Beach) to Sholtz, 12 July 1933

I am a widow left with 3 three small children[.] I draw a widow's pension from the county of $12.00 per month to live an feed clothes four of us by shoes and to prepare for school[.] I will have 2 in school this year [illegible] going up and I dont see for my life how I am going to start my children to school.

We have a family wellfare oco.[office?] here but they absolutly do not help us mothers drawing pensions whatsoever.

I have a sister in West P.B. Fla she said that [s]he heard you say in one of your campains down there that you was going to make these pensions a state pension and give more to each mother. Mr. Sholtz if there be any way to help up I prey that you will for not only am I in this stand point of liveing but several of others here in this city.

We can not feed our children and clothese them on $12.00 per mon. We are in and awful condition and hopeing you can take some stepp to help us. for all of us mothers sure did support and did all we could to help you[.] and now what are you going to do to help us in return.

Hopeing and praying that you can do something to help us with these pitiful children that havent got a father to look too. I feel that you will. Closing with hopes and thanks to you Mr. Soltz.[19]

Mrs. Bessie Mallett (St. Cloud) to Sholtz, 4 August 1933

You surely must be aware of the financial conditions of the Schools in Florida. I understand that is most of the Schools only a 4 month term will be possible. I am a widow, unable to get any employment—no income and a boy of 16 to educate and support. I am denying myself in every way possible, to put him through the last 2 years on High School, so that he will be equipped to earn his own living, and also if necessary to help me.

If school should only be a 4 months terms, this would mean 4 more years at School, and that would be a tragedy. For Gods sake find some way to finance the school for two 8 month terms, which would enable him to get thru in 2 years.

We have splendid roads all over Florida. Why waste money where it is not needed.

Other projects too, could be left over. Certainly they give employment, but a sum of money sufficient for school needs, should also be included. The boys of today, will be the men of the near future, and we want them to be well able to "carry on." Loafing on the streets, produces laziness, vice, and leads to unsatisfactory conditions.

44

Not only myself, but <u>all</u> parents look to you for help. Surely you will not disappoint us? <u>It can be done.</u>[20]

Miss Marion Hamilton, re: Mrs Amy Price (Pomona) to Sholtz, 12 August 1933

Their is an old Negro Woman, who lives not far from me, and who is blind[.] she had ben blind eleven years and is a widow. She has one son to look to for support, and he has a family of his owen with seven in family. And I wants to no if the state would give this old woman a pension? or something to help her[.] she is 76 years old and have ben liveing in this county 30 years[.] her name is (Amy Price). Thanking you for whatever information you will give me.[21]

Mrs. Lillie Kennedy (St. Andrew) to Sholtz, 13 August 1933

please pardon me for writing you but it is all the way I can find my way out of Suffering and trouble as I am a widow and deef in both ears and near Sighted and unable to do much hard work and have too children to look out for[.] I am asking of you to help us a little if you can get up some money to get us some clothes and Shoes we will not tell any one where we got the money and we would be So thankful to you[.] my Son don't get work Enough to do to keep food all the time[.] I have one Son and Daughter both belong to the Church and good respectble children but they have no clothes and Shoes and our beding is all worn out and unable to get cloth and have no cook Stove[.] now I want you to try and get others to help you send us some money and the good Lord will help you out some way[.] I am 53 years of age and do all that I am able to help my self[.] I will say again that we will not let any one know that you sent any thing to us. I am your friend and hope to here from you[.] You can send the money in money order and mail to St Andrew Fla Mrs Lillie Kennedy.[22]

Mrs. N. S. Lamb (Chattahoochee) to Mrs. Sholtz, 16 August 1933

I am writing you asking you to do me a favor. We are out of work and have been for a year and a half.

My husband has asked for work here at the state hospital every week or oftener and cant get work. he also asked for even a negro job. and I know he is a good man and has a good repetition.

Mrs. Sholtz this is the favor I ask of you. I have a nice crocheted bed spread. I would like to sell you. I hate to sell it but it looks like I have just got to if I can for I am in need of some money for food and other things.

If you will buy it you sure wont regreat it. I will take $25.00 for it altho it is worth much more.

I know you have plenty [of] pretty nice things but I value it a lots for it was hard work to make it. So if you dont want it please advise me of some one els you think would be interested in buying it. Not that I want to sell it, but it is a case of have too if I can.

Hopping to hear from you by return Mail.[23]

Mrs. Elsie Alvis (Jacksonville) to Sholtz, 17 August 1933

Why can't you pass a law to prevent strong able bodied working men and chronic loafers from beating an elderly widow woman out of the little left her after 40 years of unceasing toil when they do not care if she lives or dies? After raising her family she is expected to contribute all she has to raising theirs. One year ago this Aug 7, My husband dropped dead after three years illness. I was left alone, one young daughter[,] stenographer etc; out of employment. We had a small grocery, ample for our needs, and in his pockets was a roll of Masonic receipts (Orlando 69) and also receipts Junior Order Am. Mechanics. Out of these last I was allowed burial expenses. So I had the little store and more than enough owing me to pay all other indebtedness. Most of this I was never able to collect. There was then over $1,000 due us. Since then others have been added to the list. Men with good jobs who know I am a hard working worthy widow get me in spite of all I can do. Seldom much, but enough to consume my little profit, as my store is small, no market, probably $500.00 stock and so I continue to drop behind in my wholesale accounts.

I was figuring this morning and my obligations were $150.00[,] my assets counting cash and sound accounts about $60.00. So I went after doubtful money. long overdue. Out of over $25.00 owing me by the customers I called in I secured $1.00. My young daughter stayed in the store. She wanted to wash, and one place I went the lady (?) was sending out her wash. One child she had half grown and she, plenty strong enough to be continually on the go. There should be a law to force people to pay just and honest debts, instead of buying cars, and gasoline, and radios, and beauty treatments, and glad rags[,] while the people they owe have neither cars, radio, or clothes, and only by the honesty of a few do they have enough to eat. and when they can no longer run a store they can camp on someone's door step that will let them and be buried by charity, when they die. It isn't fair. I work 16 hours in my store. Rev. J. T. Boone my pastor asked me how many hours? and I said 16 in the store an hour for personal duties 2 hrs for cleaning etc; one for meals. And what bothers me he said is "what on earth you do with the other four?"

[signed] Mrs. Elsie Alvis, member, Retail Groc. Association (N.R.A.)[24]

Fraternal organizations such as the Masons offered their members life insurance and burial benefits. In an age before the widespread availability of life insurance, poor and working-class families considered the death benefits of the fraternal orders critical to their families' financial well-being. Individuals often had memberships in several different orders, each offering small insurance policies.

Mrs. Victoria Cauthen (Hollywood) to Sholtz, 30 August 1933

Mrs. E. A. Hickson of Gainesville, Fl, Chairman of the U.D.C. Brigade No.3 asked me to write you concerning the <u>appointment of a custodian or care keeper of the Confederate Memorial at Ellentown, Fla.</u> She said the present custodian was a northern person and the U.D.C. want a southern woman for the place and she thought I had the personality to suit the place.

I was born in Lancaster Co., S.C. in 1876 and came to Suwannee Co. Fla, in 1882. I commenced teaching in Suwannee Co. in 1895 and have taught two hundred seventy-eight months in this state. <u>What is the appropriation for taking care of the memorial?</u>

If there will be an opening for a new keeper please consider me an applicant for the place. I am a widow and have no position at present.

Refer to Mr. James A. Lewis Mayor of Hollywood Fla; County Supt. Charles M. Fisher Miami, Fla; Supt. W. T. Newsome, Live Oak, Fla; Mrs. J. R. Klepper Hollywood, Fla.

Thanking you for anything you can do for me and hoping to hear from you at your earliest convenience.[25]

UDC is the United Daughters of the Confederacy.

Mrs. Peter Lanzl (Venus) to Sholtz, 23 September 1933

we could not pay our taxes this year. My husban hasent ben very well for the last three years[.] he is not able now to work at any work[.] he is 69 years old to so expect we will have to lose our home. if you cant help us to save our home seems like he is gitting to old to have to loose our home[.] so please see if you cant keep our home from bing sold for taxes. it has ben mitey hard going for us[.] we have our daughter and her three children to take care of[.] we git a little relefe money but the eats runs mity short at times so do the cloths to. My husban and my self and all so my daughter needs cloths and no way to git them.

Now Governor Sholtz will you pese save our home for us. We live in Glads [Glades] but we git our mail at Venus.[26]

Mrs. William N. Goodman, Miami, to Sholtz, 9 October 1933

This letter is to say that, owing to our inability to pay our poll tax, we are <u>very</u> much disappointed not to be able to vote to-morrow on repeal and other issues coming up for election. We took great interest in these issues, but when it was necessary to pay out $4.00 for poll taxes for me husband and myself, we simply could not spare it. Now, we are in comparatively comfortable circumstances. Own our home, do not want for the necessities of life, but like many others, our income, (which is not steady) will not permit $4.00 for poll taxes. We have three children, and had just spent over that amount on school books and supplies / another expense I do not see is fair in view of the county taxes we pay. I could give many reasons as to why we or any other family in our circumstances cannot pay poll taxes. We are told by those politically and patriotic-minded that we are under obligation to vote on vital issues, and they continually complain about our indifference. But I wish I could give you some idea as to the humiliation, defeat, and isolation we feel as election is coming on and we cannot vote.

And while we are on this subject, I would like to add that I think (and so do others) that voting should be made not only easier, but less complicated, so that the average person does not have such a confused, and apprehensive feeling upon going to the polls and casting the vote. From what I can gather, the ballot to-morrow looks about like a crossword puzzle. Only a politician would know how to mark on such a ballot. We are too busy trying to earn our bread and butter to study sixty or seventy politicians to cast a vote for a simple straight forward question like repeal. My mother goes tomorrow to vote for repeal. She is sixty eight years of age and does not have to pay poll taxes. But how can she handle a ballot like that? And yet I am told that if it is not marked correctly the ballot is thrown out. Just because she does not know about all those petty politicians is not to say that she does not fully realize the importance of repeal.

We also were going to vote for repeal. But this county will never attain the strength and unity it hopes to, till all our laws are simplified and made secure from selfish personal interests.[27]

"Repeal" here refers to the effort to repeal the 18th Amendment, which established national prohibition. Florida ratified the 21st Amendment, abolishing prohibition, on 14 November 1933.

Mrs. Mary Porter (Miami Beach) to Sholtz, 5 November 1933

1930 census: She is 68 years old, a white widow, and working as a live-in housekeeper.

as I am trying every chance that may prove successful to me to secure funds to build me a house for a home on 2 acres of land I have in Jefferson county Florida near the town of Monticello. I am going to write and ask you if there is any chance through the farm loan or any other thing provided by the Government or State. I lost every-thing I ever saved in Miami. As I could not save my home here on account of a big mortgage. However it is the result of the loss of all my earnings in life. And when I was able to work. I am at present working as maid in this hotel. And I have one daughter—other than that I am alone. I was born and raised in Madison county Fla. if I can secure enough money to buy the material needed I want to build me a Home and go back on the farm[.] I can earn my living gardening and chickens and I can pay this money back in small payments for I am sure I want be able to do the work I now do for much longer. Please do something for me if its only small. I will be so thankful for your help as for any sugestion

Very kindly thanking you for any help.[28]

Miss Oretha Murphey (Lakeland) to Sholtz, 9 November 1933

I realize you have a lot of worries etc. and I hate to bother you, but my parents, sister, and I are in such a condition something has got to be done regardless who it worries.

We have always lived an honest life & paid our debts, taxes etc. until now. My father is 65 years old & can not find work enough for us to live. He had a little work but hasn't now hoeing Orange trees at 3c per tree. He managed to buy our groceries (by skimping) with that. My sister works here in a Restaurant that use to pay her as much as $25.00 per week but now does not pay her enough to buy clothing with. I use to work in a Restaurant but as times grew dull was laid off. My sister & I have always helped Papa pay taxes and gave he & mama money too. Now we can't help our selves & Mama got sick & we got in debt $400.00 of which we can not pay. I have faithfully tried to get work with out avail. The failure of the 1st National Bank helped to put us in this condition, as we had skimped & did without clothing like other girls wear to save a few dollars. Now we are without money & clothes, & can not get work & do not have the proper food. You people that have an income just don't realize how hard it is on we unfortunate ones. The favor I am asking you is this: We own our home & a vacant lot adjoining it in a desirable residential section of the city. The paving is paid in full. Our taxes are paid up until now and there are no mortgages. I wonder if you would help us by buying our vacant lot at a reasonable price of $900.00 We have more than nine hundred dollars in it but will sacrifice to get out of debt. If you would like to buy home & all we would sell it very reasonable too.

Our home is a seven room two story frame house, with large screened porch. Is comfortably & substancialy built throughout. This is a good buy and surely is worth your time to come & investigate. I don't want something for nothing & don't want to get through this life dishonest but we surely need help now & if you consider helping us let me know as soon as conveni- ent. Come & look this property over.

P.S. This property is located at 205 west Belmar St. Lakeland Fla.[29]

Mrs. E. C. Scott (Lee) to Sholtz, 28 November 1933

Am writing you to know if you could issue me any State Peddling licenses. With[out] any funds.

As I'm a widow have three children ages 1-5-8 yrs whom are wholy de- pending on me for a living, and a mother[,] one sister[,] one brother who is partly depending on me. Mother unable to work, and very feeble. brother too small to work. and sister is sickly.

I have taught school 1 yr. but under the new laws of Fla. I cant teach any more as I have no college training.

My husband supported us all while he was with us. But he got injured in an auto wreck and passed away five days later. and Funeral, hospital, and operation expenses taken the $1000 insurance he carried.

My children and I had to come to live with my mother on a farm but the farm is not large enough to support us all without some other help.

I've tried to get along without asking this favor of you. But seems like everything goes wrong.

So winter is knocking at our door and we have no winter clothing.

My sister is working on the Relief Force but that only keeps us in gro- ceries. Mother underwent an opration in St. Vincent's Hospital July 8 in Jacksonville, Fla. and we owe over $250.00 to the Dr's. that did the opration. besides our grocery bill and medicine bill.

I tried to get work on the relief but they said I could not work because I lived in the house with my mother and my sister working. My mother's house and farming fence needs to be repaired very badly. and if some one don't get some way of helping my sister work will go down soon.

Hoping you can grant me this favor which will not only be appreciated by myself but by all. And will thank you for your kindness. Many times over.[30]

Mrs. G. L. Anderson (Leesburg) to Sholtz, 4 December 1933

Some time ago I wrote to Justice of Peace (Sam Shiver) in Orlando, about a matter which was of great importance to my family, sending him stamped self addressed envelopes the second time, and never have received any reply.

I went personally to Judge Tally of Taveres, and his advice was for me to take the matter up with the Judge of Orange County, and I have written to him, but have not had a reply as yet.

We have had my husband's aged father with us for almost 2 yrs. He is not only feeble in body, but in mind also, very cross and hard to get along with. We have 4 (four) children, making 6 in our immediate family. And as my husband works for the Gov. it is needless for me to explain the cuts in salary he has had during the past year. However I might explain, that under the circumstances we were forced to give up our home and we now pay rent. It has been very hard indeed for us to live the past year.

Now, my husband has another brother that we feel should do something towards supporting the father, especially so, when his family consists of just a wife and one small adopted daughter.

Almost two years ago, the father gave up his work and came to Leesburg to have the two sons take care of him. Immediatly Joe (the other brother) moved to Orlando to keep from doing any-thing for the father. Since that time times have gotten worse with us, and Joe has not contributed any-thing towards helping the father, been to see him, or as much as written to him.

On or by the first of the year we shall have to make a change, and we are planning on trying to run a boarding or rooming house, and something must be done about the old Gentleman before that time. As it now is we are not only tied down at home unable to go any place, but we are not financially able to do every-thing for him, at present he needs fuel, more bed covers, and warmer clothing. While we furnish him rooms to live in and his three meals daily, we feel that we can-not do more.

Will you please investigate this for us and if you think it best, take the matter up with Mr. Shiver also the County Judge both of Orlando, and see what can be done, and at once. We wish to know whether or not Joe can be forced to take the father and take care of him for as long as we have or see that he is cared for else-where.

We stand ready and willing to do our part, but do not feel that it is fair that we do it all under the circumstances, and we do not wish to send the Old Gentleman to a home for the adged, if it can be avoided. I shall greatly appreciate anything you are able to do for us, and shall expect an early reply.[31]

Mrs. Ava Crews (Venus) to Eleanor Roosevelt (ER), 30 December 1933

As you have sympathy for people who are in need caused by the depression, I am asking a favor of you and hope you will not turn it down.

All the previous years we have been able to sell our oranges and tangerines but this year we have been unable to sell them.

51

I have about a thousand bushels in all and would be glad of.50 cents per bushel for them.

Could you buy them with relief money and have them sent to people that are being helped by the relief funds? Those employed by the relief could pick them and save that expense.

They could be shipped in bu[shel] baskets.

If you will kindly do this it would help me and my family and would those needing the fruit also would put that much more money in circulation though the amount is small.

If you would consider this please do so at once so I will know I can depend on it.

Reply from secretary dated 11 January explains that ER "does not handle the relief money that is allotted by Congress to the different agencies designated by the President, and she has no money to spend personally for relief purposes."[32]

Mrs. Margaretha Doyle (Lake Worth) to ER, 20 December 1933

1930 census: Listed as Margareta, she is 52 years old and the wife of Albert, who works as a laborer on a truck farm.

Hope and Pray, you will not class me as being very rude, very forward by asking this request. I am a cripple, hurt in an Auto accident on Feb.28th 1931 and it left me on crutches.

Was suffering great pain and in misery caused by my teeth, that on July 1st 1933, the Palm Beach Welfare Society of West Palm Beach, Fla., through Mrs. John Foltz, had all my teeth extracted, my condition has improved, but I fail to receive the required nourishment without teeth. The Dentist asks $135.00 for a set of teeth that he guarantees to give permanent service without any fault or change.

My hearing is impaired, there is a new devise that they allowed me to test and I can hear a whisper, the cost for both ears is $75.00 at reduced rate. What a God-sent Blessing it would be, if I could receive the needed help. Have a Typewriter and thus be able to gain my livelihood, but as I am, I am handicapped and the Welfare has no funds to grant my needs, so I could help myself.

Dear Madam Pres. perhaps you can advice me in what way or manner, I may obtain the needed help.[33]

Mrs. Virginia Clements (Jacksonville) to ER, 7 January 1934

Pardon me for troubling you. I guess you remember me writeing you once before this. I was in trouble about looseing my little home. I had a loan on it and asked you to help me out, so I guess I have lost it.

I hate to be so persistent and ask for your help again when I was refused. Just two old people 72 yrs old and no way to help ourselves. Mr. Clements has been paralized since last May cant talk or walk. I cant begin to tell you the worry and trouble I have had; just how I have stood up under it I cant tell.

I left Macon[.] a friend paid our way to Jacksonville, Fla thinking it would help Mr. Clements. The Goverment is helping so many things cant you get some help for me? $10.00 or $15.00 per week would be wonderful to help me pay rent and get a little something to eat, or any thing that you are willing to give me would certainly be appreciated. I owe a big Dr's bill nothing to pay with. If you could know what I have gone through with I believe you would help me. If you would help me every week or once a month. If you send anything dont make it public. I am poor but proud. I have seen better days.

Hope this wont fall on deaf ears.[34]

Mrs. J. W. Hicks (Jacksonville) to ER, 14 January 1934

I will drop you a few lines in Regards to the old age pension[.] I am 70 and my Husband is 80[.] if you can help us in that way we would sure be proud of it.[35]

Mrs. Aline M Kraft (St. Petersburg) to ER, 21 January 1934

The kind note of recommendation that you so gracefuly send me, last spring, has been a great help, to my Daughter, to get a position for which we are both most sincerely greatful to you.

May God Bless you and Strenght you, and our Beloved President, and 1934, be the best you ever know.[36]

Mrs. Vivian G. Chavis (Jacksonville) to ER, 22 January 1934

1930 census: She is 26 years old, African American, and a teacher in the public schools. Her husband, Joe, is a hotel waiter.

I your humble subject am asking pardon for taking this opportunity to write you a letter. I have read of all the wonderful things you have done for us, you are the only one I mean First Lady of the Land to show your regards to the poor.

It is our greatest Blessing during this time to have your honorable Husband as our President, if it were not for him we the poor people would not have a chance at partial living.

My Dear Mrs. Roosevelt, I am asking you would you personally notice the contents of my letter and give me your advice. I am a school teacher in the public school in Jacksonville Fla. School #104 Duval Co. My salary is $50. per month[.] I am the mother of a son 14 years old in the 9B grade, a boy scout, and is a member of the boys patrol. I have a nephew 6 years old[,] rent to pay, insurances to keep up and I am attending a college in a nearby city St. Augustine Fla. I have to have a graduate State certificate before July 1935 or else I will not be able to continue to work in this state[.] I am in debt of $300.

My salary does not come near to keeping up my expenses. I was sure you would advise me if there is a government fund that a teacher can borrow money and have a reasonable time to pay it back. We can borrow money here but not enough to get out of debt and length of time to pay back. I have read so many, so many things that you have done so in confidence I am writing you. I read in the papers if people were in vital distress to write the president or some one in Washington.

I hope Mrs. Roosevelt, you will be able to help me as I do want to complete my course so I will be able to continue to teach as I do love my work.

I will thank you for what ever you may do to help me and I will assure you it will be appreciated to the highest. Thank you for even reading this letter[.] please let me have a reply soon.[37]

Mrs. L. E. Parrish (Bradenton) to ER, 22 January 1934

1930 census: Ida is 48 years old and white, and she works as a stenographer for the city of Bradenton. Her husband is a conductor on a steam railroad. Their daughter is 14.

I realize you are constantly getting all kinds of letters from all kinds of cranks, but when we write you we do not feel that we are included among the cranks, but that we are appealing to a personal friend.

I am not seeking for newspaper publicity, as I should be very much embarrassed if anyone should know that I am in a position to appeal for help, and I can assure you if you should see fit to come to my assistance in anyway nobody would ever be the wiser, and the newspapers would never get hold of it to make capital out of it.

I have a daughter ready for college, but owing to the financial depression of the past several years my husband has been out of work practically all the time, and I myself only receive $75.00 per month as stenographer, so you can see that I have very little to pay out on college expenses. My husband is a railroad man, and is cut off all but about one or two months each year in the winter season; but he was unable to secure any help from the present federal relief works going on account of me being employed.

Now my proposition to you is as follows:

I have an old fashioned diamond brooch—having five pendant diamonds —which has been valued at approximately $250.00; also a ½ carat diamond ring worth $175.00. I have found a good college in the West where $500.00 will pay this girl's tuition and most of her expenses for two years by working for part of her expenses. What I am asking and petitioning of you is— Won't you give me $400.00 for these two pieces of jewelry in order to enable me to give this child two years in college. Of course I know that you probably have more jewelry now than you want or need; but the pin is really a pretty thing. I don't want charity and am not asking charity.

You probably will ask why I don't sell this jewelry to some one here, but I do not want anyone to know that I have to sell it, and then there is no one down here that is financially able to buy it. Should anyone down here want it they would want me to sell it to them, both pieces, at such a fearfully low price that I would not be justified in selling it.

This daughter that I write of is not my own child, but is an adopted, but I desire to give her just as good as if she were my own child. She is only 18 years of age and wants to take nurse's training in a hospital, but the heads of the hospitals write me that she should be 19 or 20 years of age before entering, and that if she can have two years in a college on a B.S. degree that she will be better fitted for hospital work and gain higher positions in the profession.

[P.S.] In my morning devotions when I pray for the President of the United States I always think individually of him by name.[38]

Mrs. Joseph Fleeschman (Tampa) to ER, 24 January 1934

1930 census: Listed as "Fleischman," Alma is 36 years old with five children at home. Her husband is the proprietor of a men's clothing store. The family is white.

Pardon the liberty I am taking in writing you but I am seeking some information and I know, dear "Lady" that I can rely on you just as the multitudes are relying on your honorable husband. I am one of the many unfortunates who lost my home and business and bank account during the Hoover Administration. Was in business in the same location here for eighteen years. After the banks closed here, I borrowed money on my home to try and save the business and in 1930 lost them both. Now what I want to know is this: Is there any way I can borrow enough money from the government to buy a small home and let them take a mortgage on same as one can purchase wonderful values to-day in Florida. You see the government would be secured as they would have a mortgage on the house for the full amount. I can purchase a home to-day in Tampa for $3,500.00 which was originally built during the boom for $10,000. There any number of them. I have six children and I would love to own my own home once again. I can give you the best of references of character and standing and would thank you so much to investigate this for me.[39]

Telegram from Mrs. B. O. Ramsey (Miami) to ER, 24 January 1934

Disregard letter sent you today by air mail. Husband got painting job thru influence of friends this P.M. Anything said might cause him to lose job. Sincerely and thank you.[40]

Mrs. Carl C Bennett (Miami) to Sholtz, 26 January 1934

Please afford me the courtesy of reading this letter through. I know you are a very busy man and this is a desperate measure I am taking but I feel the circumstances warrant it.

Have read your speech "Real Opportunities and Possibilities in Florida" and want to cite you a case.

My husband and I felt the same as you about it, so we invested all our cash in a [licence] tag for the past seven years and now I am begging you to pull the strings to get us a permit to drive our car for 60 or at least thirty days, we can't possibly buy a tag and our chances to get work will be 100 % better if we can use the car. My husband is trying to get a sales-man job and he can't do any-thing without the car.

Won't you please help us as we really are deserving and I have tried to show you that we are not trying to do any-thing in the world but ask you to please help us help ourselves. It is not as if I were asking for money, it would be so easy for you and it business, thinking if we tried hard we would have a living income for the future[.] We have not been able to make expenses although we have done our very best, now we are faced with the problem of trying to sell out and get a job.

My husband cannot do just any work as he is a disabled veteran of Foreign Wars (file#c-1106818) for which he receives the munificent remuneration of $14.85 which we are sincerely grateful for, but could be more grateful for more, he never asked for any compensation at all until uncle Sam refused him a job on account of physical disability in 1928.

We are well born, 100 % American citizens, honorable and respectable, we do not want charity. We are anxious to grasp some of the "opportunities," but don't know how, it seems.

We have lived in Miami over eight years and to prove that we are really respectable ask Wayne Allen, assistant to Fred Pine, he lived in the same town I did before we ever came to Miami, ask Mr. Shively an associate of the firm Hollywood, Inc., my husband worked for him.

Until one of us gets work we will have to eat on the $14.85, of course we won't eat much but we don't mind that, our land lord will trust us as we have paid rent here for over a year.

We have paid $17.50 for an automobile[.] would mean a new lease on life for us.

My husband does not know I am writing this[,] he would say you wouldn't even read it, but I believe in leaving no stone unturned to accomplish your purpose, even if you refuse me I shall have the satisfaction of knowing I did my utmost. You will never know the desolation of losing your savings just when you thought you had a real future, and struggling all the while.

I can't go home and leave my husband to fight alone, he needs me to keep up his morale, his clothes and his health by feeding him healthful if cheap foods.[41]

The state used car tags as a revenue measure, which caused considerable public dissatisfaction during the Depression years.

Mrs. J. A. Suggs (Newberry) to Sholtz, 29 January 1934

1930 census: This is probably Genera Suggs. Her husband, James, is 54 years old and a farm operator. Genera, 55, does not work. They are white.

I am writing you to see if I can draw a little pension, for I am cripple and have been for twenty two years. With sore legs not able to work any at all. I have three little girl children. I am sending two of them to school. Trying to gieve them a little education, and I need help very bad. I am down most of my time and cant walk a bit. My home doctor here says he cannot cure my legs. I have been to several others and they say that they cannot cure them. If there is any further information you would have to have I can get up the names of town people you if you need them. I am 58 years old. Please let me know by return mail what you will do. I am very poor. Thanking you for your kindness.[42]

Miss Margaret Huggins (Bradenton) to ER, 1 February 1934

I do not wish to be classed as a "sob sister," but since 1925 I have tried to get a college education and succeeded in getting a little over three years of college and normal work. I prepared myself to teach and this is my first year. My salary is $40.00 a month and having an eight months term, after May 4, I will be without work. The outlook for next year in the teaching profession is gloomy.

. . . Last summer I directed games and contests for the 4-H Club girls camp and also the camp for the Home Demonstration Women in Baldwin County, Alabama.

I am twenty-five years old, five feet-four inches tall, and weigh one hundred twenty-seven pounds.

I sing and read.

I wonder if you intend having camps this summer. If so, will there be any place at all into which I would fit.

It would make me very happy to know that I would have something to do after May 4. Brothers don't like keeping younger sisters all [the] time.[43]

"Normal" schools were the general name for teachers' colleges.

Mrs. Emily Smyre (Miami) to ER, 7 February 1934

1930 census: She is a 62-year-old white widow, living with her brother, a laborer in a dairy.

My father fought all through the Civil War. men in with first [drill?] helping to fight one of the last Battles. his name is Samuel Mcleason. he was a good solder never was in and [any] trouble never home to see his mother, only one or 2 times. My great grandfather Samuel Carr[?] fought in the Revolutionary war. I Emily Smyre am Daughter and grand Daughter of thise good and nobel soldiers. I Emily Mcleason Smyre, I am old and not able to work, no childring no husband to work for me no income in the world. Please help me to get the old age pension so I can live. I am 69 and not strong never in my life[.] my husband is dead, and he did not leave me one cent. I saw in Miami Herald where you are in favor of helping the poor old people, and thank god that I voted for Mr Roosevelte God bless him and you. I am old a widow living in Miami Florida because I am too poor to get back to my home land in western NC Ashville. I have worke hard all my life have been standing over a sick brother, try to work for him and [illegible]. My life is so sad and lonely[.] 2 lovely babey die [illegible] my husband he die in 1895. I have worked untill I cant work no more. Please get me the old age pension.[44]

Mrs. Maude Lewis (Miami) to Sholtz, 9 February 1934

I am writting you for instructions & help as I no that you are in position to do so. first I must congratulate you for the good thing that you are during for the people of our state. Thank God for such a Gov. I am a colored woman with eight children, my husband left here about four months ago to try to find work. A man here taken him at a certain place[.] the man came back & is still here & my husband havent yet been heard from[.] We have been married twenty nine years & have not had any trouble[.] My husband put a deal of wood in this man place[.] the man told him he would not be able to pay him until he sold the wood. I dont no what to do of course he could have deserted us but I dont believe so. this man said he taken my husband about 80 miles to a saw mill, but I am told that he is not there. I havent been no where to look[.] I dont have means to do with. I dont have work sufficent to support the family[.] one of my girls got 3 days every two or three weeks sewing. I cant keep up my rent. I do want to do what is right. Please advise me best.[45]

Mrs. Mozell Sears (Lake Wales) to ER, 9 February 1934

I guess you will think this letter is like a storry book but it isn't[.] it is true[.] I know you do not know there is one on Earth as I but nevertheless I have seen your photo in the papers so much and looked at your pleasent face so much I desided to have a little talk with you as I feel that maby you could help me just a little. About 16 teen years ago my husband died and I had 5 little children and the Red Cross woman in Jesup Ga where I lived she kept after me untill I let her send 4 of my children to the Atlanta Ga Children home Society and there they adopted the 2 little girls[.] the oldest girl come to me and my boy he is now married so I know where both of them are but the 2 that are adopted the home wont tel me a thing about them[.] I have wrote several times and asked them and they say that they do not know about them and that they have no rite to even inquire about them[.]

the oldest is 22 years old the 5th of next August and the other one will be 19 teen the 12th day of Sept— I want to see if you could help me locate them[.] I think it is quite unfair to Punish a Poor mother as they have me. I would of tried to have found them but I am Poor I havent the money to seek for them and I got the thinking that maby you could help me in some way[.] I hope this wont be a Burdon to you eny[.] May the loving God of heaven have been wounderful good to me all these years to keep my heart from Breaking[.] I hope if you can not help me eny way that you will write me a line eny way[.]

I hope to hear from you some time soon[.] will thank you so much[.][46]

Mrs. Nancy Thomas (Brooker) to Sholtz, 11 February 1934

Just—a few lines I feel that—I know that—you are doing your—part toward the Justice of the aged people while our officers here in Alachua County say the compensation wont go to any under 70 years of age[.] if I live untill September 14th of this year in 1934, I will be 70 years old. has been a widdow 8 years. has ben disabled to work since April of last year 1936. Need Dr's care but so destitute cant afford it. Also have two orphan—children one has neather father or mother. A little girl. The other a boy near three year old its dady diserted its mother before it was born it and its mother is here with me and her health also is very bad[.] I have six children living or course but none able to own a home. Its about all they can do to look after their own family's. If I could get a little pension to help these little children along and buy medicine for my self. I apreciate the help that you have already ben to our counties and I.m quite sure you will still be more help[.] may the Lord Bless you in all your endeavors.[47]

Mrs. Elizabeth Lucas Bacon, Colored Children's Home, Nursery, Kindergarten and Community Mission (Jacksonville) to ER, 1 March 1934

Your very pleasing answer to my letter in which I wrote you concerning my work as Supervisor of the Colored Children's was happily received.

In reference to your wonderful husband, our great leader, I am happy to tell you that while the world was celebrating his birth day my little family of orphans and dependents were praying for the health and safety of you all.

In these awful days of depression we are still cheerful though we have lost our little home which was built with the money that my late husband received from the veteran's bureau. We had been promised ten years to pay for our home but were forced out of it with no consideration.

We have now in our possession the contract to a piece of property with an indebtedness of $300. We are anxious to secure this property for our Mission Work and would love to have our building dedicated as a Memorial to you, who are doing so much for the distressed of this world.

Our children would be happy to come to Washington to sing for their "First Lady" if it were possible.

In closing, I am praying that you may find it in your heart to give some consideration to the work which we are struggling to foster for our poor people.

May I hear from you soon?[48]

Mrs. J. W. Haudenschild (Greenacres City) to ER, 12 March 1934

1930 census: Carrie is 33 years old. Her husband, John, is a truck driver for a water company. They have a boy and a girl. The family is white.

Dear friend, If I may call you so. I am comming to you with a rather funny thing mabey to ask but I thought since you have done so many wonderful things you could help us.

My husband has been out of work for some time, but not soon enough to register when required by N.R.A. but we have our home here all paid for and have tried to hard to sell it, but the real estate market here is filled with homes for sale.

We have a nice little 5 room stucco Spanish type home with 3 50x135 ft lots with some fruit, & lots of shrubbery completely furnished. We would like to sell and put our money in a small fruit & poultry farm in Maryland or Virginia where we can help ourselves and our 3 children.

I thought probably you would know of someone who would be interested in this place. We are only 7 miles from the Palm Beaches, 4 miles to the ocean, & 3 miles to city of Lake Worth.

P.S. My husband is a carpenter, & probably could get work in most any northern city in the spring. And I am so homesick. I don't like it here & him out of work sure doesn't help any.

I was born & raised in Ohio & so was my husband & it seems the hills are calling.

Please try & sell it for us if you can, and I sure will bless you.[49]

Miss Doris Isabel Eddy (Miami Beach) to Malvina Schneider [secretary to ER], 24 March 1934

I have been watching with great interest Mrs. Roosevelt's various activities and it has been suggested to me that there might be some place for a person like myself who is interested primarily in the social aspects of the many constructive enterprises she is so generously undertaking.

I am driving North the first week in April and I would deeply appreciate the opportunity of discussing this matter with you if you would give me permission to make an appointment with you when I reach Washington. I am free to go any place where a worker might be needed and I would be satisfied, in a financial way, with just enough to take care of my expenses if the work was of the Social service type.[50]

Mrs. Mary E. Nodin (Ybor City Tampa) to ER [undated, but reply dated 2 April 1934

1930 census, indexed "Nodine": She is 73 years old, living with her daughter and son-in-law. He works as a boilermaker on a railroad. They are white.

I have sen in many papers the good you have don among the poor. I am not asking charity[.] I am 78 years Old[.] i can still croshet bed spreads they are made of the best cotton thread[.] I have sold them before the Depression for 40 Dol[.] i have two on hand the pattern is the dubald arrow one is white and one pink fast collar[.] if you could rekemend some body that could aford to buy them[.] I put one hundart and 2 Dol in the Ybor City bank[.] that bank closed and i have no money now[.] I have sold many spreads during good times[.] I can not sell any now the people have no money to buy spreads[.] If you are not to busy and could do me that favor i sure apreciate your kindness.[51]

Mrs. Lizzie Peters (Graceville) to Sholtz, 17 April 1934

1930 census: She is 43 years old, white, and the wife of a farmer.

I have a husband and he is so mean to me and my kids[.] I wish you would give him a job[.] he gets drunk and wastes ever thang we make[.] gits drunk and trys to shoots us and trys to cut us with his knife and has run off ever one of my kids But t[w]o. and I have to tried to part from him and he want leave and he said he was not going to buy us nothan [at] all to eat or ware or if one of us was to die he would not put us away. He is a stap-father to my kids and I have no kids by him

His name is L. B. Peters[.] I am praying and hoping you will do something with him soon.[52]

Miss Josephine Longo (Tampa) to Franklin D. Roosevelt (FDR) and ER, 21 April 1934

I am a contestant in a closely contested circulation drive being conducted by The Tampa Daily Times, our popular evening daily newspaper. The Times is giving away seven 1934 Sedans to the seven highest winners at the close of the contest, Sat. April 28th. There is a Buick, a Dodge, a Studebaker, two Chevrolets, a Plymouth, and a V-8 Ford.

I am working hard and would love very much to win one of these valuable prizes which I can readily turn into cash. At present, sixty contestants are in the race, and all working like Trojans to win. It is really a close race.

I graduated with honors at Hillsborough high school in Tampa at the close of the mid-term last January. I was also elected Jan. 12th the prettiest girl at Hillsborough. Jan. 20th, I was elected by popular acclamation, Queen of the Air at an Aviation Pageant and Celebration in Tampa. On Feb. 10th, I was elected Miss Latin America from among entries representing the entire Latin population of Tampa which is approximately 49% of the total population of our City of 110,000 inhabitants.

My paramount ambition is to always bring Honor, Glory, and Prestige in any and every way I possibly can to Our City, Our State, and Our Nation. My Father has been an employee of The Metropolitan Life Insurance Co. in Tampa for the past seven years, and is a loyal and active Democrat.

I sincerely feel that apart from any personal interest that may motivate a desire on your part to help me win one of these handsome and valuable awards, you will also find that a subscription to the Times a worthwhile investment in itself. The Times is a big newspaper of Florida, and has been, and is a loyal supporter of Our present National Administration, and all of Our Presidents policies of economic recovery and reconstruction.

Each subscription gives me so many votes, and the cars are awarded to the winners having the seven highest vote scores on April 28th, one week from today. The subscription rate is 2 years $15.60 giving me 280.000 votes; 1 year $7.80 giving me 135.000 votes, 6 months $4.00 giving me 65.000 votes.

Words cannot express how deeply gratefull i shall always feel for a subscription from you, and if you feel that you want to help me win one of these valuable prizes, kindly send me your check or money order by return mail made out to the Tampa Daily Times, or to myself for a subscription to The Tampa Daily times. I will be so happy if YOU will help me win.[53]

Mrs. Edgar Barber (Miami) to ER, 7 May 1934

I want to write you a few words regarding the Old folkses pension. I do so much wish that my poor old husband were getting a little money each month to buy the necessities of life to keep us in a little comfort the few more years the Lord has allotted to us. Too old and weak to earn anything now. And I am an invalid from heart trouble. We each have a son but neither can spare us anything at all at this time. We are living [on?] a few dollars we had from the sale of our little home[,] not many left now. Oct. 18th I'll be 80 years old. There isnt any body wants to aid us. All selfish. I wish you would talk up for the pension please.

Standard reply, dated 12 May, signed by "secretary to Mrs. Roosevelt"

Mrs. Roosevelt has asked me to acknowledge your letter and to thank you for writing her.

She has always felt that some provision should be made to take care of those who have worked hard during their lives, and through circumstances over which they have no control find themselves in need in their old age. She has endeavored to do what she could toward attaining this goal, and hopes that the day is not far distant when the problem will be satisfactorily solved.

At the present time, many of the States have enacted Old Age Pension legislation, and those who live in such States are able to obtain the benefits allowed them by applying to the State officials.[54]

Mrs. Flora A. White (Columbus, Ohio) to Sholtz, 8 May 1934

1930 census: She is a 57-year-old white widow, living with her 78-year-old mother in Orlando. She does not work.

I would like to ask you if there is any appropriation ever been made for Policemans wife's in Fla. In 1917 my husband was killed in Hillard Fla. while on duty. I have <u>never</u> got anything and I sure have had a hard time. I only live around for my "keep" and sometimes not as <u>good.</u> I am 57 years old an of course I not in position to get a job that would pay me <u>much.</u> Please let me know about the above. As I feel I should be intitled to <u>something.</u>

[P.S.] I have lived in Orlando, Fla. ever since 1917. except for a few weeks when here. In summer.[55]

Mrs. Sam J. Wolf (St. Augustine) to ER [undated but reply from secretary dated 9 May 1934

I am writing you to get some information as a possible way of disposeing a valuable heirloom which has been handed down to me through three generations of my family the last one haveing it was my dear Mother gave it to me and I regret very much to loose it but my husband has been out of work so long and I now have my daughter and grandson to take [care] off and I am trying to help the later to finish his education.

The articles consist of a very handsome Old Spanish style fan made of mother of pearl in laid with gold and hand painted and the necklace is of gold and black onyx stones.

As regards to value I would not put on the fan as it is over one hundred year's old and experts have said it has a great value, and the chain has been valued at thirty-five or more so after you seeing them you could get a real value as to their worth. I would not send them to any one else, but seeing so much in the paper's of your goodness trying to help people in these trying times, I thought I would write you. I am not asking you to give me any thing, but in your position in life you may be able to assist me in the object. I have in view to prepare my grandson for the battle of life. he is now seventeen.

If satisfactory to you on recept of your reply, I will send them to you registered.[56]

Mrs. Alma Daniels (Stuart) to Sholtz, 11 May 1934

I am writing you in regards to Mothers Pensions in this state and to explain something to you and for some advice.

(3) Three years ago in Feb I became a widow by Death and the County Board Promised me a Mothers Pension of $45.00 a month and for a year they give me $10.00 a week and then turned my case over to the Wellfare and for a time give me orders to different stores in town[.] some times the order would amount to from $2.00 to $6.00 dollars a week and then my case went to the Fedrel Releaf and they cut me to $3.00 a week and I could not buy food

and clothes for 5 on $3.00 per week. So I got a job keeping house for a man out of town and now they are giving me trouble about it wanting to take my children and put them in a home. Will you please advise me to weather they can do any thing or not. We have plenty of food and clothes and dont have to ask the welfare for help. And the children are in school. Waiting for a quick reply.[57]

Mrs. M. A. Johnson (Williston) to Sholtz, 11 May 1934

I will take pleasure in honoring you with a letter, and want to explain to you how the work are going on here of the F.E.R.A. to see if you can explain to me how they are to manage. The F.E.R.A. work in Leavy County Said State of Florida. The questions I want to ask you is this Why the mens that does the heard labor that actual needs it and havent got nothing to look to but their labor for a liveing is cut down to only 12 hrs per week. Which only means $3.60 per week for him & family to live on Pay Doctor Bills & but clothes regardless to how many in the family and the office peoples Graftes gets paid for 6 days ever week. for it looks Reasonable that the mens only gets $3.60 per week and have to pay Buss fair out of that. It looks like the offices peoples could do their work in 12 hrs and only get paid for 12 hrs for I am the mother of four childrens. See if you think you could if you was the Husband of a wife and farther of four childrens live on that per week. and take care of drugs bills and pay Buss fair out of that also and expect these mens to work like fighting fire While they are working for this amount. You see the offices people is getting the money, while the laboring man is sheeding sweat & blood. Would you call this a fair deal as would you call this the peoples in the offices grafting on the laboring mens & government. all those mens that goes on these buss to work is on duty at least 12 hrs per day. Which to make the thing look right and even he is on duty from the time he is on that buss untill he gets back home. for the benefit of that job. which if a man goes on duty & pays his way on his time it looks like he might be allowed to come, in on the buss time, to make it even you see he makes 36 hrs ever other week then he only gets pay for only 24 hrs for 2 weeks which equals 12 hrs per week[.] it makes him 18 hrs per week & only gets pay for 12 hrs. They allow one man on the job at the place they calls Yankee Town to carry a pistol on the job and wear it with a holster. They claim that he has got bonds on it even if he has he could do just as much harm if he gets mad on the job as if he didn't have bonds[.] if you send a Secret service man that no one knows I will Show him this & more. J.W. Whitener supertend his Parents Raised him well enough not to have no respect to the white mens. He nick names the laboring mens & calls them gators & snakes or else he

65

threw his self away sence he left his parents. So please give the poor laboring mens Justs for you are the Judge. you have to give Honor to get Honor. if a supertend cant honor a laboring man as a labor enough to call him by his name like he is a human you know it looks like he is not fit for the job. So I will close with many thanks.

Please hold this letter on file till writes calls for it. Notice. They claims if any of the hands writes in how they are manages this work they would fire them off the job. Regardless, how bad they need this work. Thank you very much for your attention.[58]

Mrs. B. T. Hopkins (Tallahassee) to Sholtz, 23 May 1934

You no doubt in times like these recieve letters from all sorts and conditions of people who hope to attain some end with your help or through some recommendation of yours.

Whether my appeal to you will be of the same nature as many others you recieve I do not know but I do know that you can render a real service in this case and at no risk to your politically, finanacialy, or otherwise.

I am a woman 58 yrs old. I am not able to go out and work, but I know the poultry business. I have a market for all the poultry and eggs I can produce.

I am asking you to help me get a loan of $50 to get started, or some one to put the cash up and I do the work and go 50–50. I am not asking for charity —if I can get started I can pay back all that I borrow.

All I want is a loan or some other help to make the start—it requires a certain amount to pay for chicks, feed and so forth.

G. C. Hodge, County Agent, says that poultry are not farm products and that the Government cannot loan money for poultry production, if they are not farm products, then what are they?

We are on the dole list. I want to get off of it and be self supporting. All we get from the dole is enough food to keep us from starving, there still remains the rent to pay, clothes and other things equally as important.

As you are the head of relief work in Florida, I am appealing to you. Those lower down will not help me. No use to refer this to the local E.R.A. County Agent or other Officials as I done worked at all of those sources without results. It seems as if there should be some way for competant, industrious people who deserve to be self supporting to become so.

If you please Sir do something for me or help me find some one who will help me. It is important that I get started at once.[59]

Mrs. Josephine Sutton (Bluff Springs) to Sholtz, 1 June 1934

1930 census: Mamie Stafford is 64 years old, white, and the wife of Edward, a farm laborer.

I am writing this letter for my mother. She wants me to tell you her condition. She is 69 year old and have a broken hip & arm and have'nt walked any going on 5 years[.] She is in the invalid's chair and has been for and has been for in Aug. 22nd will be for 5 years. And she wants to know if there would be any way of her getting a pension[,] a old age pension or a disability pension[.] I am all the support she has got and I do all I can for her and I have a daughter to support to and the Emergency relief helps us some[.] We get $1.35 a week for us three. I got a sewing card when there was work and we have no shoes or clothes. And if the work dont start up again soon I dont know what will become of our little faimly. And I am in debt now for grocies and Mr. Sholtz will you please write me and let me know about the pension for my mother[.] If we could only get some shoes and clothes because my mother is in need of shoes & her crippled she can wear shoes & Mr. Sholtz I am a voter of this county[.] I helped you out all I could in you election because I thought you was the right man to be our Gov.—so please write me soon and hoping I will hear some good news as we don't never have a dime to spend only a $1.35 order a week.

P.S. My mother's name is Mrs. Mamie Stafford. Excuse the pencil as I have no pen and ink.[60]

Mrs. E. A. Tucker (Hotel Flagler, Jacksonville) to ER, 4 June 1934

I am enclosing a letter to your husband allong with some other letters so that my sons injuries can be verified & if you could help me in any way to get my son in a Hospital my obligations & thanks to you would be for the rest of my life[.] I am allso enclosing a report from our Dr at home that he gave us when they Xrayed him; just a few days after we had one made, they made the second one of him at the [illegible] Lake City Hospital & the Drs there wanted to do some thing for him, but of course they couldn't without an order from those in charge.

Hoping that from the bottom of my heart that you can spare some of your time in trying to get a mother medical treatment for her son.[61]

Mrs. L. D. Glenn (St. Petersburg) to ER, 5 June 1934

I have learned just recently that charity profits by the total receipts from your radio talks at the rate of $500 a minute.

Personally, I am on that list at present, much against my wishes; but a nerve trouble which manifested itself on the skin has made it impossible to appear in public in any line of work for many months until I am dependent on a $3 a week dole for groceries. Have no income. No home of my own, and alone since the War. Will soon be sixty-one, but have the credit of eight years.

Am able bodied, active and keep abreast of the times. Take care of all home duties. Also, have the care of three vacant properties, while owners are north. What savings I had are now exhausted, and nothing in sight. My object in writing you is to ask for a loan of the amount paid you for two minutes broadcasting, or $1000, as recently reported.

This will enable me to reimburse those friends who made it possible to take violet-ray treatments for said trouble and which has greatly improved same. Have made my way out in the world since fifteen, and I find this extremely humiliating, but not inclined to cry over spilled milk, even tho the odds are against me.

None of my relatives, scattered far and wide, are able to more than exist where they are, so I am writing the President also to consider our two hundred acre Neb farm for conservation purposes, as it is not paying the rent, and hardly the taxes, since that awful long drouth has hit it.

Another thing I can do with part of loan I'm asking is to get possession of five acres just outside of the city limits and thereby have a place to which I can move whenever owner wants this, as it is a salable property.

I am very close-mouthed on private affairs, so there is no danger of any one hearing <u>how</u> I got out of the dilemma if you decide to assist me, which will be appreciated.[62]

Mrs. Edna Funk (St. Augustine) to Sholtz, 12 June 1934

1930 census: She is a 33-year-old white widow with a 14-year-old son. She does not work.

I am a widow with one son eighteen years old. He works with the C.W.A. and makes $3.60 a week. I have a large two story house and lives up stairs. Have a morgage on it for $2000. Now the Peoples Bank is foreclosing. I have tried to get the government home lone to take the morgage over but they refused. If I could get it I could pay it back by keeping the downstairs rented. I have absolutely no place to go, no people to help me & if they take my place from me I don't know what I will do. Have owned my place for 21 years and have worked hard to save it. Could you help me in any way. Would appreciate an answer and any suggestions you can make.[63]

Mrs. M. A. Nutt (Biltavern Hotel, Tavares) to ER, undated but reply dated 15 June 1934

I have some property that I can not keep the taxes paid on but I would like it put to some good use.

I had thought of a home for old people. Then when I read of so many young boys hoboing it occurred to me that there might be some way to finance an Industrial home, not prison for some of them[.]

I can not afford to give the property free but would make it a bargain.

The hotel is 79x76 ft. with kitchen 2 story brick 30x30 ft (see card) enclosed[.] There are 30 bed rooms[.] The hotel is furnished.

The land is less than a mile from hotel 200 acres & 100 3 mi out. I had a 12 acre grove just beginning to bear when the Govt has it sprayed for the med fly and killed nearly 400 trees & I could not afford to reset the trees[.]

There are seven lots with the hotel about 300x150 ft.

I would like 30,000 for the hotel & 300 acres which would clear up the taxes on that & tax & mtg [on] my home & leave me enough to live on.

If there is a fund that could be loaned to the boys & they taught to farm & build small boats I think they could pay back the cost[.]

Judging from what I read you like to help the needy and are in a position to know what is needed most. That is why I am writing to you.

If you are favorably impressed let me know what your plan would be. If not interested no harm done. I am a widow 75 years old.[65]

Mrs. W. P. Briggs (Miami) to ER, 15 June 1934

I have read with increasing interest your many & various efforts and suggestion for the betterment and welfare of others and while I am unknown to you, am taking the liberty of writing on a subject that I am hoping may receive your sincerest consideration. I am a widow 66 years old, with a young son 19. Three years ago he graduated from high school, with high hopes of a college education. I lost my little income during the depression and am unable to pay his expenses at any college. Of course there are many southern boys similarly situated, needing financial aid, and for them and my boy am asking that you use your efforts in helping solve this problem. Unfortunately the Conservation Camps lack an educational feature & naturally kept out many boys who otherwise would have taken advantage of them. Miami has suffered more during the depression than any city I know & I have been unable to get a loan for my boy. There isn't any work here for an untrained boy and unless one has a profession or vocational training 'tis impossible to secure a position. Southern colleges, unlike northern college, are not endowed, and it would amaze you greatly if you knew how many young boys here are absolutely without education. I believe every boy should have an opportunity and I feel some one should be willing to make a loan to nice boys who need & want an education. I beg your pardon for intruding on your valuable time but I do feel you are as much interested in helping young boys succeed, during these strenuous times, as any other worthwhile objective you have at this time.

Thanking you for any effort you may make in helping these underprivileged boys, I am sincerely yours.[66]

Mrs. M. L. D. Trimmings (Jacksonville) to Sholtz, 25 June 1934

I am a Negro teacher of many years standing in the state of Florida, was born and reared in Suwannee Co. Received my training in the elementary school at Live Oak & my training later in the Fla. State Normal & Industrial College in Tallahassee, Fla.

I have taught continously for forty odd years and am still trying to hold my position in Oakland school Jacksonville, where I have taught for 14 years.

My application for a Teacher's pension was filed in Prof. Cawthon's office in the Spring of '33 and I have written several letters asking the Board for consideration without any favorable reply.

Mr. Cawthon said that the state was minus of sufficient funds to consider any more applications when I wrote him; therefore I am writing to him again today.

I have taught in many counties in our state, as my records in Mr. Cawthon's office will show. My physical condition is very poor, I have high blood pressure and severe nerve trouble.

I am re-appointed to my same position which I have held for 14 terms in the Oakland school in Jacksonville, but my nerves are all wrecked and I am asking of you to please say a word in my behalf as the Honorable Governor of our fair State. Any consideration from you will be highly appreciated. I attended summer school at Bethune Cookman last summer but I am unable this summer. Yours for education.[67]

Mrs. Louise Longley (Miami) to Sholtz, 9 July 1934

My reply to you to ask your advice in my troubles[.] I Louise Longley desire a information in my troubles at this present time sir my home is taken away for taxes by the Select-Securities Co. please sir advise me what I must do. I have children and no where to go[.] work is dull[.] nothing to do[.] please give me your undivided attention for mercies sake[.] I desire to do the right thing if you will give me a chance[.] I am looking up to you for your advise[.] do please let me know from you what I should do[.] believing you are a governor of sympathy please let me know what I must do in the nearest future and where you lead me I will follow[.] to see me in my poverty Strickten condition read the thirty second psalms first and second verses[.] from your humble servant.[68]

Mrs. M. A. Peden (Little River) to Sholtz, 6 July 1934

1930 census: She is 82 years old, white, and head of a household of eight (adult children and their spouses). Her children include a farmer, a fisherman, a bus driver, and a truck driver.

Will you forgive an old woman for addressing this letter to you, but I am anxious to know what is going to be done about the old age pension. "I have had several letters in regard to the matter," it is what they plan to do but don't come to the straight point. Now may-be you would be so kind as to tell me the truth, 'is the old age pension bill going to help the old helpless people." I am 88 years old. been in Dade co. Fla. 82 years. "at one time pretty well fixed." Sold most of my homestead and lost quite a sum in the banks going busted and taxes ate up what I could get saved up, till I had to let things go and just make a liveing if a poor one. Now my back has got so bad I cannot do any hard work only just mess around. I am depending on my children for support and you know that is hard, so I am makeing so bold as to ask you if there is any chance of us old folks getting any help if only five dollars a week would be a God—send to an old woman like me. I had three sons in the Navy in the war. Two of them come home well, but one was almost a wreck, I tried to get an alotment for him[.] They said he could get one, I wrote to the war—department[.] They wrote me in reply. But it done no good[.] we could get to no settlement so let the matter drop. He was in the Navy hospital at Key West and under a Doctors care for a year. "he is still no good for hard work" but up and going now[.] I am going to live in hopes of hearing something good from you, "yes I am a widow," and an old Grandma "at that." But my family cant help me much[.] times are so hard, and my married-children have familys of their own to care for, I know, I sound silly, "but you will understand; God bless you for any help of any kind.[69]

This letter has eccentric punctuation, which I left intact.

Miss Clifford C. Whitaker (Crescent City) to Sholtz, 11 July 1934

1930 census: She is 11 years old, African American, and the daughter of Carey and Minnie Whittaker. Her father is a farm laborer.

I'm writing you to ask if you please help me to enter high school this term. I'm a poor colored girl was born in the [state] of Fla. in Putnam Co. May 2, 1918. and confessed religion in May 1928. In the Elizabeth Baptist Church.

My father and mother both are living. But are not able to send me to school.

I'm 16 years old. And in the 9th grade[.] my purpose is to be a nurse because the U.S.A. may go to war. And I can help with wounded soldiers of my country.

If I only had clothing and a few dollars I could go to Pal[a]tka.

My father takes care of his aged mother and 6 children. I'm the oldest child. My father is 34 years old. And don't have an education.

My mother had a small chance and can read and write a little. I'm willing to work but there isn't any work for girls to do.

Answer soon.[70]

Mrs. Annie Parker (Sarasota) to Sholtz, 15 July 1934

1930 census: She is 31 years old, white, and the wife of Alfred, a fisherman. She does not work.

I hardly know how to begin my letter to you. And I dont know why I thought of writting you unless it was just God's will[.] My husband has T.B. and has been in the hospital in Oteen N.C. for 18 months[.] He wonts me to go to see him and that is why I am writting you[.] I only get $24.00 a month from the Vet adm. And I have four little children the oldest just 10 years & the baby just 3 next month[.] The Doctor said not to let my husband know any thing that would worry him and so I have been writting him we were getting along just fine but we havent been since last may[.] dureing school I draw a mothers pension of $15.00 per month & with the $24.00 from the Government I did manage but that mothers pension has stopped and the FERA has been giving me $2.50 per week but yesterday Mrs. Wells had to stop that since I draw this from the Gov. Mr. Sholtz I have to pay $3.80 insurance & $1.50 light bill & $1.30 for water & $1.20 for chicken feed and my medican runs around $2.00 a week so my grocie bill cant go far[.] I have lost my health & the FERA woulden let me work. Now I am just writting you all this so you will under stand I am not asking help from you but for only one thing I want to go to see my husband[.] I dont want to disapoint him for he will know then that I have told him a story about getting along good. and he means all to me[.] I would give half my life to be with him. Now in over 13 years we have never been parted only while he was in the hospital[.] I have no father[,] he is dead & my mother is old & I have a stept father he is old & it is all he can do to give us something to eat[.] I own my home and I have friends but all are like my self[,] have no money[.] Mr Sholtz for $35.00 I could go & see my dear husband and spend a week if you can help me. I know God will bless you—now you can write Mrs. Wells head of the FERA and she can tell you ever word I have written you is true for she personaly knows me & knows all I have written you to be true[.] please dont let any one but Mrs. Wells know I written you. I dont want any one here to know I had to ask for help for some one might write my husband and it would worrie him and might cause him to leave the hospital and cost his life[.] he may

72

have to spend 18 more months there[.] please Mr. Sholtz if you can help me to go see my husband let me hear from you soon. May Gods blessing be with you & yours[.][71]

Oteen refers to the VA hospital near Asheville, North Carolina. FERA was the Federal Emergency Relief Administration, one of the first New Deal work relief programs passed by Congress during the famous First Hundred Days. It was designed to be short-lived and was replaced by the Works Progress Administration and other larger work relief agencies.

Mrs. Carol Capes (Miami) to Sholtz, 19 July 1934

In a moment of desperation, I appeal to you for assistance in a matter of grave importance, which I have hither-to been unable to execute.

As the mother of eight living children, and a widow for eight years, I earnestly beseech you, not to ignore my letter, but to read it carefully and thoughtful and to immediatly make such investigation as you may deem necessary to varify every statment contained in this letter. and I do emplore you to device some plan where-by I may be enabled to consummate the deal as perscribed in the here-with—enclosed letter.

For eight years I have been the sole support of my children and my aged mother who is now in ill health. There is no one living to provide for then except myself. I cannot fail in my obligations.

Governor Sholtz I am not an object of charity. I do not ask a gift. But I do earnestly solicit a loan with bonafide security. I wish to purchase an apartment house from which I may derive an income and also pay for the property.

In the past I have been a strict and adherent of the Roosevelt's predoninant policy of "keeping the money in circulation." Too much so. For now I find myself entirely with out funds. I have exausted my every resource. My house rent is in arrears. My gass and light bills two months in arrears. My larder so empty it is pitiful. But I am not going to give up. I am no mere child asking for foolishness. I am a mature, sane thinking woman, striving incessantly to fulfill my duties to my dependants. I have perfect health, and plenty of energy. I can make a living for my family if given an opportunity.

I have always endeavored to find the bright side of every cloud. I love to live for the sheer joy of living. My children are happy care free and obedient[.] all as attractive and as intellectual as the average. They love their mother above all else and I must not fail them. But candidly, I do not know what will become of us all if you do not come to the rescue.

True we have local loan companies, both Federal and otherwise. They lend for beautifying & repairing homes, for construction purposes & for refinancing. None enclude my particular kind of "need."

The average person would be discouraged & disheartened at the numerous rebuffs I have received this past month in my unrelenting efforts to procure the loan which would spell independance for my self and little family.

There is no law authorizing a loan for purchase money. What am I to do? I have no other alternative but to appeal to the superior executive of our State for a solution of this vital problem.

By way of introduction I am enclosing a picture of myself taken last Saturday.

I have seen, and admired your pictures in the papers, and read certain articles you have written which created a sincere respect for your intellectualism. Your article appearing for the "Mothers Day" publication of the "Herald" was to me most commendable. Only a "mother" knows the trials, as well as the joy, of Motherhood. Especially is this true when one had to be both mother & father as has been my case for eight years.

I believe implicitly in the humane side of your nature. That you will be able to visualize conditions & understand how imperative it is that I have funds at once to provide food & other necessities for my lovely family. and I do believe that the necessary money will be forthcoming before my option expires the 25th of this month. I must give the owner a first Mortg. back for $2,800.00 and can only offer a second mortg. to you for the $1000.00. If you would rather lend me $3,800.00 and take a first Mortg. for same I would be only too glad to arrange it that way. I want you to feel safe. This apt. bldg. I want to buy is of concrete & tile construction built in 1925 & withstood every storm with out flinching. It is worth twice the price Mr. Barkdell is selling it to me for. He has made every concession in my favor to make this deal possible. I withdrew from the P.O. the last dollar I had in the world and paid as earnest money. You will not permit me to lose it, will you Governor Sholtz?

Forget about the difference in our stations in life. Regard me as a friend and a political supporter. We all owe each other a little consideration. I will return your favor to the very best of my ability, and you will feel gratified some day for this favor you extend on an unknown friend. You will never have reasion to regret being a humanitarion in this particular instance I assure you.

You know our Government is lending billions. The P.W.A. spends $5,000,000 per day. All I ask is a small loan. You will arrange it won't you Governor Sholtz? Many gamble more than this on the horses. Surely I am of as much consequence as a horse.

I have four daughters, four sons, two sons-in-law, two grandsons and one granddaughter. I still feel as young as any of them, but I simply can't carry on any longer with out this material assistance I crave.

Let me remain a cheerful and efficient mother by making it possible for me to continue to provide for them. My dear old mother is so sweet, and gentle, and patient. She knows my funds are very low but does not dream I am penniless. She is so worthy and good and I must not fail her.

You, Governor Sholtz, will never have done a more worthy deed, or one which will be greater appreciated, that to grant the request I entreat you to make now. I am entirely at your mercy.

Please do not refer my case to any local charities. The idea of being a charitable object is most repulsive to me. I have always prided myself upon my ability to provide for my family and can do so now with this little help.

I will continue to be optimistic until I receive the essential aid I crave from you and then my ecstasies will know no bounds.

The time of my option is short but you will act quickly I am sure.

It may seem inconceivable that I should entertain such a degree of confidence in your attitude toward my "cause." But the "cause" is so justifyable, & the need as urgent, and my confidence in you is in my proportion.

Not—with—standing your vast executive duties you will find a few moments to write me a personal letter of encouragement, to the effect that after you are convinced that every thing stated in this letter is true, you will arrange a loan. My family & business proposition will bear the most rigid investigation.[72]

Mrs. Mary I. Cortino (Mango) to ER, 7 August 1934

1930 census misindexed as "Cortines": She is 50 years old with two children at home. Her husband, Ignacious, is a grocery merchant.

I trust you will pardon me for writing you, but I am a member of the Woman's Club, also the Home Mission, and I am on the Welfare Committe. There is lots of girls and elderly ladies that do not attend church as they have no decent clothes to wear, and I appeal to you for aid. I thought that among your many friends, there might be some that would have something in their wardrobes that they had discarded and would help some sister that was less fortunate than they.[73]

Mrs. Johnnie M. Dupont (Tallahassee) to Sholtz, 7 August 1934

I am writing to ask a favor of you. I am a widow woman with two small children with poor health. My husband deserted the children and I in 1926, without a legal cause[.] left us on my people until 1930. he came back from Daytona Beach Fla during that time he never sent the children not one penny or nothing elce[.] he was the cause of me loosing my health I was perfectly dependent. he had a good position making a good salary[.] My parents was living we didn't bother him in no respect left it to his honor[.] since then they both are dead. in 1930 he filed a suit for his divorce. I didn't object of him having it but I wanted him to support his children and do until yet as I know it is nothing but right for him to do so[.] I stuck by him as a wife and mother for his children as long as he would let me[.] I have proof by both the best white and negro people where we lived in 1931 when we was called in court. through my attorney we asked the court for $20.00 each month for the support from him for the 2 little children. they only granted me $12.00 each month. he has never gave it as he should he gave it like he wanted to Hon Gov. we haven't had justice since it begain. And now he only want to give his 2 children $10.00 per month and I have to pay attorney fee out of it each month the sum of $2.00 for collecting it. Which only leaves $8.00 per month for the 2 children $4.00 each to pay rent and get provisions. he has a good job now operating the commasary for the clay co of at Midway Fla. he also owns a right new Chevrolet car bought from the Chivorlet of this town[,] boards at the best Boarding house Mrs. Annie L. Shepherds of this town[,] wears as fine clothing as any man[,] haves what he wants[.] yet he dont want to support his poor little children[.] they have to try to sell peanuts help get food[.] Pres J. R. E. Lee of the F.A.&.M. College will tell you the same as he has bought from them to help them. So Hon Mr. Gov. through my attorney Mr. C. W. Gregory we want to try to get their support raised to $20.00 per month[.] I want you to please see can you try and have it raised to that amount by the Judge who put the charge on him Hon Judge C. Johnson[.] I only want justice thats all. Hon Gov if you will help me to get it through I will never forget your dear kindness towards me and my poor little children as we certainly need help.[74]

Mrs. E. Stewart (Daytona Beach) to ER, 14 August 1934

You will pardon me but I am desperate & don't know wich way to turn[.] Now this is not charity I am asking for, but if you will take time to consider it.

I am running a little Rooming House but have had no Business and I have not been well for some time, and I see an operation ahead of me. two years ago the 2nd of June I had my left Breast taken off and I am afraid there will have to be another. I am 70 years old and no one to give me a dime[.] sorrow [sorry] to say I am one of the Forgotten Mothers[.] now I do all kinds of sewing knitting crochet [illegible] but there is no sale here[.] the place is to small. I have some Beautifull quilts and if you would allow me I would like to parcel post some of my work so you could see and if it does not apeal to you just send it back at my expense and if the Prices does not suit you, you fix them to your likeing. I know you are a just lady. I cant ask for aid have to much Pride left altho I have been liveing without a lot of merry things. I so often think of the little [lines?] my mother taught me.

What matter if the road be filled with brier,

If waking later I am more like thee,

For I am thine—to fashion as thou wilt—

Just teach me how to know and follow Thee.[75]

Mr. & Mrs. John Ogden (Key West) to FDR, 20 August 1934

1930 census: John is 26, Lena is 19, and they have a 2-year-old son. John works as a "chauffeur" in a taxicab. They are white.

This letter is to greet you with an N.R.A baby girl born Aug 15th 1934 and also to Honor you by giving her the name of your wife Eleanor Ann. This is the only way to show Thanks to you for what you have done for us and every one in the U.S.A. and hope the good can continue.[76]

Mrs. S. P. Scranton (Palatka) to Sholtz, 26 August 1934

I am asking a little information from you. I am an Heir to some money from my Mother's Estate of which my Father & I were the sole Heirs. And my father went away 11 yrs ago, and has not been seen or heard of seince. And I heard that he was destroyed by water. I am a poor white woman and have a cripple husband and 5 small children[.] gov please look this mater over and see what you can do for me. My poor husband is a cripple veteran and is in a bad condition physicialy. My husband has been cut off in his pension from $27.50 to $9.00 a month and we cant hardly exzist. Please let me hear from you as early as possible.[77]

Mrs. Mary Wolcott Collins (Mrs. J. Purser; Lakeland), to FDR and ER, 27 August 1934

Will you please listen to my plea?

For the past three months our income has been cut off through the caving in of an oil well in Oklahoma City.

On the fifteenth of September we stand to lose our furniture as we have borrowed three hundred dollars on it. we have also borrowed money on my engagement ring to buy food and will lose the ring on the fifteenth.

School begins on the seventeenth of September and our three children will be unable to enter. Two are high school students and one junior high student.

We are raising quail under Florida Game Breeders License number 4.

We have forty-eight pair of breeding quail, about two hundred fifty young quail are still in the brooders.

We do our own hatching in an electric incubator, which has four trays, each tray holding two hundred twenty-five eggs. There are four hundred ninety-four eggs in the incubator. The laying season is about three or four weeks longer.

What I wish to ask of you is: Do you know any sportsmen or sportswomen who have large estates or hunting grounds, whom you think would be interested in buying our quail or quail and equipment and let my husband and me operate the quail farm on a salary? We should prefer a place in Georgia or Florida but would go any place.

We have had two seasons of experience and we feel that we can render honest and intelligent service.

My husband has perfected an egg turning tray which will turn all the eggs in one tray at one time.

He also has perfected an electric thermostat which will control the heat within one fourth of one degree in the brooders and a condenser is not necessary for its operation.

These inventions will not be sold with the quail equipment. However if we should be allowed to operate the quail form for any one we are willing to use these inventions which will save much time and money.

We should be glad to sell these invention but haven't the money to patent them.

I am inclosing a few pictures of the laying pens, rearing pens and brooders.

Something must be done at once or we will lose everything. There is nothing against the quail farm.

We live on a rented place.

We should be truly grateful for any assistance you can give us.

Reply from secretary dated 1 September says that ER is gone and will bring it to her attention when she returns.[78]

Miss Eliza Barnett (Orlando) to ER, 28 August 1934

1930 census: She is 64 years old, working as a dressmaker doing "piecework." She is living with her brother and sister, who are both widowed. She is the only one working.

Pardon me for intruding on your valuable time but I have been wanting to write to you for some time and tell you I have enjoyed your letters in our Sunday paper. Your letter in last Sundays paper was just splendid. I think you have the right view of things & I want to thank you for the interest you have taken in the common people[,] so much more than any of the wifes of our former Presidents. And I also want to thank you for the interest you are taking in the Old Peoples pention and I want to ask you to urge Our President to do all in his power to put it through. I know he is such a buisy man I wouldnt bother him with my request but am trying to reach Him thru you. I am a woman 70 years of age I have no income have no Home only as my friends give me So I am in need of the Pention The Dr. say I will soon be in an invalids chair if I dont get treatment for my Back[.] I have a little saving to begin the treatments but it wont last long & I have no one to whome I can go too for help. I received a copy of the National Furom edited by Dr. J E Pope. he advocates beginning the Old Age Pention immediately paying them out of various Federal relief funds[.] I trust it can be done. What a great relief it would bring to many of us old people who are needing help <u>rite</u> <u>now</u> and many of us havent had any benefit of those various relief funds that others of the unemployed have had. And while I have rejoiced that they have had this generious help I feel it is our turn now. and why should we have to wait till Congress meets in Jan. & then it would probably some time before we could get it when Our President could speak the word and Lo it would be done[.] you see He has done so many wonderful things we think he can just press a button & "Presto" it is done. I know there are many Old folk myself included would be grateful it we could get relief Soon & I believe He will do all he can for us. Thanking you & Him in Advance and Praying God's Blessings on you.[79]

Mrs. Daisy Grant (Vero Beach) to Sholtz, 5 September 1934

It may seem strange But I have read and heard of so many good thing that you has done for the poor people[.] I thought I would rite you and ask a favor of you[.] I has organized a canning club among ourselves to can up some of the suplus vegetable for our need[y] ones[.] We are being helped of course but not enought that would do verry much good and our cuminity are in need of things to eat that the club could prepare if it was able to purchase some eqiuptment for that purpose such as a Sealer, Canner, and other things that it will take for the purpose[.] I dont know just how to ask you for this[.] But what I can hear of you you will be glad to give this enformation[.] it will take about $50.00 fifety dollars to get thease articales need which ever way we can do for you to help us we will be glad to do so[.] hope to hear from you soon[.] I remain sincere. [signed] Mrs Daisy Grant, colord[80]

Mrs. Alice B. Stewart (Miami) to ER, 15 September 1934

1930 census: She is a 61-year-old white widow, born in England. She lives alone and does not work.

I just dont know how to write you. Because I do know you are a very busy lady.

I have followed your travels over the country and know you must be very tired and must have rest.

I am a Widow and seventy years old this Nov. And have lost all my loved ones through death. My Husband died in Michigan and left me enough money to last me with care.

Have lost most everything through others and the last was $3000. to the Christian Science Church in Orlando Fla. Our Healer of that Church said it was the safest place to have money.

My Certificates have become due two years and dont get eny interest.

They dont even write me about them eny more. My Taxes are coming due. and I have no insurence on my home. And I just dont know what to do.

I live near the Miami River and its a dead end Street and cant get eny roomers, have tried all summer.

I cant do hard work because I give out quickly. Oh Mrs. Roosevelt if I could only get my Three Thousand I would be so happy.

I am a Prespreterian and dont know eny thing about The Christian Science Church. Came to Miami because it was warm and cant stand the cold of Michigan. Dear Mrs. Roosevelt can you see eny way to help me get my money.

I have tryed a Lawyer but it takes money for one. And I must live. I would be so Thankfull if you could see a way to advice me about it.[81]

Secretary to Mrs. Roosevelt to Mrs. J. P. Howland (Live Oak), 15 September 1934

The original is not here; a staff note says the letter was referred to Reconstruction Finance Corporation

Mrs. Roosevelt asks me to acknowledge your letter regarding the bowl you wish to sell her. She regrets that she is unable to comply with your wishes, but owing to the great number of articles offered to her, she finds it impossible to purchase anything in this way, nor does she know of anyone who would be interested in purchasing it.

However, in an effort to aid you Mrs. Roosevelt has referred your letter to the proper authorities for consideration.[82]

Mrs. Louise Baxter (Miami) to ER, 26 September 1934

1930 census: She is 55 years old, was born in Virginia, and is the wife of a real estate broker. They are white.

Help my boy to help himself—he is so ambitious and honest and splendid in every way anyone would be proud to call him "Son." But we have not the influence to get him with the Co. he is so anxious to be associated with. Just a line or word from you and the Pan American Airways Inc. would give him a position. No matter how small the position all he wants is a chance to work hard in the Co. and make good. He already has his application in and has talked to them in reference to the matter but one can't get very far without influence. My son John Matthews Baxter is a graduate civil engineer Virginia Military Institute Lexington Virginia[,] clean morally and in splendid physical condition with the exception of his eyes—as he is a great reader and student and has to wear glasses. He is hardworking and honest to a fault if just a thing is possible—he is unmarried and can give the best of references both local and out of town people. He is entitled to the best as he is so [illegible] and considerate of other people. I beg of you my dear Mrs. Roosevelt help me to help him. . . . No doubt you know my cousin Lela Hamersly who married the late Robert Roosevelt of Sayville L.I. New York—and my first cousin has just recently been made an Admiral U.S.N. His name is Henry Ellis Lackey and President Cleveland gave him his appointment to Annapolis. . . . I have the greatest admiration for you as a wife and mother and I am sure you will understand. Your great illustrious husband we all love and pray for at all times.[83]

Mrs. Emma Minor (Manatee) to ER, 27 September 1934

1930 census: She is 62 years old. Her husband, Jefferson, is a 69-year-old truck farmer. They are white.

I am writing to you [for] information. Could you tell me any place I could find a market for a crocheted bed spread. I have just finished one that is beautiful in design and work. It has a lot of the pop corn stitch[,] is 92x108 in not including the 3½ in hand tied fringe. It is made of No 12 4 ply bedspread yarn. I am asking $75.00 for it and it is very cheap at that price. I am a widow 66 yrs old and my health is poor owing to a bad heart. and such work as this is the only way I can make anything. I have a son 36 years old who was injured in birth and has never been able to do anything for himself. It is hard for me to find a market for my work here. I am trying to keep my home but just don't know sometimes what to do. if you can give me any advice or suggest a marketplace where my work could be disposed of I would greatly appreciate it.[84]

Mrs. Mary Wolcott Collins (Lakeland) to ER, 5 October 1934

On the 27th of August, I wrote to you and President Roosevelt, requesting that you use your influence to help sell our quail and equipment, to one of your sportsmen friends.

As the need is so urgent I am requesting that you please help us immediately if you will.

In my other letter I sent a few pictures of some of our equipment. Our Breeders License is number four.

We have been asking twenty-five hundred dollars for all quail, equipment, and three electric incubators.

We have fifty pair laying stock, about three hundred young quail, old enough to be released, and quite a number of young still in the brooders. I can't say the exact number without counting.

Should you be able to influence a buyer, we should like to operate the quail farm, wherever it might be situated, if possible. My husband and I have had two seasons experience and feel that we can give honest and intelligent service.

Reply by secretary dated 5 October: Mrs. Roosevelt has asked me to acknowledge your letters, and to tell you she is very sorry she cannot be of assistance in the matter about which you write, but at the present time she does not know of anyone who might be interested in buying the quail and equipment. I am returning the pictures you sent, as I thought you would wish to have them back.[85]

Edith M. Hirst, managing director, Florida Association of Workers for the Blind (Miami) to ER, 6 October 1934

I wish to thank you for the attention given my letter of Sept. 14th, which you referred to the Library of Congress. Mr. Ashby has offered me a list of the blind readers of Florida, which will help some.

It is a source of great comfort to know that the First Lady of the Land can and does find time to attend to what must be a mountain of correspondence.

As in the case of the lion and the mouse, if I can at any time be of service to you, command me.[86]

Mrs. Virginia Wilson (Lutz) to Sholtz, 18 October 1934

1930 census: She is 35 years old, white, and the wife of a salesman for a chemical company.

Will you help us? for we surely need help. I will tell you our circumstances as clear as possible.

My husband is working a small grove here, for ten dollars per month, which just keep's us existing, but we are trying to stay off the relief as it is so much better for our little girl here in the country, and the majority of relief live in close tenement houses in Tampa. Our greatest problem now is that we expect a child in December, early part, and we have'nt the means to get any necessary clothing or pay the Dr, which is $50.00[.] We have no bed clothes at all, and will need some soon, especially blankets.

My husband hopes to get a better position soon, but that doesn't help us now. He and I both nearly barefoot, and it seems like the burden is almost more than we can figure a way out of. There are just three of us, a girl five years old. The doctor says she is very enemic from lack of nourishing food. So if you can help us any way, we would surely be so grateful. We are willing to do anything right to stay off relief. If we can get some help until we get our feet again, I'm sure there will be a way to repay you. So will hope and pray for an answer.[87]

Mrs. Iola E. Faudel, R.N. (Dade County Hospital, Miami) to ER, 22 October 1934

In desperation I am turning to you to ask if you will assist me in some way to make a loan of $500.00 I have steady work now, and can it off at the rate of $35.00 each month—including the interest. For over four years I was without work and my debts grew to these dreadful proportions. My husband was killed in an accident nearly seven years ago leaving me with a baby seventeen months old and another child expected six months later. These children are well and strong and are now in school.

I have just received a raise in salary, and the assurance that I shall continue in the position, but this multitude of small debts is driving me insane.

If you would be so good as to help me to make this loan so that I could settle each of these debts and have my mind at ease I would be so grateful to you. My salary is now $80.00 a month, and I will gladly pay what ever interest you feel is right-to get my affairs in order—so that this terrible strain of worry may be abated.

Please let me hear from you, and I trust that you or your wonderful husband will tell me where I may borrow this money. I shall be glad to send you the names of people who have known me over a period of years—and who know that I keep my word.[88]

Miss Helene Meriwether (Lakeland) to ER, 22 October 1934

1930 census: "Helen" is the 15-year-old daughter of Frank and Emma. Her father is a truck farmer. The family is white.

My one ambition in life is to take a trip to Washington and to visit you. I have had dreams of going there and they seemed so real that when I wake up, I'm disappointed; although I have the greatest confidence in doing things I longed for.

I will be the happiest girl in the world if I could make that trip in my dreams real.

I'm not working and I don't see anyway of my getting there. And yet, I have a feeling there is a way.

I take such great interest in you and the president that I hope I'll get to meet both of you.

I am having confidence in getting an encouraging letter from you.[89]

Mrs. Louise K. Spencer (St. Petersburg) to ER, 22 October 1934

Please speak and write a word in behalf of the Townsend old-age revolving pension plan, for Florida. I am the <u>unemployed</u> 73 year old widow of a Presbyterian minister. I taught 36 years and was still <u>employed</u> in my beloved profession, when in 1921 my husband and I both had "flu." He died, and I have been too frail to teach ever since—besides the powers that be, say: "Too old." My husband left me a little bungalow, where I still live, with a $3000 mortgage, at 8% and a few thousand dollars life insurance, but the depression and bank failures swept that away. A semi-invalid, spinster, sister 76, lives with me and shares my poverty. We are, for the most part, "cheerful idiots" but when real sickness and death come—well what then? Possibly the Old Age Pension will be God's answer to that. My case is just <u>one.</u> There are thousands of us. Do help us. Thank you![90]

Mrs. Frank B. Warner (Kissimmee) to ER, 22 October 1934

1930 census: Emma is 61 years old and white, and she was born in England. Her husband is a farm laborer on a truck farm. Their 10-year-old grandson lives with them.

It filled my Heart with gladness when I read in Orlando Sunday paper Sentinal Star of your favoring the Old Age Pension bill. I will say if your agitation of it [it] should go through.

The blessings of Future Generations would decend on you & yours through all generations to come. just think what I could enjoy doing of ever so small pension. I could pay my church dues[,] red cross dues[.] I could give my Grandchildren 5c instead of 2c for collection. I would not be afraid to buy a poor benighted child a pair of shoes so he or she could go to Sunday School. And look like others.

. . . Just to think what we could do We old folks. The little ones would not be tempted to take that which is not theirs. It would empty prisons and insane asylums. What a wonderful world it would be to all. People would not be driven to breaking of Law.[91]

Mrs. John Ogden (Key West) to ER, 29 October 1934

I am going to have little Eleanor Ann Baptized who has been named after you and want you and the president to be little Eleanor Ann's God parents she is now 2 1/2 months old. I will send you a picture of her next month. I am her Mother and I am criple in my right foot.[92]

Ruth Parker (Ft. Myers) to Sholtz, 29 October 1934

I am writeing you Being a old timer being born and raised here in Ft. Myers[.] My grandfather Capt. F.A. Hendry was one of the first to settle here. And my grandfather served in the congress in uper and lower house. And now I am writeing you to see if you can help me to get a job looking after the Indians down here in the Everglades[.] I know them all and they all know me. And I, do a lot now for them and I thought perhaps through you I might get a good job[.] I am a widow and I need a job and I sertainly would apreciate your asisting me to get the job. I sure worked for you in your campane and I will again. I have scores of relation here and they are all voters. And if you run again I will sure work for you again. As you have proved out to do all you said you would in your talks. And another thing I want to mention in this FERA work such as this tick business. that's all right in some way. But these stations at bridges that is just throwing money away for they don't serch a car just flash a light in trunk in the car lift the rumble seat and say you head [on][.] they don't know whats under the seat of a car. It is just fine for the dairy. But they will never get rid of the tick as all the wild deer[,] coons and Opossum have ticks. And I sending you a cliping and I have been all over the Everglades for weeks at a time and have never seen any wild horses[.] This is another money scheme. Somebody will make some money out of it but will not get a wild horse out of it[.] the Indians say there is no wild horses in the Everglades[.] I ask Cypers Billie yesterday if he ever sees and [any] wild horses[.] he said no there is no wild horses in Everglades. Now I will look for a reply hoping you can get me the job looking after the Indians and I will do you a good favor in your next run if you run. I hope you will pardon this long letter but I just wanted to you to know that I apreciate you as a govner[.][93]

Mrs. Tilla Silcox (Jacksonville) to Sholtz, 3 November 1934

1930 census: She is 37 years old, white, and the wife of a laborer for a lumber company. She does not work.

I am sorry to have to trouble you with my personal affairs knowing the many responsibilities which you have, but I am forced to do this, as I feel that you are the only one to whom I can call on for help. I am a widow with two school children ages (12) and (10) yrs. I have been sewing for the F.E.R.A. until (3) weeks ago when I was cutoff entirely from work on account of my getting my mother's pension of $9.00 per month from school board.

I have tried every where for work also putting in my application for teacher in one of the nursery schools here which pays $2.50 per wk. but I have failed so far to get any results. I have taught (10) yrs. in school in this State. I cannot understand why old experienced teachers (especially mothers) are not better qualified for such teachers, than young high school girls which they seem to prefer.

My father and husband were always tax payers in this State and I cannot see why I cannot get placed some where in this work so I can support myself and children.

I am asking you to aid me if you can for we are realy going hungry. And now that winter is coming on, we need fuel and clothes, as well as rent.

Hoping to hear from you soon.[94]

Mrs. Lonnie R. Ray (Clearwater) to ER, undated but reply is dated 6 November 1934

I am writing to you to see if you would let me make your linens for you[.] I can make all kind fancy work[.] I need the work so bad am sick with a goiter bad heart and bad knee[.] I half to walk with a cane so it hard for me to do any thing only what I can do setting down[.] I am a widow have lost ever thing that I had in building loans[.] I have a son Harry Alvin Echard on the U.S.S. Saratoga[.] he don't make enough to help me mutch he give me what he can but I half to pay rent[.] I ought have something done for my goiter but have not the funds I don't wan't anyone to give me anything[.] I wan't to work for what I get[.] I have some beautiffull quilts that I have bin triing to sell but have not had any luck[.] If you like I send you a sample of my work[.] please help me if you can[.] I surely be thankfull to you[.] I am sorry to half to bother you.[95]

Mrs. Rosa J. Jones (St. Petersburg) to Sholtz, 10 November 1934

I wonder if you would take time to drop me a line, explaining a few things, I would like to know. I am a native of Fla. never been out of the state. I am a widow woman. My husband died in 1916, leaving me with three girls to raise. I worked awful hard to raise them. In fact I just broke my self down. They are all three married but I am having to live with my youngest Daughter as I am not able to work and make a living for my self. doesn't the State of Fla have money set aside for the purpose of taking care of such as I.

doesn't the state give old widow Ladys a small pension when they become disabled to work. I dont want to go to the poor house. I want to still live with my daughter but would like to be so I could at least buy my own medicine and a few things for my self. My son inlaw doesn't complain one bit, but on the small wages he makes I just feel like I am imposing. he is only second class Boatswain in the U.S. Coast Guard. just transferred over here from Ft. Lauderdale Base 6. I notice there is old mens homes and pentions for old men but never here of any help for old ladys and I know is other states they have a pention for old Ladys[.] would you please write me and explain these things to me. And tell me if the State of Fla does have a pension and could you aid me in getting it. Please answer soon.[96]

Miss Wilhemena Hernandez (Winter Park) to Sholtz, 11 November 1934

As all other means of advice and help failed me, I humbly turn to you.

I understand that the government is aiding students to return to school to prepare themselves for lifes work. I have interceeded as best I know how, but have failed to gain the correct information. Will you please help me? I am a former student of Bethune Cookman College at Daytona Beach, Fla. I have completed my freshman year and am left with one year more before I am efficient to start to work[.]

For three years the depression has robbed me of the privilige of completeing the Jr. college course and of acquiring a B.S. degree.

My parents have done their best and I feel that now if only I can get this one years work completed, I can and will help them.

I am very much interested in small children. Tho' I have been unable to work with them in elementary school, I do have that pleasure once each week at Sunday School. But the time spent is so short.

If you wish to learn about my work, write to Bethune Cookman College where I completed my 12th Grade and freshman year College work. I am gratefully appreciative to you for any aid you might give.[97]

Mrs. Kate Wood (Tampa) to FDR, 13 November 1934

As one who is depending on you to bring our nation back to prosperity, and having the utmost confidence in your judgement of what would be best for the country at large, I ask that you make the "Old Age Pension" the subject of a radio talk in the near future, thus shaping public thinking in the matter.

In my humble opinion, it could bring greater relief and happiness to the greatest number of people, than any other method that could be adopted.

In closing I would like to say that you hold my highest regard, and deepest admiration for your fearless championship of the cause of humanity and I ardently wish you could ever remain at the head of our nation.[98]

Maude (Mrs. E. R.) Ensey (Walton) to ER, 22 November 1934

1930 census, misindexed as "Eusey": Maude is 35 years old and white, and her husband, Edward, is a truck farmer. They have three children.

I'm writing to you because after reading so many of your articles in different magazines I believe you can help me, and gracious knows I need it.

I have a large Bible 221 years old which I want to sell. Could you tell me the value of it?

I couldn't sell it here as I live in the country and every one around this neighborhood are poor but respectable (including myself).

I wish I could sell it, for how we need the money just now for a hundred different things that are so necessary to make a family happy. I have two boys 1 girl.

I do not know why I had the audacity to write you but pardon me if I've intruded. You are such an intelligent lady, I know you can tell me anything I want to know so that's why I'm writing.

If you want me to, I will mail it to you for your inspection.

What an honor to me if you would buy it yourself & how proud I'd be to tell the world about it. Oh how I hope and pray some thing can be done with it.[99]

Mrs. Betty Bryan Holtman (Tallahassee) to Sholtz, 22 November 1934

It is drawing near to Thanksgiving and though that is only one day in the year and I thank you in my heart each day. I will take this time to express my thanks to you and I doubt if you will ever realize <u>just how much I thank you</u> and how hard I try to show you through diligently applying myself to my work, which you very probably know nothing about, how I appreciate your kindness.

This year, has been a struggle but I just cannot imagine just what it might have been without my position.

May God bless you and keep you—always as fine and as big as I think and believe of you.[100]

Mrs. Gertrude M. Brightwell (Miami) to ER, 24 November 1934

1930 census: She is 49 years old and white, was born in Canada, and is the wife of James, a real estate broker. There are no children at home.

I see by the newspapers that you have bought a new set of dishes for the White House, and not knowing what disposition is or will be made of the old ones. I wonder if it would be out of place for me to ask for a piece or two of the old set, just for a souvenir or for sentimental reasons.

If this request is out of order I hope you will forgive my ignorance, but if I would be so lucky as to get one of them, I'd be a very happy woman.

Reply from secretary, 1 December 1934: Mrs. Roosevelt can not help because it is government property and not at her disposal.

Mrs. Ida B. Rosemond (Palatka) to Sholtz, 26 November 1934

1930 census: The family is listed as "Rosman." Her husband, Julius, is a 39-year-old farm laborer, working in Lady Lake. She is 25, has four children, and does not work outside the home. They are African American.

I am appealing to you for aid in a cause that is of vital importance to me and my family. We have been residents of Florida for about twenty eight years and have always been law abiding citizens, tax payers and registered voters of our race (negro).

For the past four or five years times have been extremely hard with us; most of the time my husband has been unemployed and I was teaching in Jacksonville for from fifty to fifty four dollars a month.

This year I was not reappointed, altho' I have a Graduate State Certificate which was issued in August. I taught thirteen years in Jacksonville with a third, second and first grade certificate respectively. Now since spending so much for improvement, I can not get much work there. No reason was given me for my being pul of the school system of Duval County.

However I am teaching in this place for forty dollars per month and my three children are dependent on me. My husband works when he can get it to do. But has nothing definite. He is a contractor but can not get much to do. I am hoping to have a girl graduate next summer. Then she may be able to help us.

Now we have tried to get relief work but were always turned down. Have never received aid from the government in any way. The home is mortgaged and it becomes due January 1, 1935. The house is valued at about $3000 or $4000 and we are very anxious to save it.

We have been to the Home Owners and they refused to take it up for us. We applied to them the first or second week after the office was opened in Jacksonville and they said we were not in distress. We went again last spring and they told us that the man who has a mortgage on the home would not take bonds. The sum that we owe on our home is $750.00 Seven hundred and fifty dollars. My husband went again to the Home Owners last week but was again turned down.

Please consider our appeal and make it possible for us to get this project financed by [the] government. We lost our home by fire about three years ago and had to rebuild and refurnish it. It was insured but not covered by insurance.[102]

Mrs. B. D. Vaughan (Lecanto) to ER, 2 December 1934

1930 census: Rose is 22 years old and married and has a 2-year-old son. She was born in Illinois, to parents who came from Poland. Her husband is a brick mason.

I am writing this in behalf of the Old Age Pension Law which we (my husband & myself) think would be good as we know what it is to have to help our parents at times when we have our own children to think of. My husbands parents are both past sixty and have not been able to get work to take care of themselves all the time and it falls on us to divide our little bit my husband makes working on the FERA to give them a little to eat. My father would also get something from the pension and I know he surely deserves it as he has raised four children and none of us are able to help them much. We are trying to get started in a poultry business here but it is very hard to do so, as we would like to have something in our old age so as not to have to depend on our children as my husbands health isn't very good.[103]

Edith H Frazier (Zephyrhills) to Sholtz, 4 December 1934

1930 census: She is 40 years old, white, and married. Neither she nor her husband is employed.

Our Civic Club Respectfully requests information as follows. Has Florida a law which prohibits husband and wife from both drawing salaries paid out of tax money? If so, please quote act, and describe how we can call for remedy. Assuming such a bill has been passed does it apply to postmasters and post office clerks, or if one holds a state job can the other be postmaster.

Again assuming can both teach in public schools? Or Can a school trustee appoint his brother's wife as a teacher, and another trustee be appointed janitor, in this case a bargain seems to have been made between trustees. In this vicinity several families are employed 100% while others are starving no hope to divide the jobs, and request the removal of all women employed, except those supporting their families.

In this city, the wife of the city clerk teaches in the high school, family 100% employed. Several cases of both husband and wife teaching. One case husband operates store and farm, wife teaching.

One case husband state job, wife postmaster, several cases Spanish war pensioners drawing big relief job salaries.

Another case husband asst postmaster wife clerk in same office, no dependents. If these jobs are divided among needy families it will help wonderfully, and we are asking <u>how</u> it can be done.[104]

Mrs. W. H. DuBose (Bartow) to ER, 14 December 1934

I am writing you to ask you to Please use your influence in every Honorable way you can to Secure a Pension for us old and Disabled People. I am 66 years old and my Husband is 75. and we hav worked hard and lived hard and hav raised eleven children and one Died in infancy. Now they are all Married and got families except our Baby Girl and one son who is allmost an invalid and the girl is not strong either one of them could hardly make their way if they could get work to Do. But they are our Sole Dependence now. the others can hardly make a living for their families. We Dont get any thing now from the Relief as we are not able to work and the State & County says they cant Do any thing so you see what our Prospects are for something to live on medicine for our Many infirmities and so on. We Realise that there are thousands of others in same condition—lost of them even worse. so we feel sure you will Do all you can to help us out that we may well Secure for the Necesities of life for what little time we hav to live[.] thank you. and may God Bless you and your Noble Husband in your efforts for the Betterment of humanity.[105]

Mrs. F. A. Norton (Laurel Hill) to Sholtz, 17 December 1934

I am writing you again. I hope you got a favorable reply from your friend. I am suffering worse than I was when I wrote you before. wont you please have some thing done for me. have me operated on so I can do something for my little children[.] wont you help a suffering woman. Governor Sholtz I know you will give many marry x mas presents. wont you please let an operation be a x mas present to me. I would be so happy if I was operated on and get relief. please have some thing done for me. If you will have me operated on I will pay you every dollar of it back and interest on the money till I get you paid[.] I have a cow I can sell when summer comes and she gets fat. I will pay that[.] I will pay all along till I get it paid if I have to send as little as a dollar at a time. I may get to pay you every dollar of it before the summer is over. Governor you can depend on what I tell you. please do something for me. Governor my husband voted for you. he done all he could for you. wont you please have me operated on[.] I will pay you every dollar back and interest on the money till I get it paid. I have prayed so much for relief[.] I hope I will get it. please let me hear from you soon.[106]

Mrs. Charles A. Stephens (Miami) to ER, 18 December 1934

1930 census: Charles is an assistant supervisor in a chain grocery. His wife, Minnie, is 59 years old and does not work. There are no children at home.

I have been admiring the interest you are taking in the welfare & comfort of the multitudes who are underprivelged and in distress, and it is in the interest of the old people, that I am writing you briefly and sincerely hope it does not bore you greatly.

To be personal, my husband and I came down here from Chicago a few years ago and suffered all the depressing things that Florida endured about five years longer than the general depression. not from any fault of ours. Mr. Stephens is not successful in getting employment the past three years on account of age which leaves us dependent on children and a little help from the F.E.R.A, thanks to you all.

Perhaps your families have no old people and if so they have never felt the sting & humiliation of depending on relatives to get by. While our relatives are good, but they also have their troubles and it crushes our spirit and takes away our independence that old people so much crave and deserve.

I think I am voiceing the opinion of millions who might be brought back to courage & complete independence from any kind of charity if the Townsend pension bill could go into effect.

It would do away with poorhouses which cost tremendously (as figures show in one of the enclosed clippings, and I believe as many are claiming that by millions being compelled to spend their $200 monthly & creating such a stir of buying & circulation of money that it would end the depression very quickly.

With that amount they could afford to give up their jobs & young men have all the employment.

As it is in many of the states, as you no doubt know, the pension are so small that the poverty stricken condition still exists & in the case of needing Doctors[,] nurses & operation, they necessarily are thrown back on charity or suffer along without care & comforts. If you will pardon me I will enclose a few clippings thinking perhaps in your busy life, your attention has not been given to the many ways old people may be made comfortable & happy & independent through the passing of the Townsend pension bill.

I am 64 yrs old and my husband 68, alert & keep in touch with modern affairs. Should the Townsend bill pass & you ever get to Miami I would be happy to have you look us up for a little chat & a cup of tea (come any way whether it passes or not).

Taking it for granted you will be patient with this long epistle and that I may hear that your influence helped to cheer the saddened old people.[107]

Mrs. Ida M. Kunze (St. Petersburg) to ER, 19 December 1934

1930 census: Ida Kunze lives in Wyandotte, Michigan, and is a 60-year-old white widow with a 27-year-old son at home. She owns her home, and her son is an electrician.

I am using this opportunity of writing you asking you to use your influence in regard to the Townsend Old Age Revolving Pension Plan.

I realize you are a very busy person yet giving much thought to the forgotten men and wimen of today.

I am a widow sixty five years of age and having raised a family of three fine young men and one daughter. three of them being university graduates. My sons at present time unable to earn a living for themselves or family.

My house is in the north in Mich. where I have been a taxpayer for thirty five years. at present all I have to look forward too is taxes interest on debt on my house, which I have been obliged to give up and look for work.

Last winter at twenty below zero I occupied a room with no heat and walked through icy streets for work.

My self nor family have never asked for nor rece'd relief, consequently the New Deal has never benefited us in any way. But we have retired hungry and cold.

This year some friends made it possible for me to come to Fla. with promise of work, of which I have had but very little.

I am at present living from 25¢ per day.

I am only one of many such mothers who have toiled to both make our country, not what it is today, but what it ought to be, and have a little joy and comfort in our declining years, but instead facing next to starvation and despair.

So please use your very best influence in favor of The Townsend plan and help put it across and bring about smiles instead of despair.[108]

Mrs. Fannie Conley (Ocala) to Sholtz, 21 December 1934

1930 census: She is a 20-year-old African American laundress. Her husband works as a truck driver for a lumber company.

I am beging you to give me Justice. I cant get any satisfaction here. a man Clarence Dempson had ben pening my cow. he live near by me. while I were sick my cow were killed in Clarence Dempson field near his house. I were expecting the cow to be fresh with a calf in about sixty-60 days. There's some under cover doing about my cow. I tryed to, but I couldn't get a warrent taken out for them. Clarence was put in Jail one night[.] he said he paid $28.00 and they turned him out. I do not under stand what's that for. I didn't know that there was any law to rob a widdow woman and pay a few dollars and get out of it[.] Clarence said his brother Isrel sold my cow. I am a poor widdow woman[.] I want Justice, and Satisfaction for my cow. please yours for wright. Mrs. Fannie Conly, rt2 Box 195 Ocala Florida. These Family of people has a bad reputation[.] my other cow came home with her tail cut off. and one of her leg cut near off and my Turkeys came home with rocks tied in cloth to their necks, and my hogs Ears bit off by the dogs, and they killed my Turkey. They told me they are doing my things this way. I've ben here all my life and have never did any body any harm I am a poor widdow woman. please give me justice my writs and satisfaction. I only wish you know the history of these people. They have robed me. Something must be done.[109]

Mrs. J. L. Bailey (Bradenton) to Sholtz, 30 December 1934

hope you receive This Letter as a True Friend as I know you should know how to advise me in this matter[.] if a man Deserts his family for no reason onely Just another woman dont you think it should Be Just for him to Be made [to] support his first children properly. when he Deserted me my son was 2½ years of age my Daughter 6 months old. My son is now 14 and my Daughter 12[.] I have worked hard and Lived honest[.] there isnt anything against my name[.] I send the children to school and They have plenty to eat[.] I have Been sick a Lot and The children have to[.] He's never did very much for Them but married a woman with 2 children and has raised Them from small children and helped send one to College. he has quiet a Bit of property and drives a fine car all The Time and has real good clothes and still he Doesent want to help Them. he sometimes send 15 dollars per month wich he was supposed to pay when The children were small and pay a Larger amount when They were Larger But They were several years did not pay anything.

I will estamate to you The expense of Keeping up my children[:] rent 7.50 per month grocries 5 dollars per week insurance 1.64 per month for them 1.50 for lights 1.50 for water Besides Thier own and Dr Bills medicine and clothes[.] please consider This letter for my sake. and advise me the amount he should pay for Thier support[.] I have to do for Them and I cant even afford clothes for my self decent To go To Church. he is able to support Them as he should[.] if you will Just please spare me Just a wee Bit of your Time to rite to me and anser my Letter I surely will appreciate it.[110]

Mrs. Della Harper (Orlando) to ER, 31 December 1934

1930 census: She is a 61-year-old white widow, living on a farm. There are three children at home, including a 24-year-old son who works as a plasterer.

I have been reading your articles concerning the old age relief. I am so thankful that you feel interested in the old people for they are the greatest suffers of to day. Therefore I am asking you to please use your influence with The President an Congress to get the Townsend relief bill passed as it will bring relief and happiness to so many dispondent and broken hearted people[.] This plan will not only make the old people independnet and happy but will inable them to relief so many others that are striving to help themselves and their dependents and cannot through no fault of their own[.] I am a native borned Floridian 66 years of age own my own home but cant get a living I mean the necessities of life[.] I do not crave riches but only a living & comforts[.] I shall be waiting anxiously the results[.][111]

Chapter 3

1935-1936

The year 1935 represented an important turning point in the New Deal. In that year the Works Progress Administration (WPA) was established, and the Social Security Act was passed. Under the direction of Harry Hopkins, a former social worker who had once headed the relief effort in Roosevelt's New York, the WPA came to be the federal government's largest work relief program. With an initial appropriation of more than one billion dollars, the WPA attempted to deal with the vast unemployment problem facing the nation in a more systematic and comprehensive fashion than had previous programs.[1]

Of all the New Deal's work programs, the WPA offered the largest number of people assistance. In March 1936 nearly thirty-two thousand Floridians had jobs with the WPA, compared to fifteen thousand in all other federal work programs combined.[2] For men, the WPA generally meant construction work of some kind. The WPA focused its attention on building public works of local benefit, such as schools, bridges, hospitals, courthouses, and roads. Florida's WPA built more than eight hundred public buildings, including a new gymnasium for Florida A&M University, a new high school for Cocoa, Florida, a civic center for Daytona Beach, and many others. The WPA constructed more than six thousand miles of highways in the state, and Florida led the nation in airport construction.

But women could not obtain heavy construction jobs. In the 1930s Americans could not envision this kind of labor for women. No one in the federal government was advocating using the relief programs to change American views on women and work,[3] so the WPA had to find other work relief projects for women. Some were white-collar jobs, such as indexing census records and interviewing surviving former slaves. But the single largest work relief program for women was in the WPA's sewing rooms—more than half of all women relief workers were assigned to the sewing centers.[4] Workers in the sewing rooms produced clothing, linens, uniforms, diapers, mattresses, rugs, and a host of other items. They were distributed in a variety of ways. Some were given directly to relief recipients. Others were made for charitable institutions such as orphanages, or public institutions such as hospitals and schools. Sewing-room women sometimes made items for their own use. Local organizations often approached the sewing rooms with specific projects, such as costumes for a school play, graduation dresses, or band uniforms.

Women of a certain age especially considered these sewing jobs critical. Very few jobs of any kind were available to older women, a point the WPA recognized. One district director wrote: "Because of the age of a great majority of our workers and the lack of previous training in those things which modern industry demands we must inevitably reach the conclusion that in most cases private industrial absorption will be extremely difficult for them. . . . the constant demand for well-trained youth makes the present lot of the average W.P.A. worker look hopeless."[5] Middle-aged women were keenly aware of their situation, and their desire for sewing-room positions was intense. The letters in this chapter reflect that desperation.

The second major reform of 1935, the Social Security Act, addressed some other problems long noted with work relief: the elderly, the disabled, and the mothers of young children who could not benefit from most work relief schemes. In October 1936 nearly ten thousand Floridians began to receive monthly checks from Social Security's Old Age Assistance program. (Half the funds came from federal money, the other half had to be contributed by the county.) The amounts were small—in Florida, the average monthly grant was $11.36 in that first year.[6] But the program did remove thousands of elderly from the county relief rolls, where their monthly checks were usually even smaller.

Passage of the Social Security Act did not end popular support for the Townsend proposal. As the letters in this chapter clearly illustrate, many Townsendites condemned Social Security's retirement insurance plan for its low payment levels, for its exclusion of large numbers of citizens (such as agricultural and domestic workers), and for its exclusion of those remaining outside the contributory system (that is, those who had already retired before the system had been implemented.) Although the Townsend movement lost some steam after 1935, it certainly did not fold and Floridians continued to write to Washington expressing their support for the plan.[7]

As the New Deal reached its maturity, letters to the governor and to the president began to change. There were still letters from desperate women who seemed not to know where to turn. But many correspondents now began to show a level of experience with and understanding of the variety of relief programs available. Rather than write a general plea for help, they wrote about specific problems with specific programs. Numerous letters were to complain that others seemed to be getting more benefits than the writer. Just as the New

Deal was maturing, so was the general public's understanding of the system. The tone of the letters begins to change, as women grew more confident about their rights to relief.

Mrs. Bessie T. Bender (Centralia Hotel, Manatee) to ER, 18 January 1935

No doubt you will be surprised to hear from me but however I hope my epistle will not reach the waste basket.

I have been real anxious to know how you felt towards the old age pension. Knowing what vast influence you have, the first lady of the land. I am very much interested in it, as I will soon be 57 years old—no income and not able to do hard work. At present I am helping to can grape fruit but the plant is so wet inside don't think I can hold out much longer. I lost my husband 18 months ago my two boys up north married barely making a living. I nursed a lady in Baltimore about 4 years ago[,] an invalid[.] she has since past on. Would love to have something to do up there now but people no longer employ at 50 any more. I would certainly appreciate it if you would use your great influence in assisting to pass this from so on as so many of us are greatly in need of it. I am willing to do work of any kind that is honorable— something that is light. Would love to hear from you.[8]

Rena M. Briggs (Mrs. G. W.) (Orlando) to ER, 18 January 1935

I am appealing to you to use your influence with the President for some substantial relief for the aged poor. Why not try the Townsend Plan? It surely is no more "fantastic" than most of the projects enacted during the · present regime.

Steadily has existence grown more difficult for the laboring class, which I represent. Prices soaring and no increase in income.

Why should not we, as well as you, be allowed to educate our children and grand-children. Our mothers are just as dear to us as yours to you and why should we not be allowed the same privileges which you enjoy?

Please allow me to cite just one case (of many) in Orange County, Florida. An old mother, destitute and no longer able to care for herself, appealed to the county for aid. The County [poor] house is filled and no room for her there, so she was sent to the JAIL where she did have some food and warmth. Is there anything more pathetic than that?

Now our President is presenting to Congress recommendations for a pension of thirty dollars a month (maximum) for destitute and aged people who have paid their taxes for the past five years. Is that the kind of a help-mate, or servant, that we have in the White House?

We feel that our trust has been betrayed. The people are awakening and will not stand these conditions. Please help us.

Am also sending appeal to the President.[9]

Early-twentieth-century local governments continued to rely on their jails for housing the homeless and the destitute, a practice that originated in the nineteenth century. See, for example, Gilles Vandal, "Nineteenth Century Municipal Responses to the Problem of Poverty: New Orleans' Free Lodgers 1850–1880," Journal of Urban History *19 (November 1992): 30–59.*

Mrs. W. G. Adams (Baker, Okaloosa County) to Sholtz, 25 January 1935

My husband got into a little trouble and the Judge give him a fine of $20.00 to get up in 30 days and we can not get it. we have no way of making any money at the present. he has a family of six[,] his mother and others to help look out for. and all we have is what he gets on relief work. and that just for bread and other groceries[.]

we have a little farm, are making preparation to make a crop, have already begin plowing and getting the land ready for cultivation. and I have no one except my husband to plow and go ahead with the business and if they send him off now it will just leave me in a mighty bad fix for I can't plow. and the children are girls and we are sending them to school. we have already got our fertilizer to make a crop. and I am asking you to please get the Judge to give him a suspended sentence and that will give us time to make something to get the money. we want to pay the fine. but we are poor people and can't get money up right now. but you can get the Judge to please give us some time to make it, and if they send him off to work it out, it will leave me without any help or anything to eat.[10]

Mrs. Barton Page (Arcadia) to Sholtz, 9 February 1935

My husband is in jail or rather on the county road. and I would like to get a little advice from you. He got out on a final cost bond for $50.62[.] He paid $20.00 and owing to not having much work he was unable to pay the rest of it. So they picked him up and put him on the county road. His sentence was 90 days or $50.00[.] The Sheriff and Deputy both said that they was giving him credit of $20.00 and when he worked out the remainder at [$.]30 a day he would be released. I figured it up and it would take 102 days to work out the remainder $30.62 at [$.]30 a day. I carried it before the board of county commisinors and they were in my favor they said there was no justice. and he would only have 90 days if he had not paid any thing. So they agreed to give me back the $20.00 if he had to make the whole 90 days anyway. But the Deputy Sheriff Frank Platt would not agree to give the money back or a shorten his term to 60 days either. My Baby has been awful bad sick and I am in awful bad circumstances[.] I will have to depend on the county for food until he gets out. I believe they will either have to shorten his sentence or give his money back. So I am writing you for advice so I will know just how much credit he is entitled to. He was took up and put on the county road the Second day of January. Please notify me at once what to do[.]

P.S. my husband was sentenced for possesion of whiskey[.][11]

Mrs. Ruth Altman (Lakeland) to Sholtz, 19 February 1935

I would like to ask you if it is possible for my mother to get the Widows Pension. She is not really able to do any work out side, as She has been doing all these years.

She has three small Children in School and no way of Support, as I am leaving home by Marrying. She has been a widow for eight years and we girls have stood by and helped but now we are not at home.

I certainly would appreciate it if you could help her a little.

The Children have had to stay out of School <u>two</u> years and pick berries any thing that they could get to do, but they are going this term. My mothers name is Mrs. Eva MacMillian.[12]

Mrs. Frances Schley Fort (New Smyrna) to ER, 22 February 1935

No doubt you will be amaised at my cheek but when one is desperate we do many things we would not do—conditions here since all fruit froze are bad & people are actually in need of food. I have made a very pretty lacy spread & hope to sell you—it is well worth 50 dollars. I am an old woman[,] 85 in March, & make my own money[.] I used to make & sell hand-made Baby clothes, for the past 3 years people have had no money for such—so I went to crocheting & knitting—the spread is made of Columbia knitting cotton 45 cts a hank. I am a great admirer of the President, he has such a kind pleasing voice, just know he is a christian man. Excuse the cheek[.] trust your secratary will let you see this—for I would appreciate an answer from you.[13]

Mrs. Susie H. Reddick (Sarasota) ER, 21 February 1935

I am writing you because you are in sympathy with the poor people, also because like me you are a mother.

I am a mother of five children. I live in a small town here had to send my children away for High School and college.

My husband is a minister and I am school teacher, community worker, of course housekeeper.

We are struggling to educate our children with the small salaries we get.

Three of my children were away in college, in fact the two girls and one boy in High School. My oldest daughter who is a senior [in] College, is suffering of a mental nerveous collapse, caused from worrying over finances and a very heavy schedule. She passed the first semester very creditably and from all evidences I thought that she was perfectly happy and well. I received a telegram from the College stating her condition[.] when I arrived I found that she was suffering of a brain storm. We were compelled to take her from the (school) college home, in fact she is enroute home now by auto and I am on train now enroute to be with her.

There is no place for doctors [illegible] here where I can place her. I feel if I could get her in a sanitarian for Mentally disturbed people I believe she would get well.

She is young, 19 yrs. and I feel optimistic about her. I have no money, but I have a city lot in Atlanta that I would sell in order to have this child treated. My heart is broken, if I loose this child, I do not think I can live. Will you please, please, help me.

Mrs. Roosevelt, I am writing you this because you are a friend to humanity.

My daughter is B. R., Senior College class of Spelman College. She has attended this school since she was fourteen. I must have some help in my distress. This letter is personal and I trust that it will not be made public. Please let me hear from you at once.

Yours, an anxious and heart broken mother.

P.S. I am enclosing a letter that I recently got from my daughter in order that you may appreciate her type and worth. She assisted Prof. Roberts, in Psychology, and helped her self in school. You will note in this letter the number of papers corrected and how she was to receive FERA. It might interest you to know that she volunteered her services as a stenographer last summer at a training center (FERA) Clark University, one of Mrs. Ambrose Warburton Projects.

I attended the first training center at A[tlanta] U[niversity] last summer. I can refer you to Miss Ernestine Friedman, Mrs. Amber Warburton who know me personally, the latter a former teacher of mine. Miss Florence Reid, Pres. Spelman College, Dr. Jno. Hope, Pres. A.U. Atlanta Ga.

We are living 60 miles from Tampa, and I am wondering if you would get for me a Psychiatrist (I trust it's spelled correctly) at Tampa to look after this child for me. All of this must be done at once.

Please, help me. I believe you will. Trusting in God and believing in you, I am very appreciative.

I am writing on moving train.[14]

Mrs. H. N. Lewis (St. Petersburg) to Sholtz, 22 February 1935

I have a very grievious complaint to make about the many hours the poor working girl works, from ten to twelve hours a day here in St. Petersburg. I trust that you may be able to do something about it quick. Girls working especially in cafeterias. They are compelled to work <u>seven</u> days a week with <u>not one day off, no time.</u> It is more than a human being can stand. People who dine at those places remark how tired those girls look. It's the disgrace of Florida, to this grand U.S.A. that they have no <u>laws,</u> regulating the working mans hours. And the employer takes this advantage for the greed of the almighty dollar, blood money <u>with out shame.</u> What kind of law makers have you in this state? They the employers have no regard for the N.R.A. I've made the complaint there.

P.S. Kindly forward this letter to the law makers of Florida I don't know just who they are.[15]

Mrs. J. R. Marlowe (Miami) to ER, 26 February 1935

I feel a delicacy in writing you, but knowing that you are noted for your kindness and generosity, I feel sure you will come to my rescue.

I have a grandson who is quite talented, and a very bright, ambitious boy, but has not had the opportunities that he deserved. He is in the eighth grade at the Miami-Edison high school.

He is very anxious for a musical instrument, his choice is a Merrimba. What do you think of this instrument?

I am a widow, fifty eight years old and have no income, and after meeting my neccesary expenses, I have very little to help him, but have managed to save some for the purchase of the Merrimba or some other instrument.

He has a father who is very dissapated and therefore cannot depend on him for the boys future.

Any amount you will be kind enough to donate will be appreciated more than words can tell.

I know it will be a great lift for him in the future. Please consider helping him. I am sure if you knew him and his circumstances you would not hesitate.

Any kindness you favor him, I assure you will be kept confidential.[16]

Miss June Gardner (Belleview) to ER, 23 March 1935

1930 census: She is the 25-year-old daughter of James and Margaret. Her
father is a carpenter. Her mother owns and manages a "custom hatchery,"
and June works for her as a clerk. The family is white.

The news papers say that you use all you income from your broadcasting
to help ones in need. And that you recently purchased a furniture factory to
give more people work.

I own a baby chick hatchery here in Summerfield. Fla. and until recent
years did well hatching for the farmers and flock owners. Since the freeze
last Dec. that cut out the fruit crop.—as well as a large part of the trees-the
people have nothing to pay for their custom hatching, or to feed the chickens
on after hatched. We have done share hatching for as many as wanted to risk
raising chicks.

Just last week when crops were looking good, we had a dust storm-on the
12th.—that simply blowed crops away.

One of our customers that have bought chicks each year, came and got only
50 chicks as he could not see his way clear to buy, he said his water melon
vines was hurt bad, and that he had forty acres in tomatoes just coming into
bloom, that the wind and dust had swept them all away, it is too late to plant
see again, he was trying to get plants. but so was every one else. These people
do not want to be on the relief, they only want somthing to work with.

I am the only support of my widowed mother, as we make our living doing
custom hatching for others and selling baby chicks, we put up this building
of hollow tile in 1925. we have lived here is this county 25 years next Dec.
we have about one acre of land just across the R.R. track from the depot.

I am wondering if you would see your way clear to buy my hatchery property and give these people credit for one or two seasons for chicks or custom-
hatching, so they can make good. we used to hire help, but we do not get
enough business now to do that so we try to do the work ourselves. We have
put more than twenty thousand dollars in land, buildings and equipment, I
would be glad to take half or what ever it was worth to you for the above
mentioned purpose. I will soon be thirty years old and had to stop school
at 15 years of age to work in the poultry business, so did not get to finish
school. if you or some of your friends will buy my hatchery, I can then finish school, and my mother can live while I am going to school.

I have not seen where you have helped people this far south, will you
please do so now, these people are nearly all democrats and are all for you
and Mr. Roosevelt, but with these hard times here right now & with Senator
Long begining to speak in the south, it takes such a little thing some times to
turn peoples mind. and the situation here now is not a little thing by any

means. will you show Mr. Long and our people here in the south that you are just as willing to help them as you are to help ones in need up north.

The helping of the ones that need help in Florida and the whole south will bring more votes to the right one, which is Mr. Roosevelt, than several times that amount of money paid to high priced campaign managers, as it will get right with the voters, let them see that you are with them to the finish.

Think this over and if you do not care to handle it, perhaps some of your friends will want to do so, we can give you refferences as to our standing and business and will say right here that we have kept the property clear of all debt, can give a perfect title and abstract to the property, and will show or tell the ones that you place here to operate it all I know and our list of customers.

And somthing else, our family has had many many years some paper money in Confederate bills some $10. $20. and $100. and one $500. bill[.] we had not expected to ever part with it, can you or some of your friends use some of these, at what ever you think they are worth, or do [you] know where I can sell them?

This letter goes to you with our best wishes and our prayers.[17]

"Senator Long" refers to Huey Long of Louisiana, a candidate for the Democratic nomination against Roosevelt and leader of a swelling grassroots movement.

Miss Theo E. Anderson (Jacksonville) to ER, 4 April 1935

1930 census: Theo Anderson is the 15-year-old daughter of a gas station owner in Dunnellon. The family is white.

This may seem to be a very unusual request to you, but I want to ask if you would permit me to work at Warm Springs, Georgia? I am very interested in that kind of work.

Although, I have had not training in the care of crippled children, I have a brother, now sixteen years of age, who had infantile paragysis when he was thirteen months old. So you see, I am interested in all crippled children. I am not writing just for a job, but because I want to do something I think would be worthwhile, something I would enjoy doing.

I am twenty years old, and can furnish a doctor's affadavit that I am in good physical condition to carry on the work that I would have to do. I am a high-school graduate of the Dunnellon High School, Dunnellon, Florida, also took a Commercial course in Part Time School here in Jacksonville.[18]

In addition to FDR's well-known retreat home at Warm Springs, the facility also housed a clinic for the treatment of polio. See Turnley Walker, Roosevelt and the Warm Springs Story *(New York: A. A. Wyn, 1953).*

Mrs. Marie Hosmer (Tampa) to ER, 7 April 1935

Would it be too much to ask you advice on a very technical situation. I am a widow and have a 77 year old aunt lef on my hands to care for as her mind seems to leave her at times every five minutes[.] she has a little income but I will have to count every cent as I only lost my husband two years ago[.] I had a little money but is getting smaller fast[.] I have on hand my mothers Paisley wedding shawl silk and fringed very nicely kept and 56 years old. How could I make the most money out of it and could you advise me as to who would be honest and where I could find the best honest deal?

I hope you can give me a gleam of light on my very perplexing situation.

My dear Mrs. Roosevelt and kindly first Lady I thank you now in advance for eney advice and guiding hand you may lend.

PS. Please advise me of a safe old coin sales place. Thanks.[19]

Mrs. E. L. McIntyre (Tarpon Springs) to ER, 7 April 1935

I would like to appeal to you to use your political influence, now that the Public Works Bill has been passed, to give our trained men on the Direct Relief some of the good Positions that are to be given out. If those jobs are given out by our small town Officials as they were during the C.W.A. they will not be given to our men who are unfortunate enough to have to stay on the relief roll all the time, no matter how capable they are. The best positions at that time were given almost without exception to men not on relief rolls, some of them already employed, while skilled men on relief rolls were ignored because those Positions came thru our town Officials. I am grateful for what we have gotten, it has meant food for our three children, but my husband is a skilled workman, and we would like a chance at a job that would let us respect ourselves and give our children some of the care that has been so badly neglected.[20]

Mrs. C. M. Meridith (Ferndale) to Sholtz, 10 April 1935

I am asking you for help[.] my daughter has been in the state hospital 5 months and I have not seen her and I wrote to the Dr. and ask about her condition and he said it would be sometime be fore she would be able to come home and she keep on writing for me to come to see her and I have not got any money to go to see her and I am asking you to send me some money to go to see her as I wont to see her so bad and the Dr. said maby it would help her if I come to see her for she was not able to come home[.] my husband has not got any work. and they is 7 of us in family and just what he makes it takes it all for us to live[.] and send me some money Dear Friend so I can go to see her and I ceartainly will preashate it and also will pray for you in my pray as I trie to be a Christian. tell Mrs Sholtz if she has any cloths that she dont need I would be gladest if she would send me a few things[.] I have one girl 3 years old and one girl 4 years old and one boy 7 years old and one girl 18 years old and the rest of the children is all grown[.] tell her if the cloths are old Ill be the gladdest in the world to get them[.] Hopping to here from you soon and hope I get help.[21]

Shorthand notes on letter from office staff: They will give her clothes at the local welfare organizations.

Mrs. J. C. Scott (Jacksonville) to ER, 15 April 1935

I heard your talk on music, not so long ago, which give me the idea of writing to you.

I have one very old violin (two hundred and nineteen years old). Written on the inside is the following—"Antonius Stradivarius Cremonenlis Faciebat Anno 1716."

I thought you might know some one that would like to own it or of some museum or Music Hall & Conservatory that would buy it. I understand there is quite a premium on a violin like this.

I would apreciatte an early reply since we need the money and I want to give my boy music.[22]

Mrs. Frances M. Bye (Tampa) to ER, 17 April 1935

I do hope this reaches you personally, as it is from you I am seeking advice.

However, should it go no further than a secretary, hired for just such purposes, I understand, I hope it will remain as I write it, strictly confidential.

My problem, which I seem to be unable to solve, concerns work. I do not ask for a job. I am asking advice as to how to get a job under the circumstance in which I find myself.

I feel, that in order for you to understand the situation more clearly, I should go into detail to some extent.

I was married at the age of 17. I was in my last year of high school. After going thru the past six years of depression, having two children, yet getting along unusually better than many young couples, my husband left me. He had managed to find a position in Florida and I, and my two children were coming to him when my oldest daughter and I were hurt. She fell from the car and I jumped after her thinking to be of assistance, I suppose. I returned to the home of my parents as soon as I was able, I had recieved a broken leg and severe head injuries, and had been there, but a few days when my husband, he had returned soon after I was hurt with father and mother, told me he was leaving.

A short time ago he wrote asking me to bring the children and come here to him.

Feeling that even though the feeling, which had once existed between us, was dead, I owed it to my children to do so, I came.

I have found that it is all rather hopeless. I am sure we are better off separately.

My problem now is this. He has a job, very poorly paid and should I return home he can contribute but very, very little to the children's support. Mother and Dad are in no position to care for us, and I [illegible] feel I was being fair to return to them with no means of support for myself and children.

It is utterly impossible, particularly with my limited education, to find a position in my home town, Alliance, Ohio, where all my family reside, with the exception of a married brother and sister.

Can you send me information as to whether there are any government jobs available for one in such a position as I find myself? If so, will you advise me as to the best way in which to procure said position?[23]

Mrs. W. R. Adams (Dade City) to Sholtz, 25 April 1935

Please advise me if there is a law to Protect my children so the[y] wont be put out on the Street. My husband has been on the Relief roll for almost two years and during that time we got behind with our rent (4) four month.

My husband was sick last summer in Tamp Hospt. we have three children in High School. now we just received notice to vacate the Property on the Second of next month. we have a real nice garden which almost feeds us. and the Taxes has not been Paid on Property where we live in (5) Five years.

My husband was borned and raised here in Pasco Co. a hard worker & sober. will refer you to Mr Geo Weems. He knows the whole family. Please do something about this at once.[24]

Miss Rose Elizabeth Lynch (Quincy) to Sholtz, 1 May 1935

I am writing this letter to request you to kindly give me permission to draw a small Pension each month to help support myself & to buy the Medicine I need to keep me from being Bed-ridden.

I am a young woman, single & living at home with my widow Mother on our little Farm six miles north of Quincy, Fla.

I have been suffering from Epilepsy ever since I was a child & as I grow older the attacks continue to grow more severe.

I am now thirty-five years of age, white.

My father has been dead for the past ten years & I have been living with my mother trying to help her earn our living, but on account of my sickness she could not go out to a regular position & expenses count up so rapidly when you hire help on a farm there is no way to meet them all without other help at times.

I have just found a certain medicine that has given me more relief than anything else but I cannot afford to buy it & the fruits & other foods the doctor advises you to eat while taking it for best results. So I am asking you to kindly give me a note to draw a small pension to help support myself until my health improves. Hoping to hear from you soon.[25]

Mrs. J. M. Brice (The Stewart Hotel, Lake Wales) to ER, 2 May 1935

If I didn't know you were a friend of the working woman, I would be afraid to ask you to please help me out in this contest, I do want so much to win a prize, as I have spent the money (in my mind) for a hundred and one things—that I need so badly.

I love you very, very much and am always to interested in all you do and write. You are just wonderful.

I used to have a home of our own and a large farm too and through Broken Banks, Cotton Mills that failed where we had our savings we were forced to give all up. But my Husband who is 62 years old and me close behind him we have been very happy in doing the next best thing we found to do, and we are in this hotel working every day, that is why I though[t] you might give me a few suggestions to write about (A famous woman) namely Miss Frances Perkins.

The contest is about famous women and she is among the names included in the word-picture. I had no trouble finding her name and I do think she is doing a splendid work, if I only knew how to say it, also if I knew some of the fine things she has done, and where she was born.

Please can you help me arrange about 75 words about her. Oh I would be so happy to have you do this for me and then I will be happier to win a prize.

I am tired tonight. We had such a large crowd in the hotel for the Sunrise Concert at The Bok Tower in this place. People come from every-where to hear the Bells (Anton Brees plays them and he finished up the season today at 4 P.M. He will come back to Mountain Lake in December to play another season.

I wish you could visit the Singing Tower it is one of the loviliest places in the world. Come down to see it Mrs. Roosevelt and stay at our nice little hotel, we have such nice people to stay with us, and Mrs. Stewart our manager knows all about the Tower and it's Construction as the builders lived in our hotel during the buolding of it.

In the Sanctuary there is an enclosed marble resting place for visitors that the kind neighbors gave to Mr. Bok in memory of their love and there is this little verse on a marble slab at the entrance that you see every-body copying,

"The Kiss of the sun for pardon,
The song of the birds for mirth,
You are nearer God's heart in a garden,
Than any where else on earth."

There is a lovely spot always out there for it is well kept, the folks that live in the at the MT. Lake are very wealthy and are so generous with it to keep the Sanctuary every-thing that is lovely and inviting. People come from all over the U.S. to see the Tower.

I am enclosing the little set of rules so you will understand how they ask the questions and what depends on the little notes given to those who try.

I can never thank you enough before you send it even. I trust I have not used too much of your valuable time, but you will not be able ever to know just what it will mean to me.

I remain just The Pastry and Pantry Woman for Mrs. Steward. I am so glad I can do this work and can please her.[26]

The Tower and Gardens, located in Lake Wales, was built by Edward Bok, author and longtime editor of the Ladies Home Journal. *Francis Perkins served as FDR's secretary of labor, the first woman to hold a cabinet position.*

Mrs. Emily Lahrman (DeLand) to Mr. and Mrs. Sholtz, 12 May 1935

Pardon me please for taking this liberty in writing to you. As my son Walter Lahrman is a friend of you also in politics I thought you would take an interest in me. Am 73 yrs old and through the awfull worries and troubles of last winter was afraid I would lose my mind cannot stand it much longer. All I have is my little home which I share with my daughter and grandson no income and although my daughter has the reputation of giving the best shampoo, scalp treatment and manicure here she made a mistake in refusing an offer last fall[.] she is without steady work. All tourists that have come to DeLand have praised her work and every one says she has such a pleasing personality[.] wish it would be possible for you both to meet her and see for yourself and get aquainted. Do think with your influence it would be possible for her to go on. Do you think you would be over at your Daytona home in the near future that she could meet you there? She could take a taxi over. Surely there are enough good women and men here in DeLand that would help her get a shop, only a small one. I tho't probably to take shares and in that way they all would be interested and as she does good work would come to her. I believe Mr. C. D. Landis would be interested as we have lived here so many years and he is also a friend of Walter's.

Will you please do what you can and let me know if I may have hopes? This is not a neat letter but you will see that I am very nervous and will excuse me. Neither my son Walter or my daughter know that I am writing this letter but I feel that Edna must have work and she will do her best and is known to be truthful and honest. Edna could not do anything alone and must have influential parties backing her as Mrs. Reynolds has told her she would "squash" her within a week if she opened a shop after she had refused her offer[.] it was a mistake and we do regret it.

Please, please give this your attention and I shall be so grateful you will have saved the lives of the three of us as we cannot go on this way much longer[.] would you want my daughter to come to Tallahassee? Which ever you say. Trusting to hear from you as soon as convenient with great hopes I beg to remain.

We are of german descent also.

P.S. Walter was with you at the Elks convention at Los Angeles in 1929. He has a Kodak picture of both of you taken with him in the mountains.[27]

Miss Nettie Sloan (Miami) to ER, undated but envelope stamped 12 May 1935

I am a girl of 10 and like all boy sports such as baseball football tennis golf and all others[.] I am in the 6A in school and have 1 pair of pants that got too little for my brother who is 13 years old[.] I wear them to school when they are clean[.] When my sister who's 14 years old gets dresses that are too little for her I get them. I don't like dresses but have to wear them[.] I can't get a job and my mother and father havn't work[.] Can you help me get some money to buy me some pants.

PS. Pleas answer me even if you cant help me so I will know my letter got there.[28]

Mrs. Nellie Gray (Daytona Beach) to Sholtz, 20 May 1935

Wont you please do all you can to pass an old age pension bill for this State? No matter how small the amount it will help me to save my home.

I was one of the heavy losers in the crash after our real estate boom ten years ago. Then all my money was lost in three bank failures. My stocks and bonds have been sold to meet living expenses. When I could no longer pay taxes and the roof of my home began to leak I made a government loan through the H.O.L.C. Because of an accident this past winter I have been practically disabled ever since and necessary expenses have been high, so payments on the mortgage are past due. The Atlanta office has served notice that unless I can "pay up by July 10th they will sell my home for amount of the mortgage."

As I am entirely alone in the world, 72 years old and cripple from a broken hip, I just <u>can not</u> lose my home and yet I see no way to meet the payments unless an old age pension is passed. I have explained the situation to the H.O.L.C. offices in Atlanta and Washington. Now, in the mean time, what can I do to save my home?[29]

H O.L.C. is the Home Owners Loan Corporation.

Mrs. Mary E. Comer (Jacksonville) to Sholtz, 29 May 1935

1930 census indexed as "Conner": She is 29 years old and white and works as a bookkeeper in an "electric store." She is listed as married but is living as a boarder and not with a husband.

as i have been reading of Some Things concerning The Old Confederate Soldiers & Sailors home as i said when i written yu about the Relief help here i only wish i cold talk to some one like yu in Personall about lots of things like the Old Soldiers home & also the relief as there is many things that yu do not know or relize that is going on[.] i also red in the paper that only one can bee mantained at the home in a family[.] there is 4 of one family There now & has been for 10 years & the help hired they have got 3 homes & a plenty [illegible] & also all the board in Friends & Relative of theirs & that is what keep them there now[.] here i am myself a widdow & the mother of teen children been with them above for 20 year & got no home to have to pay rent & i cant eaven get a job[.] yu see there is 7 there to bee mantained by the State besides the old men there is only five of the old men There when they are all there & there is only 3 there now & has been for a month i cant understand why when i have devoted so much of my time to the conadates that i canot get Some results[.] i had a letter from Mr Stones concerning what i writes you about the relief & he said he had turned my letter over here to the Relief People that will not do me any good as i have beg them for help & work & have never got any results[.] they said becouse i had one little delagate daughter working making from 8 to 10 a week they cold not do any thing for me & now that she is married & gone i still dont get any thing[.] So what are we to do when we cant get no work or help[?] i want work not Relief help[.] i will ask of yu please dont use my name about the old home as i have worked there off & on for the past 4 years as Nurse & matron while they was away.[30]

The Confederate Home was a state-run facility for elderly Confederate vet-erans, located in Jacksonville. "Mr. Stone" refers to Julius Stone, state administrator of the WPA.

Mrs. Stella G. Bennett (New Smyrna) to ER, 1 June 1935

1930 census: She is 38 years old and white and is the wife of S. G. Bennett, who owns an "auto station." They have four sons.

It truly grieves my heart & Pride to write you in this Way. But hope you will Be Patient & Bear with My Pleadings for God a bove knows this is my true conditions. I am a Mother having fours sons ages 18[,] 15[,] 13[,] & 6[,] the oldest of whom is at present working with Western Union But hardly makes enought to take care of himself & Make Payment on Bycicle. And I have a kind & loving husband who tries to make us a livlihood By Transfering with one small truck[.] But he gets very little to do & half of time he is not able to work if he had work for he has a bad kidney trouble & at times just cant go at all[.] But Before his health got so Bad he managed to Buy 10 acres of Best hammock land 6 miles from town. of which 3 acres is clear & one acre in 2 yr. old Grape fruit trees well fenced & good well of water. (But no house) and is clear of any incumberance Now this is all we have. But god know we cant eat it & we cant live on it. with out a house.

Now I don't mean to Beg you to just give us any thing. But we really have put $1500.00 in clearing[,] fencing[,] well water. combine with purchase of land. So what I want you to do is Buy this land of us for $1000.00 so that we may live & give Husband the treatment he needs so Bad[.] This is only a small amt. I am sure to you[.] But it would mean so much to us & I Pray God in his infinite Mercy would Bless & repay you in more ways than one[.][31]

Mrs. Maude V. Duncan (Crystal River) to Sholtz, 4 June 1935

As Gov. of the people and for the people of Florida, I think you are the proper one I should write to. I have so much to say. But will make this letter as short and brief as possible. Gov Sholtz I am a mother 32 years old[,] three children 14 daughter 2 sons 12 (almost in Sept) and 7. have been married 14 years to the father of the 2 boys. The daughter is by my first husband. (died) before the birth of my daughter. Gov Sholtz if you recall last fall, I think one of my letters was referred to you in regards to my husband selling liquor in our home. Making the house (not a home) a public place to men & women and if I complained I was knocked down by him my husband and forced to leave the home and was on the mercy of the better people of this town, he helped us in no way. And the relief would not help me, because he was able to take care of us. they told me to go to the pros cutor George Scoofild. I went

112

and he waved me out of his office told me he would have nothing to do with it. my husband had been to see him. He was selling quit a bit of liquor[.] the court here will do nothing with a liquor man. And of course we know why. We all know what our sherrief does, so that much is useless to go to the sherrief. But any way he would not help us the relief would not, there was no work to be done in this small place. I was forced to humble my self to come back to this awful place where he has been meaner than ever. tells me he will not take care of us. he done very well until he though the bonus bill would be pd, then he begain to lay plans for the children and I would leave. The federal men got so hot after him he quit selling liquor for a while. But said as soon as the bonus bill passed he was leaving. he beats the children and me when he get ready[.] we are dared by him to open our mouth when he tells us to hush[.] he swore my daughter would have to leave if she was not nice to these drunken dogs that came here. says we ruined his trade. Oh its so awful. he worked on this road work here make 18.00 ever two wks. Gave me 8.00 for grocier bill for 2 wks. he would keep the 10.00 my boys with out a shirt to their name[.] I have one dress nothing else[.] I & the boys has had to pick berries to by us a few garments he has bough clothes for him self, stays out, and now since the bonus bill has not passed he has ordered another 5 gallon of liquor from the man he bought from before, suposed to be here tonight & says we must do as he wants done or get out. that he had proction from the law & he was to[o] slick for the federal men. Gov Sholtz I can not stand [it] I am afraid I will just have to kill somebody and I dont want to. But if I ever see another drunk pawing over my little girl. she says she cant stand to live here. We have no money and he wont let me take a job[.] it would only be for 10 days taking care of a lady & baby. says my place is here and if I stay here I must help sell the liquor & I wont. my friends here was dissipointed in me because I came back to him. But I had to[o][.] my people are 1,000 miles away in Indiana & Ky. They all hate him & will not help as long as I am with him. They are all just honest working people. farmers. So Gov Sholtz, what can a person do. I do want to get my children away and give them a deacent chance in life[.] Our lives are miserable, could you tell me, if there is any place in this state where I could get a loan to by a few acres of ground with a small house so I could raise chickens & vegetables[.] I was raised on a farm & Know how to to raise incubator chickens, I have tried to gat a loan from several places but no results. We would be content with a shack if we could live in peace[.] I am willing to work hard, just any where, where I can make a living for my children, of course we have no money to do a thing with there are so many cheap places around Tampa[.] would I be intitaled to a farm loan, to buy a chicken farm. I can get one for $450.00 four hundred & fifty five hundred dollars down. But a woman can not do any thing. It seems like men can do lots of things but they seems to think woman can not work. Gov Sholtz I wish you would write me & tell me where I might get my children to a place where I could make a living for them, or could you tell me, where I could get a loan [illegible] want it gave to me. I only [illegible] to borry & pay it back please for I can-not stay here and take off this man much longer & I can not do any thing to make him better, For I have my children to think off. he threatens to kill me, I have laid awake afraid to sleep. he would load the guns & tell me he would kill us all. I know I should tell this to a lawyer[.] But I have no money and no clothes to go see one. Please help me and the children[.] I am not wanted revenge[.] I only want to get away and leave him alone. For we are not wanted.

P.S. am sending a few ads for the up places for sale. If there is any where I could obtain a loan or any where you know I might get a place please let me know.[32]

> *The Bonus Bill was a precursor to the GI Bill. Unlike a veterans' pension, which only supported veterans who could demonstrate need, the Bonus Bill was to pay a bonus to all veterans of the First World War. Originally passed by Congress in 1924, the bonus was scheduled to be paid in 1945, after sufficient funds had accumulated. But during the Depression needy veterans began to demand the payment immediately, arguing that the early redemption of this promise would help put money into the economy and into the pockets of those who desperately needed it. This led to the Bonus March of 1932, where thousands of veterans, some wearing their World War I uniforms, camped out in Washington to lobby for the early payment of the bonus. Gen. Douglas McArthur, charged with clearing the veterans away from the Capitol, dispersed them with tanks and machine guns. Despite this public relations fiasco, Congress repeatedly rejected proposals to pay the bonus early.*

Mary Reeves (Micanopy) to ER, undated but reply dated 4 June 1935

Several days ago I wrote you telling you of a dream I had and how it all turned out to be the finding of a beautiful diamond broach of an ancient design and I was directed to write you and ask you to sell it for me and I did[.] But as yet I have not heard from you[.] Now this is not the rave of any crank are chain letter fad this is the real truth[.] Write me even if you will not handle it for me and I will try to get some one else as I am sure that I am telling the truth as to how I got the gems[.] I am sending you a stamp for reply[.] Please ans at once as I am a poor sickly woman an expectant mother and will need the money in the near future[.] if you handle it why you should be paid for your trouble[.] the Spirit toled me in my dream when it told me where the broach was that it was worth thirty thousand dollars[.] its the prettiest peice of jewelry I ever saw[.] please help me if you will[.]

Awaiting your reply with best wishes and prayer for your success.

PS. Excuse the stationary and lead pencil as this is the best I have[.][33]

She did not sign her letter "Miss," and she says she is an expectant mother, but the reply letter was addressed to "Miss."

Mrs. Mattie J. Story (Winter Garden) to Sholtz, 6 June 1935

May I introduce myself before making my request. I have been a voluntary worker for years, working in my community just for the desire to make others more comfortable and happy. The very poor, need so much that they never get. Now my request is this—out of the many millions spent for roads and other improvements won't you have a small sum set aside for the following specific things? Artificial teeth, glasses, and tonsils, but especially I am hoping for money to buy teeth and glasses. I have in mind several who are so badly in need of these. Our co[unty] worker can get the teeth out, and the nurses give free examination but what good are examinations when there is no money for glasses? And these toothless people are a pathetic sight. The small sum of $100.00 a month would do worlds of good or $150.00 could help on tonsils. This could be divided equally with our county welfare worker and our county nurse. This clipping attached, also many others of similar suggestions is what prompts me to write you and as a Christian woman, my prayers have gone already for help in this urgent need.

Will the Governors sec'y. please read this to him at the opportune time, only.[34]

Mrs. Ruth Henderson (St. Petersburg) to ER, 13 June 1935

This letter may be quite a surprise to you. But I have a combination bookcase & writting desk once the property of Elexander Hamilton, Secretary of the Treasurer some years ago. This desk is a very beautiful Antique—Queen Ann style, hand carved Rosewood.

I would like to sell you this desk for some Muesum of Art or Library.

If you should be interested I would like to hear from you at your earliest convenience.

P.S. I am the Mother of eight children all at home. am in need of funds is why I am selling this Antique if you wish further detail's of how I came in possession of the desk I will be glad to do so.

I will crate carefuly and ship to you if you wish to purchase this Antique.[35]

Mrs. Pearl Still (Pensacola) to Sholtz, 13 June 1935

1930 census: She is a 34-year-old widow with four children. No one in the household has a job.

I am a widow lady have three small children and am on the F.E.R.A. and will you please tell me why that Mrs. Owens and my aid want give me this cloth like ever body elce. every family here around me has got cloth from 25 to 23 yards[.] I also ask my aid to give me as she had give the others[.] she want do it[.] so if you will send some one out here to my house and see for your self the ones that got all this cloth doesnt need it so bad as my family does[.] so please tell me why my children and I cant get as the others, if you want names to find out my condishon write me I will send them[.] so please let me here from you at once[.] Many thanks.[36]

Mrs. Mary J. Lockard (New Port Richey) to ER, 14 June 1935

1930 census: She is a 55-year-old white widow. Her 30-year-old son, a line- man for an electric company, lives with her.

I have peiced a blue eagle quilt and thought maybe you would be inter- ested in buying it for one of your grand children to keep as a remembrance of their grandfather's administration. It is made of blue & white broad cloth: blue eagles being appliqued on eighteen inch blocks in white.

It is quilted in feathers and other designs. This is an original idea and I do not know of another one like it. I might add that there is not a machine stitch in it. It is all made by hand.

If you would be interested I should be only too happy to send to quilt to you on approval, as I make my living by making quilts.[37]

Mrs. Bertha Galvins (Kissimmee) to Sholtz, 24 June 1935

I am asking you to pleas help me. I am not able to work and I need Something to Eat[.] Haven got no Husband and cant even walk. the releaf is not doing one thing for me, or either the county and I need Some body to help me and I have wrote you all two times for help and I haven Ben able to recieve it yet contend Begging for help and the peoples may put me out of doors at any time[.] have no father or brother.[38]

Miss Euvah Bridges (Sarasota) to Sholtz, 26 June 1935

1930 census: She is 23 years old, white, and unmarried, and she works at a mattress factory.

I am an orphan girl and am asking you for a little aid. Mr. Claude D. Coleman of Sarasota Fla. formerly but now located in Tampa Fla. and working for the government, borrowed $200.00 from me back in December 16th

1925. I have written several letters begging him to please pay me the money he has payed me $10.00 ten dollars in the whole 9 years and 6 month. The next time he said he would pay me when he got d—— good and ready.

Now govenor I am an orphan girl and I have a blind sister to help and I sure do need the money so please help me.

I was hurt in a railroad wreck and they payed me the $200.00 and I was nurse for his two children at the time.

I have the canceled check and also the letter showing that he borrowed the money.

I certainly will appreciate any aid you will render. An orphan has a hard time in this big world now. Hoping you will give this your most kind attention.[39]

Miss Annie Ferraro (Pensacola) to Sholtz, 28 June 1935

1930 census: Anna is 10 years old. She is the daughter of Lonia, a laborer on a fish shack, born in Italy.

I am thirteen years of age and my name is Annie Ferraro. I am American born, but Italian decent, and I am in the eigth grade. I have three sisters and three brothers, so that makes seven children and my mother and my father make nine.

In beginning my hard-luck story I will tell you of our suffering. My dad has been out of work for over three years and to tell you everything is pitiful. We have been chased from one house to the other not being able to pay our rent. I also have a baby brother five months old, and another next to him, two years old, and many times even at the present they have cryed themselves to sleep for not having any milk. My dad does get five day a month from the Red Cross, but how far does that go? Not far of course. We have heard so much about you even in our school (St. Michaels) and all I hear people say is how charitable and generous you are, and I have read one of your booklet that tells how smart you have been. I'll tell any-body that you are one of the best Governors in the State of Florida. So Gov Sholtz I am asking you for one thing, and that is to give daddy some work. I am so unfortunate, at least I think I am, to see all my school friend dressed nice with good shoes, and me with the rest of my sisters depend on the poor Sisters of the convent to give us clothes. Of course I am thankful to God for what we have got. So please try to get daddy some work to help us out, and I will be so thankful to you I remain your little friend.

P.S. I will be waiting with anxiety for your reply.

P.S. My daddy is a healthy man, and I will be glad and grateful for anything you can give him.[40]

Mrs. Gertrude Humphrey (Ft. McCoy) to Sholtz, 1 July 1935

Sir I am writing you concerning my own personal needs & condition. I am a widow woman with poor health. My husband died last Sep 17, 1934 from ingue [injury] of truck which was own by Mrs. Dessie Vincen who had my husband employed fencing up land for government cattle. Mrs. Vincen and Mr. John Stephens had employed him for this works. While on the job he was taken ill an was being sent home on the truck which was huling posts for the fencing[.] it was driven by James Grontham white. Making a quick turn at a cross road threw my husband off and backed up on him breaking several of his ribs an puncured his lungs. he was taken rite from the place to the Memoral Hospital which was of no avale. Mrs. Vincen after taken him to the Hospital rushed back to me and told me my husband was not seariously injured[.] said she had an x ray taken and only 3 ribs was broken[.] said he would be home in 3 days. I beeing very weak & nervous was advised not to go but sent my oldest daughter the same night. She stayed as long as she was allowed too. he passed away shuretly after she left. Mr. John Stephen and Mrs Dessie Vincin rushed quickly to me in my excitment and one on either sid of me to try to quiet my self long enought to sigen a paper. I dident even read the paper I was broke down in greif[.] they said to me we ar your friend and came to help you we ar going to bear all expencis. They had all ready pluce his body in the white undertaker which had no accomidation for C[olored] people but had his body out in a garage[.] and I ask Mrs Vincen to have it remove to the colored furnal home[.] told me she would but fail[.] I had it remove my self which cost me $15.00 fifteen dollars. They refuse to pay this after every thing was over[.] I begon to try for help[.] I consulted a Lawyer abut it he said they taken the advantag of me and I had sign my rites aways[.] I had nothing to look to[,] no boys to take charge[.] only 2 girls[.] I was left almost in a suffering condition with only $8.00 eight dollars in cash which my husband drawn from his work the previous Saturday. I was left alone with my childrens to fathem, out my way with no helth no money. A big Dr. Bill small mortogue an my place 3 years behind in taxes. I have tried from all suces [sources] to get help but fail[.] I went to the releif offise in feb aplied for help. They told me if I could work they would give me a job. But I was not able. I ask for the rehabilation loan twice they told me they would come out see abut me but did not[.] I went to my Dr. who new my condition and was some what interested in the gov. works. He said he would notify the county commissions[.] i aughto get some help from the county. People all around me gets help from the relef that ar in much better circumstances than I. I have been a resident of Ft. McCoy Fla more than 28 years[.] you can get my recomendation from boath white & C[olored] all knows I need help. I

118

have a daughter trying to make it in school who was not able to purchas school books last year[.] made a turn studying with other children and made a grade. Now I am asking you to Please consider me or have me considered any way you see fit for I am realy in need along all lines[.] I have a good country farm home but nothing to go up on. The people of the Comunity has had to help me along[.] this year through a hard strugle I got a little crop growing on my place[.] every one I have gone to for help have fail so I do believe you can if you will do me some good.[41]

Miss Mary Gay (Apalachicola) to Sholtz, 21 July 1935

I am shure you will Bee surprised to get this but Mr Sholtz I'm Doing something I hate to do but you see I have no parents neither father are mother. The Schrimp factory where I worked has closed up and I have nothing to do. There is a small lunch room here I can rent for only $20.0 twenty dollars. If you will lone me this small amt I surely will appreciate it and do assure you I'll pay you back. Just as soon as I can posibly make it. I've bin selling toilet goods but times is so hard I can't do any thing at that I'm shure I can do well if I can only get this lunch room. would you mind helping me that much I surely will appreciate it and I'll promise you I'll shurely return your money the verry first I can possibly make[.] If you care to learn more a bout me my condition or if I'm realy worthy of help right Mrs. W. J. Lovett Apalachicola Fla. She is wife of Sheriff Lovett I'm shure you no them.[42]

Mrs. Essie Keen (Miami) to ER, 23 July 1935

With regret I write you this letter. Condition demand it. I have invalid mother 75 years old. Husband in his 71 year sick long time[.] We havent had help from any source. More than a year a go we lived in Tampa[.] a man named Jimy Trotta an Italian whom we knew was trying to refinance his home. and in his Lawyers office it was found taxes was not Paid. deal was rejected un till paid[.] we loned him the money there in office. [illegible] he was to pay in 4 days when he drew his sallery. he works for the Tampa Electric Co. has been there 23 years he sayes he refuses to pay it. we reported it to the electric co. they Promised to have him pay it after they investigated from the Lawyer name Harry Sandler representative from Hillsborough Co to Tallahassee and now the Govenor has apointed him Judge. Mr. Sandler being Mr. Trotta atorney told the electric co it was a Bonifide loan. Now it seems they all want to get out of paying it I need it so much. Mr Sanlers Office is in Citrus Exchange building Tampa Fla. is there some way a Government agent could ask the utility co to see that Mr. Trotta pays since they investigated. correct a loan. Thanks you so much. loan was $65.34.[43]

Mrs. Alice G. Collins (Citrus Center) to Sholtz, 2 August 1935

1930 census: She is 29 years old and white and does not work. Her husband is a superintendent of road construction.

I would appreciate it if you will tell me where I can apply for a widows pension to be most likely to get one. I applied some time ago to parties in Miami but so far have not gotten it. I had to leave Miami & leave my two children there to teach a little one room school here & was happy to get it but it was a terribly hard one for any woman to manage so they have to get a man. I cant get another place with out a first grad certificate & I couldn't attend summer school this summer to review on account of children & not enough finances.

Mr. Collins deserted us about 6 years ago & I can't find him & no one will help me, he doesn't send a penny & I've had an awful time. I lost my house a beautiful one in Miami & other property. My sister took all my beautiful furniture while I was ill & going thro grief of Mr. Collins dissertion, my brother who grew up with me & whom I have sent money to so many times when I was single & teaching won't send me a penny. If I could just get a pension & be help in that way till I could review enough at home to get my first grade certificate then I wouldn't need any one's help. I could go on and finish the education of the two & mabe could live with some ease of mind. This load seems to much for me to carry with out some aid in way of some pension. wonder if you can help me get it a man that will leave his family without providing some support should be put under the Jail I think but poliece in Miami say cant locate him.

I did nothing for Mr. Collins to do this. We were a happy home till he went to Ind. to work & then distrous results have followed. We were members of First Baptist Church & well thought of[.] Dr. White can recommend me or so can any of my numerous friends & Mr. Collins was living right then too. I'm having a hard struggle[.] I need help to help my self.[44]

Mrs. Annie V. Cadman (Pensacola) to Sholtz, 13 August 1935

I take the liberty of writing to you because I think and I do honestly hope and pray you will not turn a deaf ear to this until you have read it any way. I am a widow and nothing to live on (no I dont have any children at all) but my sister who is a widow like myself, and I are trying and do live together[.] she is over sixty-five and I have passed the half century mark myself, but here is what I would ask of you, now please dont think I am just a regular beggar for I am not. there is a place here in the neighborhood which is Ferry Pass. there is over two acres with a little three Room House on it and it is for sale at a reasonable price I think. now if you will get among your friends and get together six or seven hundred dollars and let me have it to buy this place you may have it when we are through with it. that is all I could promis for we either of us have any thing else and we could I believe make a little something if we had a place like that. I thank you.[45]

Mrs. C. I. Dozier (Bonifay) to Sholtz, 20 August 1935

i am writing you in Regards to one of my nieces who has Ben staying at the poor home of holmes County Fla[.] it was arranged By the Board of County Commissioners to take care of all old dependent folks who are not able to work[.] the poor house is combined in with the stockade[.] My niece was there for the Reason i was not able to take care of her[.] i am a widow woman and have no in come at all after they changed hands or Boss men. At least at the stockade my neice who was still there she could not get any medical aid at all are hardly anything to Eat[.] i had to Bring her to my home for Eats and medical aid[.] The Commissioners will not help her and i am really not able[.] i would ask you please make an investigation of it your honor[.] if you would like to make an inquiry to the County physician[.] write Dr Paul at Bonifay Fla. this old lady is not able to work and has no one to Look to for help[.] her age is 62. her name is Tilda Kent[.] would gratefully appriciate any investigation you would make to the County Commissioners of this.[46]

Mrs. H. T. Stephens (Dade City) to Sholtz, 22 August 1935

I am writing in regards to the widow's pension. We have no widow's pension in this county. We feel that we are entitled to the pension just as much as other counties in Florida. I have four children of school age who are dependent upon me for support. I don't see how I can send them without some help. We would appreciate anything you could do for us. I don't have any kind of work now and haven't had hardly any during the summer. However we might have some later on, but wages are cut and we will get very little for our work. May God Bless you in your work. Thanking you, I am your friend.[47]

Mrs. Millie Fuqua (Defuniak Springs) to Sholtz, 26 August 1935

Kind sir just a few words for I am in trouble and I want you advice on this as my husband and I lived to gather 8 years have 3 children and we separated the 9th of last Oct 1934. he beat me threatened my life also the kids too. We couldent stay with him[.] he lay drunk almost the time and now he stays drunk and they has Been siveral told me he said if he every gets me rite he was gonie shoot me. and also he runs after me tries to get me off by my self[.]

I am afraid to evan go [on] the road and I had a Peaice Bond made for him and they turned him out on good Behaver and he has not dun any thing he promised at all[.] he want help me with the lids atoll[.] I was up the auther day trying to get help from him for the Kids and he only got me $2.00 per grocers and that is all he give them since May the 1. and I have went to the Lown Mr Bird Davis Mr. Johnnie and all these in Defuniak they wont do any thing with him about it atoll[.] I am afraid to sleep at night[.] he sees me on the road any where he takes to me and he has threatened my Life so much I cant rest no where. And I sure wood appreashate it if some one wood do something with him Before its to late[.] he fault one of my cousins about 6 weeks ago and put him in the hospital for an operations[.] so I want you to help me at once.[48]

Mrs. M. J. Sapp (New River) to Sholtz, 5 September 1935

1930 census: Mathew J. is a 48-year-old farmer; Marion C. is a 29-year-old mother of three children. The family is white.

I am writing you in regard to my husband, M. J. Sapp.

He is being held in jail in Tallahassee for a board bill of $24.00 which he made while the legislature was in session.

He boarded at the Maxwell House and was promised a job and he kept staying thinking he would get something to do so he could pay his board & never did.

I am left here with five children the youngest a baby eight months old and this is making it real hard on me. I have no one to look to for anything. And my kind neighbors are giving us our groceries now. If you could take some steps in this matter and he could be permitted to come home, that would relieve this condition.

You have no idea, what a position this is placing me in. My mother is a widow and I have no people to look too. I think that you know how Sapp worked for you in the campaign and I feel that you should use your power to help him now. I think his case comes up about the 14th & if you couldnt do anything before, I feel that you could ask your county Judge to suspend sentence on him. This would not be much for you to do and you cannot realize what it will mean to us, his family.

I will refer you to our represinitative Mr. Charlie Johns or any of our county officers as to whether we deserve any help.

I have applied to the F.E.R.A. office in Starke for help but cannot get any.

Trusting that you will do what you can and thanking you for anything you will do.[49]

Miss Mary A. Brown (Hampton) to Sholtz, 8 September 1935

1930 census: She is 12 years old, white, and the daughter of a farmer.

I am writing to you because I need help, and I feel like you can and will help me. I don't expect what I want to be given to me. I just want to borrow it. I want fifteen hundred dollars. ($1500.00)

I want the money to buy my parents and younger brothers and sisters a farm. Also to have the house repaired and buy stock to farm with and a cow so the children can have plenty of milk to drink. The farm will need some fencing done on it too. I want to get the house repaired before the cold winter gets here for the house gets wet all over every time it rains. I would like to get it fixed on account of my baby brother as he is sickly and I am afraid it would make him worse to stay in a cold wet house.

There will be four children in school in just a few months now. I dont know what they are going to do for clothing when it gets cold. I could pay back part of the money every year. I have got a sister in the ninth grade that I sure want to help through school. So she wont have to quit as I did.

I am the oldest of the children and I can work and will to pay back the money. I could not pay interest on the money but I would pay back fifty ($50.00) dollars more than I borrowed if only I can get the money.

I believe if my family had a farm of their own so they could have everything they made and also the other things I mentioned that they could get along good and keep the children all in school.

Just something to give them a start is all they need as they have never had one. a home is what I think they need. I would work and pay the money back so they could have all they made from off the farm.

Please dear governor try and help me as soon as you can for the winter is coming. I will be satisfied if only I could do for them what I have mentioned to you. It seems as if out of all the money that there is to help people that I could get the amount I want so I am willing to work and strive to pay it all back just to help my family.

Answer my letter so I will know you received it and please try to help me as I sure need it.[50]

Mrs. Sarah L. Bartlett (Live Oak) to Sholtz, 10 September 1935

The storm blew so many shingles off of my house. and it is needing fixing. I certainly will appreciate it if you will send me a check for $30 or 35 to have this work done. As I havent any way of fixing it. I really need the money. As I will have to get some body to fix it. I sure will appreciate your kindness if you can help me this much. I will try not to ask you for any more assistance.[51]

On 2 September, the so-called Labor Day hurricane hit the Florida Keys. The official death toll was 423, which included 259 World War I veterans living in three CCC camps.

Mrs. F. M. Craig (Palmetto) to Sholtz, 11 September 1935

I am kindley writing you on Account of my Condition[.] I am going on 74 years of age and I am blind in one eye and almost Blind in the other and disable to work and a widow also. I need means of Buying me Medicine and clothes and my teeth need pulling and I have tried on the FERA for some help and they did not help me any and I have Been a widow 6 years and Ive Been Before The Board of County Comminsors 3 times and they put me off every time saying there wasnt any funds in the treasury[.] But Still They help, others and I have my own litttle home But I need some Thing to live on. I have Been getting a little food But thats all. I cant get clothes or medicine[.] some folks think because I have my on home I dont need anything But it isnt any income to live, please give this letter attention for I need help.

PS I have neuritus and Rhuetism to where I cant work any[.] thats what ails my eyes[.] Please look after this[.] I went Before The Comminsiors in Bradenton Fla.[52]

Mrs. Lila Robinson (Yankeetown) to Sholtz, 14 September 1935

1930 census: She is listed as "Lela"; her husband, Horace, is a 60-year-old farmer. She is 38, has eight children, and does not work outside the home. The family is white.

I am writing to ask you if there is any way of getting help to pay a doctor bill? I'll have to tell you a little about myself so you will know what I mean.

I am a widow with 8 children. The oldest is working for himself. The next is staying with a half sister (I also have 2 step children) going to high school and working for her to help pay his expenses, that is alright, I'm glad he can. The other six are wholly dependent on me, without some one happens to give them a little something. One of these six is in high school. I have to board him out as I teach on a little island where there is no high school. Nothing but a few fishermen, (that just barely makes a living) lives on the island. I teach in an old dilapidated building. (The island is Pt. Ingles island[.]) But these children need schooling

Two years ago my husband was shot and instantly killed by J. J. Dampier, you know doubt have seen the account as J. J. Dampier is in jail. My husband was a deputy sheriff. And it has certainly made it hard for me with such a large family.

124

FERA vocational education. African American basket-making class. Bradenton, 1935

CCC arithmetic class. Camp Olustee, 1935. Women were hired as teachers.

FERA canning center. Hastings, 1935

FERA adult education typing class. Stanton High School, Jacksonville, 1935

FERA vocational education. African American basket-making class.
Kissimmee, 1935

FERA mattress factory. Gainesville, 1935

FERA project, women carding cotton. Miami, 1935. Note the masks.

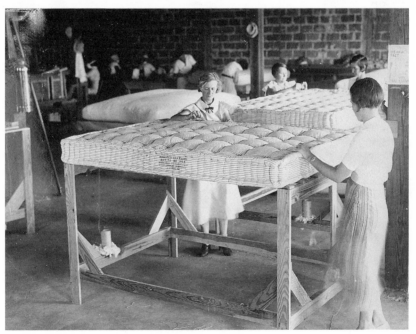

FERA mattress factory. West Palm Beach, 1935

FERA mattress factory for African American women. Jacksonville, 1935

FERA African American women quilting a comforter. Palatka, 1935

FERA project, African American women carding cotton. Jacksonville, 1935.
Note the absence of masks.

FERA project, women working on a comforter. Pinellas County, 1935

FERA leather-working class. Ocala, c. 1936

NYA vocational
school, silkscreen
printing. Ocala,
c. 1940

FERA sewing room. Tampa, 1935

FERA sewing room. Tampa, 1935. Note the older women workers.

Eve Alsman Fulmer, state director of Federal Arts Project, c. 1940

Maude Woods, superintendent of Vocational Education, NYA, c. 1940

Eleanor Roosevelt and Mary McLeod Bethune, 1937

FERA adult education
class. The oldest student.
Booker T. Washington
High School, Pensacola,
1935

WPA office. Arcadia, undated

FERA tree-planting project. Stock Island, 1935

FERA nursery school.
Brushing teeth as part
of hygiene lessons.
LaBelle, 1935

FERA adult education typing class. Largo, 1935

Franklin Roosevelt, Claude Pepper, and Miami mayor Robert Williams. Miami, 1937

Migrant worker family. Belle Glade, 1939

CCC camp. Sebring, 1938

Townsend roadside sign. Frostproof, 1939

Migrant family shelter. Belle Glade, 1939

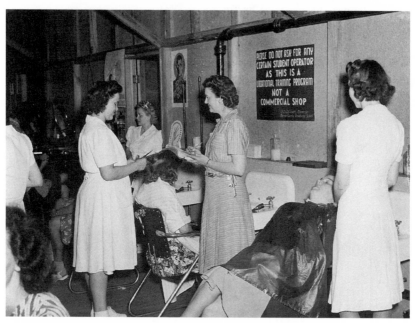

NYA vocational education. Beautician training. Ocala, c. 1940

Francis Townsend speaking at Bayfront Park. Miami, 1940

Townsend roadside sign. North central Florida, 1939

One year ago one of my children (a boy then 15 yrs. old) was tortured. Some men put handcuffs on him then set him a fire with gasoline. The child lay in the hospital 7 weeks, and lay in bed two months after he came home, he couldn't wear his pants for a little over two months after he got out of bed. So of course you know that made a <u>doctor bill</u> and that's the doctor bill I want <u>help on.</u> The person that burned him may not be 21, I don't know, but any way he was sent to jail, but that doesn't get the doctor bill paid. I felt like the officer that let them have his hand cuffs ought to help pay the doctor bill, but he hasn't, of course he didn't know (I don't suppose) that they were going to set the child a fire when he let them have his hand cuffs. But I feel like if the Government is going to keep officers that lets out their hand cuffs, the Government should help pay a doctor bill, so carelessly made, especially when its to a poor widow's child. The doctor of course wants his money and I don't know when I will ever be able to pay it. We tried to comprimise with the men, but they wouldn't compromise because we wanted the doctor bill paid. The one that did the burning said he'd serve his time out before he would pay any. The officers said they didn't do the burning and they wasn't willing to pay any. But seems to me as it was the officers hand cuffs on the child, he'd be willing to help. There was two officers there and neither one offered to do anything for the child except the other officer did take the hand cuffs off and put out the fire and then they went away not offering to do any thing for him. Of course I don't blame the officers for the burning but as it was his hand cuffs I thought he could have been human enough to offer to help and then do what he could. I will certainly appreciate it if any help can be given towards his doctor bill. Write <u>Dr. Peek</u> in Ocala, he can tell you how bad he was burned, he is the doctor to be paid, and then some hospital bill, to be paid back to one that paid that bill. Thanking you for anything that can be done. I hate like everything to ask it, but the doctor should be paid.

P.S. There is some people on the island where I teach needs help but I don't know how to get it or where, I have tried a few places.[53]

Miss Bessie Beaty (Jacksonville) to Sholtz, 16 September 1935

Will you please give one some information as to how I am going to make a living? I came to Jacksonville about four years ago and paid around $100. for a Beauty Course so that I might suport a widow mother and sister who has no income what-so-ever.

In the mean time I've tried to get work with the F.E.R.A. which seems impossible. My mother isnt allowed to register for help as I registered for work. I can not make my expenses and now I've got to pay the $12.00 license to be able to work. It seems as if our country isnt a free country any more. Mrs. Nobles[,] who is at the head of this[,] has plenty and of course she doesn't realize or care how a poor girl gets a long. I have not got the $12.00 and no prospect of getting it and I know lots of other girls in the same fix[.] now tell one what we are going to do. No work and cant even get food from the Gov't.

I was manageing to pay the taxes on some land my father left in Hamilton Co. till my mother wasnt able any longer to get the widows exemption so I supose we will loose this as I cant pay taxes any longer.

I have no one to go to for advice and your advise or any you can do for one in regards to this will certainly be appreciated very much. May I hear from you at an early date?[54]

Miss Philo. Delegal (Live Oak) to Sholtz, 17 September 1935

1930 census: She is 49 years old and single, and she works as a farm laborer. She lives with her father, who is a retired farmer.

Pardon my seaming presumption in writing you & only my great need gives me courage to do so. I will be breaf. Tell you my situation[.] I am a single woman 57 years old dependant on my labor for a support for myself and a paralized Sister. I borrowed $100.00 (one hundred dollars) this year to grow cotton[.] while my crop was late it would have met my obligations but before I could gather any of it the storm came & blew it all out now I see where They are giving asistance to the storm suffers If you could help me I feel you would be helping one that will suffer greatly if I can not get help my self & Sister[.] ask your kind consideration.[55]

Mrs. Milton Yancey Hood (Jacksonville) to ER, 19 September 1935

1930 census: Milton Hood is the manager of a newspaper. His wife, Mary, is 35 years old and white and does not work. They own their seven-thousand-dollar home.

I hesitate writing you, because I hate to bother you, and I don't know how you can help me, but, you and your husband know how to do things, so I am hoping there will be some way out.

My husband and I have a darling little bungalow that we can't finish paying for. We haven't a penny to pay on it and not any money to get out of it. We can't get a gov't loan or any kind, as my husband has no job. Has been out of work for more than four years and what we had saved has dwindled away. We should have paid quarterly interest yesterday amounting to $65.63 on $3,750.00 mtg. but could not, and I know the lady will forclose on us. She is very wealthy but is strict. This mortgage falls due in June, but unless something turns up we won't be able to pay off any and she always wants at least $150.00 a yr; paid off. Property value and loan values have gone down so am afraid we couldn't get this amount now. In fact, I know it.

My husband is one of the "White Collar Men" that has not been reached. He was a newspaper man,—and is very proud. He doesn't want something for nothing. He wants work. Our house is in need of repairs and everything we have is going to rack and ruin.

If we sell we have no place to go, but, have even been trying to sell it and can't. Everyone wants you to [al]most give them what you have. We came right into this place off our honeymoon Oct. 1925. I sure hate to move out, but, would if I could save it by renting, but, we haven't the money to get out. And there are some repairs tenants would require.

If there is anything further you'd like to know I'll be glad to confide in you, but, something has to be done at once. Mr. Hood is sick over not having any work and doesn't seem to know what to do.

We are democrats, and honest people. I will appreciate and thank you for any suggestions. We are hardly existing. This is confidential and I trust you will give it your personal attention.

Sincerely, a worried wife, Mrs. Milton Yancey Hood.[56]

Mrs. Dorothy William (Ocala) to Sholtz, 19 September 1935

I am a widow age 30 yrs. with one child to suppor age 12 yrs. and I owe debts and I am unable to pay them and I am seeking some way to get a job so I can make a living and pay my debts and I am asking you for help. I cant explain like it should be but I am doing the best I can. And I hope you will understand me. I want to get the government to buy me one acre of land here in Ocala Fla. and build a 12 room boarding house. And collect each month till the cost of the building has been paid. I thank you.[57]

Mrs. Nelia Curry (Tampa) to Sholtz, 14 October 1935

1930 census: This is probably Delia Curry, a 24-year-old African American and head of house with two children. She does not work. The census lists her as married but with no husband in the house.

I will now drop you a few lines today[.] I don't expect it will do any good but Here goes anyway. When the Storm blew so bad our roof was. Damaged. Part was blown off the rest was losened on the nails raised untill the water Just pours in. We made an apeal to the red cross. The caseworker came and measured the house but nothing was done so I went to the red cross taking a letter that our family Dr wrote for me. telling them about sickness in our home[.] My husbands mother is old and has been sick evry since the storm. I am a sufferer with the asthma and this wet house is making us worse. We can hardly cook on our stove. The red cross sent some men out here to fix the house. The man told us women your dam house don't need a roof. and that I lied when I said it did. We can prove the storm Damaged our roof. It wasent that way before the Storm[.] they put the roof on one side of our house. none on the rest of it and when it rains it just pours in. it was in the papers we understand that you said the people must have aid that had their homes. Damaged in the Storm. We thought the money was given to the red cross to help the people[.] there is to houses in my neighborhood that the red cross covered all but the porches (one woman told at my house last Sunday the Storm never done nothing to her house but She sure got a new roof out of the red cross. We are poor folks. cant hardly live and no money to by roofing with[.] It looks like the one that dont need always get the most and the Needy ones nothing. We hope you are a man with a heart. and will Do something for us in this trouble[.] I have wrote to the county Commissioners but they wont Do nothing for us. When times were good we always helped the red cross[.] now when we are in need why could they not help us[?] I ask them for roofing. that my Husband could put it on[.] They told me some people they had found out sold the roofing. The lord knows we need it to bad to sell it if they had let me have it[.] we are no floaters [we] are Tampa people[.] It looks like some times that there is nobody with hearts any more just gissards in place of hearts[.] we are eleigible for WPA work also regestered with the National reemployment service at Tampa[,] own our home and are voters[,] have been so for years[.] I expect this will find the waste Basket or if ans. will be in this way. cant help nobody[.] but hope there will Be something Done to help us. I dont know the man that came out here but the red cross does. he also said the Dam case workers Did not have say so he done as he please when he went to fix a roof. I told him we were human beings not Dogs. The Dr that has been Dr ing us has a heart[.] he will get his money some day if we ever get work to pay the Bills. will mail this to you. and hope you will Do something. right away. I will close[.]

P.S. again this morning every thing all wet in house.[58]

Miss Toots Musy (Sanford) to Mrs. Sholtz, 16 October 1935

I [illegible] sorry to write this to you but I am forced to do it. To get to the point I need twenty five dollars $25.00 and I am asking you for it as I know you have it. Your husband could give $12.50 and you give $12.50 and I know the Lord will bless you. I am a poor girl and I have got to have it for personal purposes. Please send it in a money order. If you can't send it please write and tell me. Thanking you very much and I am praying to our dear God that he'll help you send it to me. I hope you wont ever have to call on anyone like this and if you do the Lord will see that you get it.[59]

Mrs. Sarah L. Bartlett (Live Oak) to Sholtz, 14 November 1935

A Business Man of Jacksonville—told me that if I would write you, that you would buy my radio, for some of the Institutions you have. It cost me $650.00 and I will take $60.00 for it. It is in perfect shape. please help me with this for I am blind and need help. please let me hear from you at once and if you cant please send me enough money to buy me a pair of eye glasses as I need them terrible bad.[60]

She wrote $650 but undoubtedly meant $65. Shorthand notes on the letter from governor's office staff: "Write to the institutions. Regret have no state fund from which I could help you."

Miss Martha Chestnut (Holt) to Sholtz, 29 November 1935

1930 census: She is 35 years old and white, and she lives with her widowed mother and works as a laborer in a fruit grove.

am writing you in regard to the work for women. We sewed some about four day a month for about two months in the summer then were stopped[.] they claimed they put us on the direct relief only got from $2.00 two $2.50 every two weeks. Now we are notified that that is stopped and I see that the sewing project on the W.P.A. is approved and has been for some time. there are about twelve (12) of us at Holt to sew and they have only put one on, and from one to three at Milligan & Baker But all are on at Crestview and we are (12) miles from Crestview and have to get there the best way we can[.] Please tell me why is it that they will not let us work since the pragect is approved for us and also Why cant we have a sewing room here at Holt. We feel like that it isent fare like its going[.] we all really need the work and as for my self I sure need it as I have a mother 74 years old who is Blind and I am the only one to care for her and there is no work here that I can make a living[.] also have to pay three & half $3.50 per month rent for a place to stay[.] can you please advise me why this is or why we dont get work[.] I feel like you can help us out are advise us[.] so thanking you in advance. I wish to hear your reply By return mail unless you will find the notice like we all received[.] again thanking you.[61]

Mrs. J. G. McKay (Lakeland) to ER, undated but reply dated 1 December 1935

Owing to the scarcity of money in the teaching profession in Fla., and the fact that I have four children who are already beginning to look for Santa Claus, I have made up my mind to try to sell some things my father left me. He was a missionary in Smyrna for nearly 30 years, and picked up many articles most of which were destroyed when our house was burned in the Smyrna fire. I have, however, a 13th century Venetian tapestry, some hand beaten brass bowls and a Roman lamp excavated in Ephesus. I have no proofs that the tapestry is genuine except the word of a man who gave more than twenty-five years to the ministry.

Can you tell me of anyone who might be interested in buying these things? I would appreciate it very much if you could take the trouble to let me know.[62]

Mrs. M. N. McCullars (Gainesville) to ER, 11 December 1935

1930 census: This may be Maggie McCullars, a 48-year-old white seamstress. She is widowed with four sons at home.

I am writing you as I see you are very much interested in helping to take of care of T.B. now Dear Mrs Roosevelt I no of an oil that has never been put on the market a Lady was down and no one though[t] she would ever get off her bed but she is still alive or was a year ago she [is] in the north now some where I will tell this is any one will make it worth while yes I am interrested in the work but you no I am do [due] something for what I no and I need it as I am a widow and trying to make my way take care of my children[.] no have never been on relief or ask for help[.] you no how to get at this is why I am writing you so please do not think I am a Lunatic for I am just a poor widow so please help me and let me hear[.] please do not cast this a side it will be for you as for me. pleas read this and I will thank you as I am not able financialy able to put this out is why I am ask someone who is.[63]

Miss Mildred Helfrick (Miami) to Sholtz, 14 December 1935

My grandmother came here for her health. She is our only support. I and my two sisters want to go to school very much, but we are unable to pay $4.00 a week for our schooling. We have fine records from all of our schools. And are very anxious not to lose more time then we already have. Please Governor could you do anything for us to make it possible to attend school.[64]

Mrs. Lucile C. F. Wesley (Miami) to ER, 15 December 1935

1930 census: She is 38 years old and African American, and she lives with her husband, George, in Ft. Lauderdale. He is a minister; she works as an ironer in a laundry.

I have listed to your wonderful speeches at different times as you spoke over W.D.O.D. and W.Q.A.M. and I have also read your speeches in different papers which I have enjoyed so much. I am a young Business Woman (colored) and I want to do something that will be helpful to the Business Women of my Race. I have been thinking of so many things and my final decision was a Young Business Womans Club and I deside to write you and ask that you be kind enough to help me in my effort by sending me some Club Plans that I might organize this Club in a helpful way, which will be both uplifting and enlightening. I have a little girl five years old and I put her in Business school at the age of nine month old and I have spend these five years in trying to make her little Business a sucess. I am trying to raise her up in a way that she too may be of some help to her people and a real citizen in a helpful way. I am a young widow 31 yrs old and I have been a Dressmaker for 18 yrs. and I am hoping to do all that I can to make a sucess in life. My little girl sews beautiful and she is very Proud of her Business. Today she is known as Miami['s] Youngest Business Woman. I also wish you would send me a Plan that I might organize a Club for little girls from 3 yrs to 12 yrs. I am sure I will appreciate everything you do for me and from time to time you will know just how I am getting along and when Francine Marie grow up I will teach her that she owe so much of her sucess to Mrs Franklin D. Roosevelt, The First Lady of the land, who I have always felt that was the mother of all.[65]

Mrs. Cecil R. Heap (Daytona Beach) to Sholtz, 17 December 1935

My husband, Cecil R. Heap died in the Veteran's hospital, Lake City, Florida, in March 1933. I am of French descent, my husband marrying me while he was in France in the U.S. Army. He saw two years over sea service. I came back to this country with him and have raised our four children since coming here. After my husband's death, I went back to Paris, but they told me I was an American Citizen and should go back to America as they could not give me a position of any kind. I returned to America and have tried to support my children by giving French lessons and sewing.

I have applied for a pension from the Veterans Bureau, but I haven't got satisfaction yet. I am mailing to show them affidavits of people who have knone my husband before and after the war. I do not see why I should not receive this as well as other widows. The Federal Agency has been able to help me, for a few weeks, with $2.50 per week; but since more one month, I dont get any thing at all.

When my husband died, he was 100% disable and was getting a pension of $40.00 per month.

Last February, being almost in the street with my four little ones, I went, after advice of different people, to see the mayor, Mr. Armstrong. I begged him a job of any kind, asking him to help me to secure one in town, being a resident of Daytona Beach since I live there since one year and half, permanently. A few weeks after, Mr. Armstrong gave me a job in the City Hall, Water Department, where I was doing my work perfectly well. (Billing water bills) for $15.00 per week. This was a great help to me and my four children had some thing to eat every day.

But, elections came, and, for no good reason, Mr. Armstrong and Francis Mills put me out right away. I explained to Mr. Armstrong and the City Clerk my situation, alone with four young children, no help at all of any kind, what I would do now on? But, he says, he cannot do any thing. Mrs. Kemp Barbe is at my place now and has a permanent job.

I am willing to do anything to earn a living that is honest, as I cannot support four children and myself on what I am making now teaching French.

My rent is due since several months; I cannot pay anymore the Power and Light Co. and I had a notice this morning my gas and light are going to be cut if I dont pay immediately.

If it is possible in any way that you can help me to secure a pension, I would be very grateful, dear Governor, as many times I have had to put my children to bed without even a piece of bread to feed them. Christmas is coming, and it will be no Christmas for my dear little ones, in fact I am to day absolutely peniless.

Hoping that you will find some way to help me in this matter. You have yourself four children, a great heart and surely you will understand me.

Hoping that you will find some way to help me in this matter.

My husband No was: XC 2060412. My children age is: 16–13–9–5.[66]

Mrs. Gustav Brast (Longwood) to Sholtz, 19 December 1935

I am afraid I will lose my home and 5 acres for taxes. We have 130 orange trees but no fruit on account of the freeze last year[.] My husband is a P.W.A. worker on the Sanford division and [h]is wages are 22 dollars per month. I have 6 children the eldest 14 years[.] I have sold all my luxuries such as a car[,] radio and washing machine to keep the home fires burning[.] I have not even a pair of shoes to my name[.] I can get along without shoes but I need a shelter for my children[.] anything you can do to help will be greatly appreciated.[67]

Mrs. Grace Cutler Evans (Tampa) to ER, 8 January 1936

1930 census: Her husband, William, is a real estate agent. Grace is 54 years old, was born in Ohio, and does not work. They are white.

I know you are a busy woman, but have heard you say over the radio, that you were not too busy to read your personal letters, and I am making this personal.

To make a long story short, we want your husband, our President, to be reelected, and we want him to go in with a land slide, no split vote, and he will do this, if he will approve the Townsend Bill.

I am a club woman and a business woman, and I have an opportunity of knowing the trend of thought of many.

We have in Hillsborough County, Florida[,] alone more than 35000 that are pledged to vote for the Townsend candidate, and they run into the millions all over the United States that will vote for the Townsend man who ever he may be. I truly believe that ninety-five percent of these voters will vote for President Roosevelt if he will approve this Townsend Bill. Use your influence, and do not let him lose this opportunity of being our next President.[68]

Mrs. Bertie Jennings (Lake City) to Sholtz, 21 January 1936

I have received the Mother's pension for a few years. Last year I had a little trouble in getting it, but they finally paid it.

This year they have refused to pay it. I have 6 children. All the older one's are girls. I have 5 in school. I had to take the older girl out of school, in order to secure work to keep up the household, as I have not been able to work since last August.

I have not been on any charity or relief roll since the death of my husband (7) seven years ago. I have been to see them (4) four different times, and as yet, I have not received any. The only answer they gave was, that they were not going to pay it. I think the officials, of this county need an influential man to get behind them. I am very much in need of this pension.

When I first received this pension I received (2.50) two fifty per child, but last year they reduced it it one dollar per child.

If I could receive this it would help me so much as I am not working and have to depend on the wages of one girl and it is not enough.

Will you please investigate this matter, as I do not want hand-outs or charity if I can get work, and I am willing to work for what I get.

Will appreciate your kindness in looking into this matter. (Please)

P.S. Will vote for you in coming election as did before.[69]

Mrs. M. Douglass (Daytona Beach) to Sholtz, 3 February 1936

I am writing you at this time to ask a special favor. I want you to ask for an increase in Widows Pensions in this state. if we only had ten dollars more per month what a help that would be. I am living on forty dollars per month and taking care of my widowed sister. you might ask how I do that, <u>answer</u>—by <u>hard</u> work and good <u>management.</u> I mean we exist on this[.] as you well know my children have their own families to support therefore cannot help me. there seems to be money for other purposes and I think we widows should have at least ten dollars more per month.

I greatly appreciate what you have done for my son Kenneth and I ask you to please help us widows <u>now.</u>[70]

Mrs. Emma Salter (Ft. Myers) to Sholtz, 5 March 1936

1930 census: She is 33 years old and African American and has six children. She is listed as married, but she is also the head of the house, and there is no husband in the home. She does not work, but her oldest son is a day laborer.

I am writing you as my last hope of saving my place. My husband left me over four years ago with seven head of childrend and carried the deeds to the place with him. And I was thinking that he was keeping the tax up on the place until here recently when they started sending me tax and I was exempted from all my state and county tax and I thought that I was exempted from my city tax to. but now they tell me if I don't pay up all my back taxes that I will loose my home[.] also now I have a son that is able and willing to work but they just wont give him nothing to do and I am a poor old widow woman and as far as I can see now I could not make up fifty dollars in thirty days let alone one hundred and forty one dollars and ninety nine cents and I can hardly get bread now[.] if it had not been for the relief last summer I dont know what I would have done and I didn't have no rent to worry about so I don't know what will become of me if I have rent and grocery borth to worry about[.] please governer give me some advice or help me to save my place[.] My son says that there is nothing in the world that is too hard for him to do if it will help me and the place any so if you please or will, please send me your advice or tell me what I can do to save my place[.] I haven't got any money to pay my tax with and no husband[.] my son went up there with me this morning to offer to work for the place and they wouldn't accept it[.] They send my son off to the c.c.c. camp and since he been back they wont give him nothing to do and I am a poor widow woman without a husband (and I don't know how to go about seeing about no tax bills and things so I will close[.] from a widow.[71]

Mrs. Mellie Ingraham (Miami) to Sholtz, 7 May 1936

Governor I take the liberty as an old Key Wester as I know you are a friend of the Poor and Needy of KW to write you[.] I have been a tax and licence payer in K.W. for many years untill a few years ago my husband Died and I had to go out of business and since then I have not been able to pay my taxes[.] I have a Piece of land on one of the Key's left to me by my Father but am not able to Pay the taxes on and if you will have back taxes cancled and excempt me from future taxes I can get a small home built on it and support myself with growing vegatables an roses as I will be near Pirate Cove on Sugarloaf[,] a winter resort. Please let me know soon as I will be anxious to get to work.[72]

Eva Furgison (Jacksonville) to Cone, July 1936 (no day given)

This is Misses Edward and Misses Smith and Msses Ford i am putting my plead to you askin you to Please for god sake help poor Eva Furgison on the releafe to get her work card back for she is but to luse her mine[.] got nothing to go around no one to help her rent to pay and insurance to pay for her and the children and other little Bil and no help at al[.] she is to my house cryin and nothing that i can do for her i give her some thing to to eat but i eant got no money to give the poor thing to help her with her children and we is Begin you to help her in the name of the good Lord and you two for i no that you can help her for we no that you is got al pour [power] in your hand to help her for my sake and and god sake do some thing for her before this week is endid[.] would you be so Please do some thing for her in the name of the lord Please give me a letter back by male 217 Park st Jacksonville Fla. Please help her for she is a good woman but she is criple in the hip from a fall.[73]

Mrs. Etta Coon (Jacksonville) to Sholtz, 10 July 1936

1930 census: She is 43 years old and white. She was born in Georgia and does not work. Her husband, Robert, is a laborer on the county road.

I am riting you in regard of my little boy[.] he is deaf and cant talk and goes to school to st. augustine and his school will start agin in Sept and we are poor[.] my husband works with the W.P.A. and don't get but 30 dollars per month and we have six in family to feed and some times We Dont have any thing to eat and I cant have money enough to buy any clothes and my little boys teacher in St. augustine give him your address and told me to rite to you[.] so if you will please send me some money to buy all his clothes with for school[.] it will take about 20 Dollars[.] so hoping to heare soon from you.[74]

Mrs. Catherine Green (Delray Beach) to Sholtz, 27 July 1936

I am writting to ask you is there any was at all for one to get any money out of the Knight of Pythias Lodge? My husband has been dead three years and they havent paid off yet. I am a widow and have no money and no one

135

to help me and cant get what is owed to me. Please see to them paying me. I am in need[.] I dont have money to get food with. They owe one $4643 four houndred six dollars and forty three cents and they have not paid me. They owed me $600 and they havent given me any money since August 1935[.] My husband died Jan 21, 1933[.] please attend to this and oblige.[75]

Knights of Pythias is a Christian fraternal organization. Like other similar groups, it offered its members life insurance and burial policies.

Mrs. Juanita Mayers (Tampa) to Sholtz, 27 August 1936

I have tried to get a mothers penson for my two children by my former marriages. She Mrs Blossom Sack says I cant because my husbands are not dead. She read me the rules and as I understand it if a father isn't able to work mental or physical able to care for my little girl whos nine years old. I dont see why I cant get it at least for her[.] My oldest a boy 11 father I havent seen or heard from him since [A.] was 1 year[.] I have heard Mr. Colby was dead but I cant say. in closed you'll find a letter from my mother in law as to the conditions of Mr Dana G Morse[,] [D.'s] father—Governor Sholtz I have struggled for 2 years taking in washings to suport and care for my children[.] my health is breaking and I cant do as much as I used to. School Starts pretty soon[.] my children needs clothes also books. I was told by several people here if I'd state my case to you you'd help me. Governor Sholtz does my children have to go hungry just because thier fathers are not dead? Or because one isn't able to care for his child and the other to sorry to do so. My heart aches for my babies[.] it is not thier faults or mine for I have tried I've never even asked so far for one thing for my children to eat or wear. I see no way but to put my children in a home and I'd rather see them dead than in one. No matter how good a home is mothers love isn't there. my oldest is a boy [A. L. C.] age eleven[.] his father has never done one thing for him. My girl is 9 [D. M. M.] her father did do for her as long as he was able if at any time he is able to help me. Or I can do it my self. I'll stop taking the money from the pension if you'll be so kind as to help me get it and I believe you will for the people who asked me to write you, said you were a kind understanding man. Any way I have faith in you and my maker. Looking for a reply soon I beg to remain sincerely yours.[76]

Mrs. Gerda Gran (Hialeah) to ER, 5 September 1936

Forgive me for taking this liberty of writing to you. I will however make myself as brief as possible.

136

First, if President Roosevelt had not come in as he did, why US. would just have been ahead of Spain in bloody revolution. Alright you'd say common people, what do they know? Plenty, but we know things from a different Stand or view point. What I mean is this, while from your childhood on, because of your wealth, you see life from the front only, while we must, yes must, experience all tru everywheres. In other words, the Negros, the Catholic's etc. If you Mrs Roosevelt can See this, which I hope you can, and then, try to persuade Mr. Roosevelt to ponder on this, for this is more to it then you will think at first. It is not you, yourself and me but it concerns the whole Nation. Take for instence, Some of the catholics Seems to be for, Mr Roosevelt, others is against him. Now listen we are both Northerners and Southerners. The Catholics are underhanded, they work together, none is for President Roosevelt, this for, and against is their way of working, all for themself. Their password is. (The Pope is our God:) What wonderful sentiment for the rest of us. Now then, Mrs. Roosevelt there is not one family in the whole country but what they have some old enough person, or relative whom go in big, for the Townsend Plan, "Oh but we know that it, will go over." So please, I beg of you, try to make President Roosevelt see it. And dont forget that in Catholicism is no for a protestant. Too, they Townsendist say $200.00 a month, but $100.00 a month, for 60 years and over is plenty. No doubt you have studyd it out. Money in circulation, without politicians devour it before it get to where it is meant for. I am not on no relief, thank God. In ending I pray that God may lead you aright.[77]

Mrs. Alice Barton Harris (Coconut Grove) to ER, 28 September 1936

1930 census: She is 50 years old and a French teacher, and she was born in Washington, D.C. Her husband is a music teacher

I dont know you—except as everybody knows you—but I am going to ask you a great favor. Several years ago it became necessary for me to help my husband financially and I got a position teaching. I enjoyed it a lot and did it well. About a year ago it ended—so unexpectedly that it found us with obligations impossible to meet. I need badly $1000 to put things in order—and tide us over until I can find another job.

I am 58 years old—and with so much health & energy that I must work to be happy—and I feel confident that I can find something—and begin to repay you.

We live in Miami and last year I came very near getting an executive job with the N.Y.A. My friends in Washington were quite sure of it. But to my great disappointment those jobs were handed over the Y.M.C.A. to fill—at least in that district.

I shall keep on trying however, for I have reached the age when a woman needs a job more and is best fitted to fill it well.[78]

N.Y.A. is the National Youth Administration.

Mrs. Izola Evans (Freeport) to Sholtz, 22 October 1936

1930 census, listed under "Fitch Evins": She is 36 years old and white with six children. She does not work. Her husband is a laborer but unable to work. Her two oldest boys work dipping turpentine.

On Dec 17, 1935 my husband Fitz L. Evans died and left me with six children four of them are school age[.] last year I received a mothers shool pension of $7.00 per month. this school term I have not got any thing and two months of school are most out.

I have a son in CCC camp, but we got so far in debt during the sickness and death of my husband until we haven't paid out yet and unless I can get a little more help will have to stop the children from school for the need of cloths[.] Will you please help me?

If you want to know if this is the truth please write C. A. Mitchell of Freeport Fla. H Crook Freeport, M. Hatcher they all know my needs and are honest. Thanking you in advance.[79]

Mrs. Elibeth Hagler (Marianna) to Sholtz, 12 November 1936

I am writting you for information conserning my state & Co. tax. I trust you will give me at once answear to just what.

1st. I am a widow woman. Was born before freedom. I haven't eny one to I work as to help me eny. And these, tax colectors still have me pay it each year. Please attend to this mateers at once. I am never releiced from eny and have no back taxes due. Although I have a bill a few days ago, for city tax. Please, Please look to this at once.

P.S. And I am all but bline, have been for years. Can't see to do my work. Please see to me rec'd, Eexzemption Papers Please in full. I only have my 10 year old grand child to stay with me for company.[80]

Mrs. Lora Evans (Freeport) to Sholtz, 16 November 1936

I am asking if you will help me in some way. I havent had to ask any one to help me with my children so far. But I am in a condition now that it seems that I need some help. I have got three children a girl of 12 one boy 9 and one boy the age of seven, and I cant send the children to school. For I cannot buy them any clothing and they have been sick with fever and I owe a doctor bill of $11.65 and I thought probably you could or would send me some money if not mare than $15.00 it would enable me to start them to school. I am a widow and have been 5 years, and I havent had to call on any one for help untill now. Mr. Sholtz if you can send me any help I will appreciate it and I'm sure that Heaven will award you and I will not ask you for help again. please do this as soon as you can, If you can help me.[81]

Miss Christina Burns (Miami) to Sholtz, 1 December 1936

Just a few lines to see what you can do for me. My name is Christina Burns Age 16 Born Feb.16 1920. My intension is to finish High School but owing to my condition I dont know if I'll be able[.] I attends Booker T. Washington High School Grade 10[.] I would not mind if you can give me a position some where. Please don't fail me. It does not matter what the wages be[.] all I want is something to help me through school my mother is half blind, and my Father is partly Deaf and he hasn't had a job in ages so please looke after my letter[.] dont mind about the wages any thing to help me along.[82]

Chapter 4

1937-1940

The presidential election of 1936, which gave Franklin Roosevelt a resounding national endorsement, put into motion a series of political changes that would revise the New Deal and have tremendous impact on Florida. During the campaign, Roosevelt pledged to balance the budget as soon as possible. (Despite his first administration's spending record, Roosevelt had never been completely at ease with the concept of deficit spending.) After the inauguration in 1937, eager to believe that the Depression was ending, Roosevelt ordered budget cuts and program reductions. Relief programs were not spared, and the WPA had to release large numbers of workers from the rolls.

The results were nothing short of disastrous. The "recovery" was too soft yet to sustain the deflationary impact of the budget cuts. The stock market collapsed again, production plummeted, and unemployment skyrocketed. By the end of the year, industrial production was down by more than 40 percent, and four million workers joined the still-large ranks of the unemployed. By the spring, the downturn was being called the "Roosevelt recession," and it gave encouragement to Roosevelt's opponents, who smelled blood in the water and hoped to take advantage of FDR's major setback. Conservative southern Democrats, including Virginia's Carter Glass and Georgia's Walter F. George, joined with Republicans in an effort to gut the New Deal.[1]

Florida's new governor, Fred P. Cone, sided more with the opponents than with Roosevelt. A banker from Lake City, Cone had campaigned in 1936 on the slogan "Lower the budget to balance taxes rather than raising taxes to balance the budget."[2] Cone believed the New Deal had gone too far and had gone on for too long, and it was time to return to more conservative financial principles. He even refused to match some money required for federal appropriations, thus reducing the amount of outside money the state could receive for the repair of schools and other institutions.[3]

Cone likely cheered for the budget cuts of 1937. But they nevertheless had a direct and negative impact on many Florida residents, and the letters in this chapter reflect those changes. Many writers were concerned with the layoffs in the relief program, and the workers who lost their positions often wrote begging for reinstatement. Nor had the particular need for women's relief diminished. One study from 1937 found that southern women were certified for relief jobs nearly twice as often as the national average.[4] This combination of factors led to one of the most dramatic events in Florida's New Deal history: a sit-down strike at the sewing room in Ybor City. The sewing rooms had continued as the New Deal's primary relief program for women. But practical experience had by now demonstrated that the sewing rooms were not actually training many women for jobs in private industry. Florida WPA officials had to acknowledge that there were "few garment manufacturing plants" in the state, so very few women from the sewing rooms were placed in such jobs.[5] Indeed few female relief workers obtained private employment of any kind, so their WPA jobs seemed all the more valuable to them. The cuts to the program, scheduled to go into effect on 1 July 1937, provoked "considerable unrest among the workers, [and] community protests" throughout the state. The reduction "left many families with no income," wrote one official. Another noted, "whole communities have protested the release of women workers from the [sewing] centers."[6]

One week after the layoffs, women in the Ybor City sewing room began a sit-down strike. Demanding reinstatement of the released sewing-room workers and a pay increase for all WPA workers, the Ybor City sit-down was the first of its kind in the South.[7] Attempting to put pressure on the WPA, 250 men from three other WPA projects in Tampa went out on a sympathy strike. But local and state WPA officials refused to negotiate with the strikers, arguing that their hands were tied since both wage levels and hiring policies were set in Washington. The sit-down crumbled, workers began drifting back to their machines, and the strike was ended within a week's time. The WPA reinstated all the strikers except the leadership. Although several other communities had threatened similar actions, the failure of the Ybor City sit-down cooled their enthusiasm for relief strikes and no further events ensued in Florida.[8]

In the spring of 1938, Roosevelt finally moved to end the recession now bearing his name. He sent a package of recommendations to Congress that would stimulate recovery, including massive new public works projects.[9] Congress responded with the "five billion dollar" spending bill, and southern representatives managed to get farmers added to the WPA rolls. From July to November 1938, the number of WPA workers in eleven southern states increased from 461,000 to 641,000. (As George Tindall noted, this was a nearly 40 percent increase, compared to the 10 percent increase in the nation as a whole.)[10] Moreover, wage levels for southern relief workers were also raised, on average about five dollars a month.

The positive response to the new spending bill suggested that Roosevelt supporters should do well in the fall elections. In an attempt to shore up support for his program, FDR hoped to secure a more cooperative Congress in the off-year elections of 1938. The southern states, where some conservative Democrats were in open revolt, were his particular focus. Claude Pepper's primary victory in Florida helped convince Roosevelt that the South could yet be his. Pepper, in the senate since 1936, had been one of Roosevelt's staunchest southern supporters.[11] In May 1938 Pepper won a hotly contested primary against a conservative opponent of the New Deal, Representative James Wilcox. Many observers, Roosevelt included, believed this victory represented revived southern support for the president and his policies. Three days later Congress passed a long-delayed wages and hours bill that FDR had been waiting on for months. The Fair Labor Standards Act thus had Pepper's primary to thank for its passage. (Unfortunately FDR squandered this momentum by his failed attempts to unseat southern congressmen opposed to him. His attempted "purge," as it was called, served to strengthen the opposition. In the November elections, the Democrats lost eighty seats in the House and eight in the Senate. Support for further New Deal innovations evaporated.)[12]

It was not only spending policy that troubled some southerners. Many southern politicians were disenchanted with Roosevelt's position on race. Although the New Deal did nothing to challenge white supremacy and had made room for racial discrimination in hiring and wage levels, white conservatives were nervous about some recent events—many of which were purely symbolic. In 1936 the Democratic party seated black delegates at the national convention for the first time. The party actively courted black voters that fall, especially in northeastern cities, with unprecedented results.[13] Roosevelt's "black cabinet" of African American advisers expanded in number. Between thirty and forty black leaders had the ear of the administration, including Florida's Mary McLeod Bethune.[14] A federal antilynching bill passed the House in April 1937, although a filibuster by southerners killed it in the Senate. (The gruesome lynching of Claude Neal in Marianna in October 1934 had helped to promote support for the bill.)[15]

But more than any actions by Franklin Roosevelt, it was his wife's reputation on racial matters that caused conservative southerners to squirm. Eleanor was far more committed to civil rights than was Franklin, and her record on racial issues had grown increasingly public. She invited Walter White of the National Association for the Advancement of Colored People (NAACP) to the White House. She pressured New Deal administrators to hire blacks and to pay them the same wages as whites. She spoke to African

American organizations, and she lobbied to get Mary McLeod Bethune appointed to the National Youth Administration. By 1938, when she famously refused to abide by Birmingham's segregation ordinance during a meeting of the Southern Conference on Human Welfare, Eleanor Roosevelt had become a frequent target for southern politicians attempting to undermine her husband's political agenda.[16] Fears about race further hardened southern opposition to the New Deal.

By 1939 the New Deal's work relief programs gradually segued into war preparation. But the letters in this section serve to remind us that the Depression continued on through the end of the decade. For some the fear and desperation were just as palpable in 1940 as they were in 1930. Although politicians had grown nervous about the costs of these programs, the needs clearly remained. The letters in this chapter also highlight the fact that supporters of the Townsend plan had not yet given up. Despite the adoption of Social Security, Townsendites continued to lobby for their program.

In 1938 Fred Cone suffered a heart attack and was incapacitated for some time. His brother, Branch Cone, and his secretary, Ella Neill, undertook much of the correspondence of the governor's office. Some of the letters of this chapter are addressed directly to W. B. Cone or Branch Cone.

___

Mrs. Mary Cook (Crystal River) to Cone, 27 January 1937

I gess you will be surprised to heare from a old friend[.] I am the widow of Charley Cook he was born and raised in lake City fla. Charley is dead[.] he died April 26 1933[.] he was sick eight years not able to do any thing[.] I took care of him the best I could by working hard. but finley he got so sick and his mind had got bad so the doctor sent him to the state hospital at Chattahoochee fla[.] he was there one month and eight days and then he died. now I am not able to do heavy work and I need some help[.] I am sixty years old and I have no way of suport and I dont no what else to do only to ask you if you will to help me. I went to the releaf for help last June I think it was and they only give me 2 lbs of prunes and a can of beef. every to or three weeks. I told them I could sew on the sewing room but they said they couldent give me no work in the sewing room. I told them I needed some clothes and some sheets they said they couldent give me no sheets[.] that they would do what they could and that is what I told you in my letter[.] now Mr Cone I helped out in geting you in ofice I voted for you and I got others to vote for you[.] now I am asking you to help me in some way for I need help. I no of others that are geting help rite close here that are geting 25 dollars per month from the CCC camp and some have farms and are able to live with out the relief but they are geting help from the relief[.] well I no that the ofice people are to blame[.] they give to those they want to. I will close hoping to heare from you soon. I hope you wont think hard of me for writing.[17]

Mrs. Adam Tyson (Raiford) to Cone, 1 February 1937

1930 census, spelled "Tiscon": Grace is 22 years old and white and has one child. Her husband is 34 and an unemployed farmer.

On June 29th 1936 I paid Levy Alvarez 35 dollars for a cow. I kept this cow one week and the clerk of courts at that time taken this cow away from me. and S. T. Dowling fixed it with the States Attorney which is Hal F. Maines of Lake Butler for me not to have the case prasecuted and beat us out of $35 dollars and we are writing you and asking you to explain to us why the States Attorney want alow us to prosecute the case. I see Levy Alvarez every day and he dodges me to keep me from asking him for the money as I go to my work. I work on the W.P.A. in Raiford and has been for the last 14 months[.] the Dr. taken my Husband off and I went to work and I do need your assentance to help me get my cow back[18]

Mrs. M. L Armengol (Tampa) to Cone, 2 February 1937

Just a few lines from a 65 years old lady. I voted for you and all of my family knowing that you are the man we need that will look with your good heart to the aged and the poor people.

Now I am a Dr. daughter raised in wealth educated in music and languages never never new what hard times were, and that is hard to bear at my age. My father was a Dr. in the Marine hospital service, expert in yellow fever. I am a widow depending on one son that has his obligation and hardly makes enough for a family. I live in an old shack of an old bachelor and with plenty of money and now that we are so hard up he has raised the rent when he dont need it. Why can't we have a pension when we have built this country and be independant from our children? Why cant you give us old people the few days we are here a little happiness before we leave this world? We have here only grafting if you could see the office with so many employes that are not necessary and man and wife, getting good salaries and other starving.

What is that social Security act taken away from the poor worker one per cent even if they dont want to. Well I hope God will give you health and happiness, and hope to know you are going to do for us old people.[19]

Mrs. Miriam Horn (Chiefland) to Cone, 9 February 1937

I will write you a few lines to ask you to pleas try to get us Old Confederate Vetrans pension raised[.] we are old an not able to work an not

menny of us a liveing an that money was put in the treasury for no other purpose only for vetrans[.] I only draw $40 dollars a month I am a widow an is
crippled with rheumatism till I cant hardly walk[.] I cant do enny work at all
an I need medical aid[.] an forty dollars wont feed me an furnish me a house
to live in an cloths an pay no dr[.] bills an I have nothing to look too but the
pension an I dont see why we cant draw enough to make us comfortable
while we are here for we cant live much longer[.] you verry well know we
never have had a Governor that cared for the poor an I think they are the
ones that needs the help if you are a friend to the poor an them that need
help[.] please rais our pensions to enough we can live in some comfort for
the rest of our days whitch wont be meny you know[.] pleas rais it as soon
as you can as I need mine real bad[.] may God bless an perserve all the faithful an all the good deeds they do an help them that is a friend to the poor[.]
hopeing you will help us that needs it I beg to remain your humble servant.[20]

Mrs. J. S. Nicholson (Lakeland) to Cone, 17 February 1937

I am writing you in regards to work, I have been laid off from the sewing
room on account of me drawing a $10 mothers check to put three children
through school with.

I have three grandchildren myself and an invalid brother to support. I
have no other means what ever to support my family and I am 65 years old
and no way to make a living but my labor. You know it is most impossible for
a woman of my age to get work other than that.

It don't seem fair for a woman to be turned out of the sewing room. With a
family my size, when it takes the ten dollars a month to keep a roof over their
heads and other women working who are younger and can do other work.

One woman I know off has got houses renting for $10 per month in this
town but still she is working in the sewing room.

It is not a pleasant thing for a woman to have to go down to the relief
office to beg and then most of the time get turned down.

All I am asking for is for work to do and I can do that kind of work. If
they will just put me back to work I ask for nothing else.

I am not the only one that they turned out from this cause. With me they
turned out about 29 all because they were getting this pension and all of
them paying rent.

I wrote a letter to the president of which I received a answer telling me he
was sending my letter to head quarters at Jacksonville asking them to rein-
state me. This has been about four weeks ago.

They told us women when they turned us out that they women who were
drawing these mothers checks would start not later than 5th of January to

drawing $30 per month and the government would not permit two checks. Please let me know if there is anything you can do to help me get back to work at the sewing room.[21]

Mrs. H. E. Wilson (Hawthorne) to Cone, 18 February 1937

I am writing to see if there is any way you can get Mr. Landis views changed in regards to the heirs not receiving the pensions of their Mother. My Father served in two wars Confederate and Indian[.] Was wounded in both. Served full time. When my father died my mother got the pension. She died 28 day of last July and leaves four children. We put in claim for her pension of 28 days and Mr. Landis says there is no one to pay it too. I want to know if you can't ask higher court to change that ruling. I am a widow and need all I can get. We cant get the Indian War pension for the reason my mother left the home. Neighbors to us have received their fathers pension and cant see why the few that is left can't collect. I don't think either one of the rulings are fair. Please look into this and see if there is any way to help us get the pension.[22]

Mrs. Thelma Faust Read (Bartow) to ER, 20 February 1937

I want very much a position as social secretary-companion. I am a musician—play the violin, piano and sing. As a child, Macon, Georgia, was my home, and I attended and graduated from Wesleyan College.

I am forty years' young and have a beautiful, smart daughter who is twelve years old—my only child. Mr. Read died nearly five years ago.

Have traveled some, play Bridge, would like to play golf—can drive car—manage a household economically and love to entertain. A position with a person connected with diplomatic service would be lovely. Would not mind whether it be with a man and wife or just one person.

If you can aid me in finding such a position I will be greatly indebted to you. Could arrange a trip for personal interview on short notice if necessary.

Please allow me to tell you, what thousands have already voiced—: I think you are a marvelous person—woman, mother, President's wife, and benefactor—a Christian model for a wonderful Nation. And just the one for our White House Hostess. I say this humbly and sincerely.[23]

Mrs. Joanna Cain (Kissimmee) to Cone, 26 February 1937

In sending this letter from Mr. Glenn Ray and business people of the town, I will state my condition[.] I am a widow woman and son 16 yrs of age had to take him out of school but only gets part time work and only a boys wages which is not enough for us to live on. I was layed off from the sewing room last of August never had any work there since. Will you please see what you can do for me.

Attached to this was a petition signed by twenty-two residents of Kissimmee, asking that she be re-employed by the sewing room.[24]

Mrs. W. H. Fowler (Orlando) to Cone, 28 February 1937

We are confronted with a problem right now, that to you may seem such a small matter, but to us is the most important thing in our lives, that of being moved out in to the street because we have no means of paying our rent.

I saw an article in the Orlando morning Sentinel a short time ago that said landlords (in Miami) had been warned not to put out families with children as there is a state law forbidding such action. I would like to know if this is true, is there such a state law?

We are told that tomorrow we will be served a notice by the sheriff to be out in five days. I will certainly apperciate an answer as soon as possible as I would hate to be put out with no place at all to go, no money, no one to turn to.

My husband is and honest, hard working man. He will work at any thing he can get, but is just one of those unfortunate men who has done well to provide food for his family since Xmas.

Something should be done. One of the Sheriff's debuties told us that recently they had put several families out on the street.

I am trusting to the faith I have in the Governor of my state that my question will be answered in the next five days.[25]

Mrs. Norma Bell (Miami) to Cone, 5 March 1937

I am ritting you for help. I live at palatka Fla. Come down here seeking for work[.] I had a sick husband for 5 years he had a heart dropsy and on the 28th of January he died and it took all we could do to make ends meet while he lived and during his illness we got behind in our tax and I have tried to pay what money I had on them and they will not accept it and I don't want to loose my home[.] I am a widow and no body on earth to help me and beside that I am not a young woman[.] cant somthing be done or I get some Kind of favor untill I can pay them[.] I hate so bad to worrie you but I don't Know what else to do[.] I am working and if I can be allowed to pay it as I draw my money each week I will soon have it paid[.] But please dont let them sell it for I am to old to try and buy annother one[.] beside that we have owned this property 23 years and I just cant bear the idea of loosing[.] please help me it is $89.28 and I tried to get them to take $40.00 and they would not[.] if they will just not sell it until I can pay it[.] I am so very worried a bout it[.]

Please for Gods sake consider this letter please sir[.] we never had no tax trouble before and I feel like Where I have lived and been honest all my life and then no help I ought[.] My Property is in Palatka Fla Putnum County[.] My name is Norma Bell. Please if there is help or consideration for Widows I am asking for it in this address.[26]

Gula (Mrs. D. E.) Walker (Hallandale) to Cone, 7 March 1937

1930 census: She is a 31-year-old white widow with six children at home. Neither she nor any of the children has a job.

Am writing to you to ask a few questions about the mother's or widow's pension. I have been a widow for almost ten (10) years. and I have been getting a pension of $10.00 a mth. until last July when my son joined the C.C.C. Camp. I was also working at the Gov. sewing room here and when my son joined the C.C.C. Camp my pension was stopped also I was took off the sewing project. I have three (3) children at home with me and I need more than the $25.00 I get from the boy that is in camp, to feed and clothe the children and pay rent.

My husband was a [illegible] marshall, at Osteen Fla.[,] also a Co. Constable of Volusia Co. and State Fish and Game Warden for the State. He was killed by a boot legger when he went with a warrent to search his car for liquor on the 8th of July—1927. leaving me with six (6) children. I have with the help of the pension put the children as far in school as I could. Why is it I can not get a pension of some kind to help support the children at least until they are old enough to work?

I have the chance of renting a 5 acre lot and house at Lakeland Fla. for $8.00 a month. I wish to rent this place as it is suitable for all truck farming and poultry raising. But I need some money to ship what furniture I have here and to buy a stove, chairs, bed and 2 dressers any way as my furniture was stolen out of storage after my husband was killed. My husband was born and raised in Putnam Co. about about 20 miles west of Palatka Fla. Will you please see that I get some pension each month also enough money to get moved and settled on this little farm at Lakeland, Fla. I wish to leave here about the 16th or 17th of this mth. My people are helping me all they can but are not able to help enough to buy furniture and get moved.

Please give this your emediate attention. And let me hear at once. My husband was a Mason also but have never had any help from the Masons at all. Please send me some and as I wish to get my children on a farm and two raise our vegetables and chickens.[27]

Note that this is the same Mrs. David Walker who wrote to Governor Carlton 5 July 1929.

148

Mrs. W. A. McDaniel (River Junction Hardaway) to Cone, 8 March 1937

I done all one Percen could do to put you in office for governer. and you got the office. so now I am asking you to help me[.] I am old worn out have no one to do one thing for me. and have a little boy my baby to raise[.] My husband is with me but afflicted[.] he has not been able to get eny thing to help his selfe to or do eny thing for me in three years[.] they say they cant sine him on eny works for he is not able to do the work and they are not allowed to do such a thing[.] I have work in the sewing room but it is such a small sallary I cant take care of the family with it a lone[.] my house rent to pay my wood bill to pay and thirty five dollar det on me and they keep after me woring my life a way out of me and I cant do to save life more than I am doing so[.] will you please see that my husband gets a Pencion enough to care for his self. he got crippled up in machenry first and the had a stroke of par-alies and for three years he had palagry [pellagra] and his affliction calls for medcine and nerishments and I just cant care for him nothing like he need. do you do all you can to open a way for him. we have no home no nothing to help our selves a long with only my little salry of 24 dollars a month and I cant do enough to take care of[.] in the condition of his health and my health a bout gone 56 years old my self. He 55 and not been able to get him self a shirt let a lone making a living[.] he is onstly naked for clothes I have ask Mrs Monroe to help him with a shirt and overalls but she wont do one thing for him[.] I ask for a bed for him to lay on but she wont let me have one and he has not got one we only have one bed I barred a single bed for him through the winter or till I could get one but have not got it yet do some-thing soon. Mr Cone I will tell you where my husband was and what work he has on at the time of his cripple[.] he was in savannah Ga in 1918 he was working at the Pulp mill where they were making paper. he had done signed up to go to war in the next call but the war ended before they took them and he was down in bed crippled when the war ended and was a long time that he couldnt walk a step[.] we rolled him on a chair and he hasnt been very able to do eny thing sence. its been awful hard on me every sence and all the childrens have married of and left me and they dont help me a dime now for they are not able family of their own[.] the one I have with me is 12 years old and I am rying to keep him in school but it looks like I cant do that much longer if I dont get help some other way for he is out of cloths now and I have patched till they are a bout past that stage[.] let me no some way soon and oblidged.[28]

Mrs. Massie Garritt (Auburndale) to Cone, 10 March 1937

I am writting you in regard to a very imparting matter that I need attention & I feel as you can help me & I need help. Last Dec 12 They put me off the W.P.A. because I was getting $7.50 to send my kids to school from the County for 2 that were there & they expected 7 of us to Live on this amount & said that congress in April would pension us & they haft to put us off for us to get this pension[.] has they been any such Provisions as to that Part approprate in Wash for us that us widow were turn out to starve & our family suffers Dec till April[.] they was seven of us[.] Mary Norman[,] Effie Griffen[,] Eva Weatherford[,] Ruth Norman[,] Lottie Arnett & my self on this & us with family with children & they kept on women with out children & they are still working on the W.P.A. & we are still off & they wont give us no work say they cant do any thing till April when Congress meet[.] will you plese make appeal for the benefit of the widow for help soon as we belive you as our governor you should no we are in destitute & need work are help are something to go up on[.] I have a family of 7 + no one to work but my self & I can't get no imploment in the Packing house[.] I have a sick husband has been down two years helpless as to work & he need medicine & can't have it[.] me no work[.] he need food he hasn't got & unnoursh the reason he cant get any better[.] Please help us if you Possible can to get work are is they any such provisions in Washington for us are will be can you tell us[.] I watch the paper & I never save it. Please let me hear from you soon.[29]

Mrs. M. P. Wollam (Homestead) to Cone, 11 March 1937

I am writing in behalf of a dear neighbor of mine Mrs. Jean Jernigan, who finds herself widowed this morning. Probably you will remember Jean Jernigan; his widow tells me he lived next to you in Lake City. He died very suddenly early this morning, and she has five lovely children, the eldest one eleven and the youngest about 16 months of age. He was a man held in great esteem in this community and I'm writing to you direct about a mother's pension for his widow. Will it be possible for you to get one for her at the very earliest convenience.

I feel sure the people here will tide her over the present time of bereavement, but I'd like to know that she would have something to depend on each month. She's ambitious & is talking of doing typing in her home,—just so she can keep the family together.

I am also the mother of five but they are grown now, & we can provide temporary relief—but please as a special favor to me, interest yourself in her case at once—won't you?

Thanking you in advance[.]

P.S. Mr. Jernigan carried but $500 insurance; he at one time was a Mason but had to drop out, on account of expenses at home more important to him, seemingly.[30]

Mrs. Vassie Lee Hall (Westville) to Cone, 12 March 1937

I am a widow woman with one child to support. I have a father who is an invalid and nearly blind. A mother who is old and has strange nervous spells and a sister that has all sorts of queer spells—imagining strange things—I want work and have applied at the relief office and employment officials, asked for work in the sewing rooms. I have asked and asked ever since there has been work here.

My brother is worked down trying to feed us all and keep doctor bills etc. paid up. Is there any way by which I can get work in the sewing room so I could get the necessities. My boy age 10 has to stay out of school because he has no clothes. There is nothing here that I can do & bring money for necessities.

If you can help me out in getting work I will be very grateful and try my best to give satisfactory service in any work I can get.[31]

Miss Olive S. Ford (Miami) to ER, undated, date stamped as received 17 March 1937

Because you have shown that your sympathies are with the working class of people and I know you are anxious to do whatever you can to help our beloved country, I write to call your attention to the enclosed highlights of GENERAL WELFARE BILL of 1937, which is now before the Ways and Means Committee.

We live in a New Age, with new problems confronting us (one of which is the tremendous displacement of men by machines.) Therefore a NEW ECONOMIC SYSTEM must be brought forth, and this General Welfare Bill provides it.

The President is earnestly seeking a way to take care of "40 million underpriviledged Americans" without further burdening the already overloaded taxpayer. This bill would easily solve both questions for the simple reason that it PUTS MONEY INTO CIRCULATION, which you know is the secret of national prosperity.

Washington lead the way to political freedom. Lincoln led the way to racial freedom. Please use your influence on the President so that he may see his way to lead our people into economic freedom. Something MUST be done. Millions of people over the country want to try it. Why not let's see what it can do?[32]

Mrs. Jesse Tullis (Crestview) to Cone, 17 March 1937

Mr. Cone I gave you my support on election day now I am asking for you to help me. My Husband was an ideal husband & Father until he got in with a low class woman[.] they have been running around together now for 4 years.

So the 4th of January they come right here and opened up a Roadhouse I guess you would call it[.] any way they are right there together same as man and wife. And I want to know if you cant have something done about it[.] He has spent a part of one night at home since the 4th of January. Our Sheriff know about it to they just wont do a thing. And I am writing you for help as I think it is a shame & we have a 10 year old boy all so an my husband just don't care for anything. Please send men here and investgate[.] I think they will find plenty of work to do. They are running the Man Camp Tavern on the Pensacola high way. The woman is well known by all the law around[.] She is just a trouble maker. Ople Parker is a blond[.] I feel like if you would send men here I am afraid they would both go to Raiford but it is shameful the way they are doing[.] They ride the streets to-gether.

But if any one askes him are we seperated he says why no.

So if there cant be any thing done I want you to write & tell me & let the work be done.

P.S. I feel like our Sheriff still could do something if he would.[33]

Mrs. Fritz D Mayenhoff (Miami) to Cone, 23 March 1937

May I ask for a few minutes of your time. The States does every thing they can for the poor unfortunates in the State hospital. Why don't they do something for the husbands and wives. My husband was <u>sent</u> there Aug 1929. two years previous to this I took care of him which at times it was dangerous for me to do. I <u>am only</u> one <u>of many</u> like this. And I've heard many people say they thought after a few years in cases of this kind hopeless chronic paresis, There should be some way for us to be granted marriage annulment or divorce. I've seen 10 years of this. As I worked and took care of him for two years before he was sent away. I wonder if the ones who makes & changes the laws of the states will ever consider what we have to look forward to. As to another home and happiness when we can not have one of our choice. Enclosed letter. Kindly return as I use it some times as reference the last one I have from there. As I understand it takes special act of Legislature. For any thing to be done about this I hope <u>they will some time</u> think of us. As we are worse off than the ones in the Hospital. They don't realize any thing and we can not get our freedom. I've heard some very good attorneys say they thought it very unfair[.] My family has been tax payers in this state since before 1860. The Canovas and Perrys of Lake City are very near relatives of mine[.] I mention this to let you know I am a real Floridian.[34]

Mrs. Etta Messina (Apalachicola) to FDR, 23 March 1937

1930 census: She is 53 years old and white, and she was born in Canada. Her husband, Joseph, owns a seafood-packing company.

A souvenir of the dear Old South, one of twelve hundred dollars for which a cavalry horse was sold at the close of the Civil War by my husband's father Frank Messina he having belonged to the cavalry of the Confederacy.

My appreciation for the sending of my letter to the Federal Home Loan Bank Board—if it will just bring some relief to us.[35]

Mrs. Lelia Haye (Kissimmee) to Cone, 8 April 1937

I am turning to you for advice or help.

I have been living in Fla. about 65 yrs. and was living here in this part of the county when it was named Osceola Co.

I have been a widow 22 yrs. Raised my family of five children who are all grown married and have families of their own except one, and she has been paralyzed since she was 7 yrs old and I have to care for her. She is 49 yrs old.

I worked on the relief as a seamstress about 15 mo. They have laid me off because I was over 70 yrs of age. They want take me back on and the county has used up all the money and can't give me any pention untill the legislature approprates more money.

I have nothing to support myself and my afflicted daughter. I am in need now. What can I do? Did they have any right to lay me off without any support?

There was not any fault with my work[.] it was just my age.[36]

Mrs. W. V. Godwin (Madison) to Cone, 9 April 1937

I am writeing you to see if you can help me out about geting work with the W.P.A. my husband was in a car wreck Jan 16. And had to be taken to the hospittle he stayed there eight days[.] We put what money we had on the bill[.] he hasnt bin able to work and wont be this year to amount to any thing and I an afriad he will never be at himsef altogether on acount of external ingures in his lung[.] he had three are four ribs broken and his arm close to his shoulder[.] his lung punctured[.] he is 49 yeas old and it will take some time[.] the D.R. said he would be able to work some in 8 months. I went to the WPA ofice in Madison Jan 18[.] they told me all the way they could help me was to give me work in the sewing room[.] he was in bed here at home about five week[.] when he was able for me to go I went back to see about geting lined up to go to work[.] they told me my mother in law was working for us and she dont even live with us. She has all she can manage at home and is not responsible for us. I hope you can get this all adjused and get me lined up for work[.] we are poor farmers and havnt been able to get a crop planted and we havnt even got hores or a mule and we have a mortage on our place & besides all the other things we owe[.] so pleas help me out if you can.[37]

Mrs. Thelma Combs (Glen St. Mary) to W. B. Cone, Executive Secretary, 13 April 1937

1930 census: She is 30 years old. She is listed as head of the house but married. She has three children and is a laborer in a florist nursery.

I am writing you in regards to some work. I will explain my case to you and see if you can help me in any way. If you can it will be highly appreciated.

I have a boy in the C.C.C. camp[.] But I have two other children in school and the twenty five (25) dollars I get from him is all I have to pay all expenses[.] So you know if any one needs a job it is me. I have to buy all of his Dress Clothes & shoes, out of the 25.00 I get from the C.C.C. I have my application in at Lake City at the government hospital but I have been unable to get the job. I am willing to work at any thing I can get to do. I can not take an office job. But I am willing to do anything else, and anything will be appreciated.

I have not been able to get any cloth's from the relief office since school started and I have tried to get on in the Sewing room, But they wont do any thing for me because my boy is in the Camp.

One of my children is a [illegible] she needs her tonsils removed she needs glasses But have been unable to get them.

I havent any one that I can go to and tell my troubles. I have one brother, and my father isnt able to work for himself. it sure is hard to say you will take care of four with the amount of money I recieve. I will always Remember how good you were to my brother that is deceased. I really can't thank you enough.

I am trying my best to educate my children.

I will close and I sure will appreciate it if you can help me out in any way.

P.S. I hope I haven't made any mistakes in the writing.

The case worker of McClenny is Mrs Pearl Hubbard.[38]

Mr. W. D. Cogswell (Zephyrhills) to FDR, 23 April 1937

United States citizenry are truly grateful for the wisdom, acumen and humane activities you have so liberally displayed during the past four years to benefit banking, agriculture, transportation, industry, labor etc. and restored national happiness although there remains seven million to nine million in a scrap heap that are classed as unemployables on account of age and lack of positions suited to their capabilities, I refer to the aged indigents who have exhausted former savings, their homes and insurance policies are sacrificed to provide food, clothing, shelter, and in some localities fuel, are now without daily necessities.

Many are praying and imploring that you use your valuable influence to enact legislation for their relief and numberless can think of none that would be as effective as H.R. 4199, General Welfare Act of 1937, however, should there be any other or others that can be successfully applied, will you in the name of suffering humanity, please recommend immediate action, as those having good incomes do not realize the deplorable conditions that exist.[39]

Mrs. W. D. Cogswell (Zephyrhills) to ER [undated, attached to her husband's letter to FDR above]

When I read yours in Lad[ies] Home Journal the thought came to me that like Jesus had to suffer so He could understand and sympathize with suffering humanity you had to have an unusual childhood to prepare you for your future station in life. Most rich girls are reared in selfish idleness while your relatives taking you on their charitable expeditions gave you an insight on human suffering you never forgot and has caused you to become one of our greatest humanitarians and if you will carefully study the new General Welfare Act 4199 and use your influence to have it enacted you and your great-hearted husband will go down in history as having done the greatest good for the most people the world has ever known. Pardon presumption.[40]

Mrs. C. A. Gibson, widow, (Tampa) to ER, 24 April 1937

Will you allow me a few minutes of your valuable time? I just feel impressed to write to you for I've read of the great work you do for those in need. So you must be very kind hearted.

I sent the President an Easter Card and poem—wonder if he read it.

I know he has done a great deal for humanity and we appreciate it. Yet there are so many suffering for the necissities of live. O it is pitiful to see so many old people who need medical aid also food. Cant something be done? I guess there are more in Florida than elsewhere.

I feel like there is a plan that will relieve these people. Now wont you and the President study the General Welfare Act of 1937 H.R. 4199? It is now before the Ways and Means Com. and use your great influence to have it reported out of Committee for House action at earliest possible moment?

We don't see how you can help endorsing it. It then will not be necessary for any more poems like this—"Over the Hill to the Poor House."

When the Townsend Plan is passed and made a law there will be no Poor Houses (and we are now taxed to keep them up.) I feel like then I can have a square meal and not have to take meat in a capsule, as if men, millions are working for it. And we trust the voices of the people will be heard and heeded. Just give it a trial and see if it works. Read the book on the Plan. I feel like when our good President signs the General Welfare Act H.R. 4199 his name will go down in history as the greatest president we ever had. May God bless you in your work.[41]

Mrs Maggie A. Green (Groveland) to Cone, 26 April 1937

I am going to state to you my condition[.] I am a poor cripple widow woman cant walk[.] have to travel on one half on an orange box[.] have a little girl 13 years of age. and the county only gives me $8.00 per month for my support.

My husban a Confederate soldier left me a little 4 room house 1 lot of land. and he left a mortgage that is just on the verge of closing me out. And putting me out in the world with no place for me and my Child to lay our heads. Mr. A. M. Davis of Groveland has the papers over my plase and he stated yesterday that he was soon going to close me out.

So I am pleading to you for help to save me and my child a place to stay. If you please do all you can for me as I have no one to look to for help in any way. I hope to hear from you at once.[42]

Mrs. Bette Croft (Clearwater) to Branch Cone, 11 May 1937

I am writing you a letter to see if you have any weight in helping me to get on at the Govt sewing room here in Tampa, where I have been living for the past 5 years. I am just over this week visiting my mother[.] I have been registered on relief roll and have been getting the comodities for a long time. I have tried so hard when I'd fail to get work to get on at the sewing room. Their excuse was I didn't have a dependent and I know of no's [numbers] of women that are one in a hill that have been employed in the sewing room for not only mo's but years. I am completely out of work and have tried faithful to find employment but certainly have failed so far. Mr. Cone knowing you personally you very well know that my people cant take care of me because they have to look out for themselves. Even to my mother you know how hard she sewed at McClenny for a living. I realize this is Govt work but I've been told that with your and Gov Cones help from Jaxville office you could help me out. I need the work so bad I'm almost destitute to be frank about it.

Will you please ans this letter in person and let me know the returns of it for work. I will leave here about Tuesday of next week to go back home. Please reply here in c/o my mother. Thank you, Good luck, and Goodbye.

P.S. You shall remember me as (Leo & Walter Dykes) sister at your home town.[43]

Mrs. J. E. Johnson (Altha) to Cone, 12 May 1937

I am writing you in regard of my aged Father. He was 71 years old the 5th day of April, and is a preacher, but never did charge for his work. He is not able to do anything. Have lived in Fla twenty seven years was sent to raiford 10 years on the account of people telling lies. Have lived in phelam Ga eight years. I have a single sister that was taking care of an she is 46 year old and is not able to work. They were staying in pelham and was out of doors. They had no wood and had to get their water one half mile from the house. My sister had to walk four and one half miles to town and leave my father by his self. He just falls around and they only got 4.00 a mount to live one. They had to come and live with me wher I could help look after daddy[.] If you can give daddy the pension please do so. We sure would appricate it for I am not able to take care of my self have been sick all of my life. I am 38 year old. I have been to Marrianna to see about getting help, but was turned down on relief and all. My daddy has not got greese, bread, meat nor anything to live on and my sister either[.] neither have we. We have to buy all the thing we eat, wear, and feed for the live stock and we live on gravy and bread most of the time. Write to Dr. J. B. Douling, Alliance Fla for any information you want. My name is Mrs. J. E. Johnson. Address Altha Fla Route 1.

My sister name is Miss Mary Sims and daddys is J. M. Sims. They live with me.[44]

Mrs. Mabel G Braswell (Ft. Myers) to Cone, 17 May 1937

I am coming to you for advise, also aid if it is in your power to give it.

I understand Our State have a fund provided for the blind. I do not know how to go about getting this aid. So deside to call on you. Gov my mother is 84 years old[.] She is blind and I have to Sacrifice my whole life to her. I am 45 years of age my self. I can not leave her to get out to look for work. She needs me every minute of her life. My Father was 87 when he passed away[.] he was a Tax payer of the State of Fla for over 65 years. She should be entitled to the blind pension if any one is and we need it. it is true She gets a little Gov check of $40.00 per month old Vets pension but Gov you realize $40.00 dont go far when it comes to buying Medicine paying Dr's Bills and all expenses of living for an invalid. My mother takes medicine all the time. I should but can not get it. So I am asking you to advise me on this question[.] it wont be for long that she will need help, for she is now an invalid and do not have many more months to stay with me. I feel that her days are numbered now. She have been confined to her bed for over a week now not able to sit up[.] I have not had a Dr for I do not have the money to pay one. I will appreciate all you can do toward advising me how to go about getting the fund for the blind.

P.S. I have her Pension check cashed at the P.O. and they take 15 cents out of each check for cashing it. I did not think they were supose to charge for cashing the Gov. check.[45]

Miss Evelyn Herrington (Munson) to Cone, 17 May 1937

I am a poor girl and I am writing to you to ask for help.

My father works on our farm. He doesn't follow any public work at all. All the groceries that we have bought lately have been bought on credit from Mr. N. Nadeau, Santa Maria, Florida.

I am a high school graduate and I want to take a business course so maybe I can get a job and help my folks.

The business course will cost me sixty-five (65) dollars and I would like for you to send me the money for this course.

After I take the business course maybe I can get a job and pay you this money back.

It will be highly appreciated by me if you can send me the money.

The school starts to-day week so please let me hear from you real soon. The school is held at Crestview Florida.[46]

Mrs. Nellie D. Hagin (Plant City) to Cone, 24 May 1937

I'm sorry I have to bother you, but it seems that there are not any laws in Hillsboro County, on Desertion and more support of wife and child. My husband C. M. Hagin Deserted me around 3 years ago, the first year he did support me a little, but in the last 2 two years hasent in any way supported me or mine and his child, a little girl 4 years old. In 1935 I had a warrent sworn out for him, it went to court in judge sandlers court room in Tampa, Fla[.] The court ruled that he should pay 7 dollars a week temporary alimony and said if he did not pay this amount to notify them, and they would make him pay it or go to jail so I did so. but there wasent anything done about it. so in 1936 I had another warrent sworn out for him[.] again in about one month prior to the date I had the warrant taken out it was brought up before Judge Cornelius in Tampa Judge Cornelius passed it on to criminal court[.] thats been about 8 months ago, it came up about 3 or 4 months ago, but was put off for an indefinite time. The exact dates are on record at court house at Tampa. My husband C. M. Hagin lives here in the same town Plant City I live in, and is always working at something and also lives with another women, the women he deserted me for and have not any divorce not as far as I know of[.] of course I've never bothered him in any way for that, he says he has got me beat in law. so it seems as if he has, unless there is something you Governor of Fla. can do towards it. I can prove my character clean in every way necessary[.] I will close asking you to have this matter looked into at once[.][47]

158

Mrs. A. B. O'Quinn (Chattahoochee) to Cone, 26 May 1937

I wrote about a month ago in regards to a job at the canning factory. Went to see Dr. Sherell as you said to. He was very nice. and when the factory opened I was notified to report for work (last Wednesday) got in 10 hours, Thursday 9 1/2 hours and Friday 7 1/2 hours. of which I appreciated more than I can say.

Jim Lewis told me not to report back until we were notified by Mr. Freeman, so I waited. So today (Wednesday) at noon I went to a neighbor's and phoned to Mr. Freeman and asked when we would be needed and he said a few was at work today. But did not have enough beans to put the whole crew back to work. So I said O.K.

But I got dressed went up to Dr. Sherell's office was told he would be out of town until Friday. Thats why I am writing you.

Now when we went to work there were fourteen (14) called and than seven more on the next call. I was one of the first 14. and this first crew was called this morning with the exception of myself. and I am sure with the exception of one other lady and myself have their husbands in some part of the Hospital—drawing a salary the year round. I have not been up here quite two years but there has been taxes paid to the State of Fla. here and Jax. by my grandmother and my mother for the last Thirty–Five years. and I feel that I deserve a job to work for my three children and mother as I have no income. If I had a husband I would not be trying to work and keep women that really needed to work off the job.

Mr. Cone I am positive I give satisfaction with my work that's what I go there for. not to visit the toilet and labority. I dont even know where it is located. So I am taking my problem up with you. Though I dislike to go higher authorities than the hiring Boss. But it seems I am forced to[.] all these other ladies have worked there last year and more. But I am worthy of the work and need the money not to buy extra summer clothes but for my children. and I beg of you to inform the right party that is supposed to hire the help—to be sure and call me at all times. If they have work for two let me be one of the two. That is just as long as i do my part of the work that is there for me to do. and until I fall down on the job and do less work than is required by each of us to just drop you a line and let you know I am not doing my part. Than I will take a lay off by you.

Now Governor I hope I won't have to worry you any more about my little measley job. But if I do I'll be writing, Thanks a lot from one who appreciates a job for what its worth and not to just make a day of pay. Hoping for early results.[48]

Mrs. E. R. Coleman (Wauchula) to Cone, 7 June 1937

I am not writeing you as I persum, hundreds of others have done, For a Job. But for help. I am a sick Lady (Seriously) and no hope of Recover, untill I can have some Surgery Work done.

My husband is a P.W.A. Worker, and you know the same as I do That No P.W.A. worker can finance a hospital Expense. I do not know what this expense will be as I have not consulted my Physician that far. For I was or am, not able to have the work done. If you care to have me too, I will, explain the case, or better still, will get a Certificate from the Dr. It is just a Femail Trouble. But Very Painful, And if not stoped, I fear it will, (if it have not already) cause cancer. I was told by a Physician several years ago that it would. Your Honor Sir: Please give this your Sincere attention. And if you can passiable help me, It will be appreciated more than words can explain. Please let me hear at as early date as will be convenient. For while I am waiting I am suffering agony. If you can not help me, Please advise me just the same, so I will not be vainly hopeing.

P.S. Any other details you care to know I will be glad to explain.[49]

Mrs. Alice G. Sims (Port Tampa City) to Cone, 7 June 1937

1930 census: She is 34 years old and African American, and she is not employed. Her husband, Ernest, works as a stevedore on the docks.

Enclose find a notice received from the Public Works Assn. after I had applied for a job in the W.P.A. sewing room[.] I have been nursing for nearly seven years, and my health has failed so much that I am unable to do any more nursing—altho I have to work at some thing. I have three dependent children and a mother to support, and my pension is only thirteen dollars per month. Can you please advise me how I can get on in this work which I have applied for. I must have work at once.

My husband died in 1930. He was an Elk, member of the lodge in Tampa, and you can get references from both Tampa and Port Tampa about me needing work—will appreciate any thing you can help me in.

Attached was the WPA application denial stating that she was not accepted for work because she had a mother's pension.[50]

Mrs. N. J. Sellers (Marianna) to Cone, 9 June 1937

Am writing, asking a favor of you, which I believe you'll grant, when you read the circumstances.

I have asked, repeatedly, for a job in the sewing room here at Marianna, & I am always told there is no vacancy.

But since I first asked last year, there's been numbers laid off and others taken on.

I understand of course, there's not work for all, but I feel that they should give me work for a while. I need the work very much as I have 4 small children, & my husbands' income is not sufficient to keep us up.

I am perfectly capable of doing the work and our family is of thouroughly good character. Also I have asked for a few of the clothes they have there (made at the sewing room) & have rec'd only one small allotment, & that was last year. So I feel that we should have a few of them, as others get them regularly.

If you can, please send me an order, signed up in full for [a] job at the sewing rooms & a few of the clothes.

I surely would not write this, if I did not need so, & would not have asked for them up at the office.

So if you'll look after this soon, I'll thank you very much.

Our aid ladies of this city are Mrs. Sadie Bostwick and Mrs. Dickerson.

Just an order from you, with your signature is all I need to present up at the office. I'm sure I'd get the job then.[51]

"Aid ladies" refers to the local caseworkers.

Mrs. C. Moore (Umatilla) to Cone, 21 June 1937

I am writing you in regards to my condition[.] there is six in my family and I am not able to work & support them and I was talking to Mr. George D Likes in Tavorese to day and I told him I was going to write and tell you my condition and he said that was the thing to do[.] my husband has had a stroke of paralises and is almost Helpless and they have taken my commodities from me and also I was talking to Mrs. W. O. Johnson in Eustis and we people that needs help never get it[.] we do not have a social welfair visitor at all & when Mrs. Johnson had charge of the business my home & others and we got help[.] there is quite a few of us people that would be glad if you would put Mrs. W. O. Johnson back on the job. so hoping to hear from you at once and if there is anyway in the world to get help we would sure appreciate it to the highest.[52]

Odia (Mrs. J. A.) Thomas (Westville) to Cone, 21 June 1937

Willmere Watson and Mukey holds a margage on my home and are goeing to farclose in July or August and I am a widdow woman with a little grand child an orphan to raise and have no means to live only on my little farm. If you can or will help me I will sure be proud[.] I have lived here for 19 years and have raised my family here and you know what that means to me to have to leave hear[.] my children are all married and gone but one[.] I am 56 years old have high blood pressure and cant work much but can make a living here if I can stay[.] so please please help me if you can. Yours in Disstress[.]

W. A. Watson and Mulkey of Geneva Ala holds this morgage.[53]

Callie Hughes (Pensacola) to Cone, 23 June 1937

Please read this letter[.] I heard you say in yore speches that you would help us poor people all rich and poor to solve our problems and god in heaven know I need yore help[.] I have no one to look for a dime and I did work 7 months ago in the sewing Room at quincy and I got a job of nursing because I woud not haft to pay rent and I coulden get iny more after that one got well so its left me down and out and I need [illegible] chothes and dont have half enought to eat and I want you to Please Please write to the manerger heare of the WPA to let me sew[.] if I cant get on I dont no what I can do for I have tried an tried to get work and I have had to take care of my Husban for 12 years and do please write me a letter give the WPA office heare to let me work[.] I'll tell no one that you did it and god will surley Bless you[.] I am bare for clothes and I dont have a dolar to my name no not a dime but if I can get on I can live and I can do my part of the sewing that tha have to do for I [am] to old to get work like yong ladies[.] But I can do that work so do please help me out and god will sure help you[.] tha took on 2 new ones to day and said first of July tha would take on a lot more and do do Please tell them to take me on I am suffering for work.[54]

Mrs. Missouri Ergle (Island Grove) to Cone, 24 June 1937

I have tried several way of trying to get a job on the Relief and havent succeeded yet so am asking you to help me[.] I have a large family (only 10) and not any too healthy a husband and not an income of any kind just what my husband gets out and works for is all this family of ten gets[.] havent had any help from the relief in a year and half except one little batch of clothes. I live three blocks from the sewing room and would be very glad if you would see that I get a job. We are really in need and will you please see that I have a job on this relief project. Thanking you and hoping to hear from you soon.[55]

Mrs. M. A. Ventry (Greensboro) to Cone, 24 June 1937

1930 census: Martha is 55 years old and white and does not work. Her husband, Ira, is a "saw miller" in a shingle mill.

I am writing you, to find out, if you can explain, Just why <u>we</u> can't get some of this W.P.A. work.

My Husband and I are both able to work but still we can't get anything to do.

We are very much in need of clothing and grociers, and we are in a rented home, and nothing to do make expenses.

I am right here (in Greensboro) clost to sewing room and would be glad to get sewing to do. Also we live right on the line, where W.P.A. truck passes each morning.

We are both in our early 60's less than 65. Looks like we must get something some way. The W.P.A. officiers of Quincy always give us promises, but that is all we get. And we simply can't live on that much longer.

Could you help us? In some way.

I feel like you can for I believe you are a friend to the poor. And may God Bless you in all of your under takings.[56]

Mrs. Rufus Fields (Tampa) to Cone, 26 June 1937

I am writing you and asking you if I am entitled to W.P.A. work. I have tried repeatly to get on and never got any further than the head of the stairs at the Allied building. My husband works on the County Road at a salary of $12.50 per week. There is nine of us in family seven children my husband and my self. Now there being a lay off of one week on and one week off gives us only $6.26 a week. That being true has thrown us into destitution. Our shelter and water is $12.50 a month and that we have to pay or be thrown in the streets. My children are very under nurished. They range in years from 14 years to 14 months. We are very bare of clothing and every time I make an effort to get clothes and commodities from the government I get only insults. While I know numerous others who does not need them. This can be proved. I would appericate the fact to know if I am not entitled to W.P.A. works clothing and commodities. My family has been a residence of Tampa for 15 years. I am thinking the mane cause is that I give information to one Mr. Hoyt in the case of stolen government products. he Mr. Hoyt posed as a dictive [detective] for some and I am thinking there has been double crossing. Cincerely hope you will assist me in keeping the wolf away from my door.[57]

Miss Martha Witter (St. Petersburg) to FDR and ER, 26 June 1937

1930 census: She is 11 years old, white, and the daughter of a railroad fireman.

I've been reading in the paper what a wonderful break Roberta Jones has been getting ever since she came to visit you. Well, it always takes just such as that to start a person on the road to fame.

For instance, in this City of St. Petersburg you've got to have money or 2 or 3 cars or you've got to be top-notch on the social register.

It really hurts me sometimes to see how things are, because I really am ambitious and want to go places and do things. I've been going to Junior College here to prepare myself for the College in Cincinnati, Ohio where my sister, her husband, and darling little baby, Judy, lives.

Now, I'm working in a real estate office as a secretary & stenographer until college opens again in Sept.

Well to give you a little history of ourselves. My sister, Anne, and I have always been a singing and dancing team, and have appeared at places all over the city. Our teacher said we were wonderful singing together, and a dancing team has tried to make us appear many times on the stage, but it was not always an easy matter to do so.

Now, my sister was Queen of Gardialand at Cypress Gardens in Winter Haven, Fla, and has received wonderful publicity from it. Maybe you saw a picture of her in the Washington paper some time ago. Now a very prominent woman in town took pictures of my sister and I to try and get us a job posing for advertisements in magazines. She said we looked so much a like and were both nice looking and she wanted us to have a break. So maybe something will come of that.

Well, my sister's husband is a musician in Hollywood, Cal. & has an orchestra of his own. His name is Pat Kelly, but for professional reasons, they changed it to Charles Cavalier. He's really marvelous and has many chances to get in the movies. My little niece has also been offered several chances. She is the cutest little girl you ever saw. You see my sister & her husband has lived out there now for 4 years, and have many friends there. The personal manager of Madge Evans, Marie Brassell, said that she could help Anne and I in the movies if we would come out there again. You see we were there 4 years ago, and saw most of the movie stars. Maybe this will happen some day.

Well, I'm almost 19. will be August 10. I was thinking, but it would be almost impossible I know, if I could only get to visit someone as prominent as you, I would be made. I have always dreamed of something like this and I would love to meet you. I think Ethel Du Pont is beautiful and I would love to meet her and your son.

You know you would make me the happiest girl in the world if something like this could be arranged. I would just naturally be in Heaven. Do you think that you could possibly help me out. I suppose you will think I'm awful for even asking you such a thing, but I couldn't resist writing you. I've been wishing all my life that I could do something like visit the president or be a movie star. Maybe I'm overly ambitious, but I cant help it.

Won't you please try to help me. I'm of a nice appearance, and you wouldn't be ashamed of me, and I can sing & dance.[58]

Ethel DuPont was the wife of Franklin Roosevelt Jr.

Mrs. A. L. Anderson (Sneads), to W. B. Cone, 29 June 1937

Some time ago I was over there to see you about getting me a position at Chattahoochee and you gave me a letter to give Dr. Sherrell asking him to make a place for me in the sewing room. I gave Dr. Sherrell the letter the next morning and he just ignored it. He didn't give me the job nor ever any encouragment, said he didn't have sufficient money to pay any more help in the sewing room tho they did need more help. and said you knew it before you sent him that letter. So a few days later the supervisor of that department was discharged and another lady advanced to that place leaving a vacancy so I went back to see him and asked him for the place and he said he was trying to run it without another person but I know he will hire some one, so will you please write him or send me a letter to give him asking him to give me this place. because as I told you before I am badly in need of this work. I cant understand why I cant get a place over there because I have had several of the most prominent men of West Florida write them and ask them to give me some-thing to do. I have good recommendations and every one that knows me knows I am badly in need of work. So wont you please help me out in this matter or do you think it necessary for me to come to see Gov. Cone personally? Hoping to hear from you at an early date.[59]

Mrs. F. L. Deaux (Jacksonville) to Cone, 29 June 1937

I am writing to you in hopes of getting some help. I feel that you can and will help me out, as I am in a terrible position. several months ago my husband & I bought a home in So. Jacksonville as we have to take care of my mother & father in law. they are close to 70 years of age. we have managed to keep the payments up until now, but due to the fact that my husband has been out of work for 4 months we are not able to keep the payments up any longer. and they are threatning taking the place away from us. Mr. Cone this place means everything to us. We might have been able to have payed a little more on it but my husband and I both contracted malaria fever, and have had it all the summer.

What I want to know is would you take the place over and pay for it and take the deed's and give us a chance to pay you for it. you will never know how much this will be appreciated if you can and will.

and if you can't, is there someone you might know of who will. The balance of the place is $800.

I truly hope that you will give this your utmost attention. I feel sure you will help us in some way. So please let me hear from you at the earliest possible date, as we have to do something at once.[60]

Mrs. Essie Mae Connor (Miami) to Cone, 4 July 1937

I am droping you a few lines because you are the Gov. of the U.S. and can help if you will. My husban is seriously ill and I two daughters between the age of 9 and 10 yrs. old, and I havent got no one to help me. I was sewing on the project and was laid off. I went down to the office and told them my circumstances and they told me they couldn't do me any good. Today I haven't got a mouth full in my house for my children and therefore I need help very bad. They keep young women on the project who are well and don't have any children. So your honor will you please help me. I will appreciate anything that you will do for me. Please don't expose my name down because they will hunt me down here. Will you take this under consideration. I am hoping an early reply.[61]

Mrs. Rosabel Fielder (West Palm Beach) to Cone, 6 July 1937

1930 census: She is 34 years old and white and does not work. She is the wife of an auto mechanic.

Perhaps you will be surprised when you learn, just who I am writing this letter. First I must explain to you who I am. Well second I am the Warren girl, that married Reese Fielder the younger son of Mr. and Mrs. J. M. Fielder of Lake City, Fla. We separated 17 months ago and I have been trying to make a living for my self and 10 year old daughter. And for the past three months I have been out of work only fill-in jobs. I tried repeatedly for the past year to get work on the WPA as seamstress or cutter, or would like to get on the book-binding project. But every time I go up to see them I'm always thrown off, that they are not making no assignment or their quota is filled and all the time new women are going to work, and I cannot get no encouragement whatever. I need the work badly. There is Mrs. Rosalie Avaden the former Gov's sister Rosalie Sholtz from Daytona Beach. She is supervisor of women's work West Palm Beach[.] Lives in Palm Beach with parents in a $100,000 home. She is divorced and gets $100.00 per month Alimony and gets a salary of $175.00 per month. Has held her present job for two years. She also buys a new car every year. Now do you feel that she is doing right by widows who have families to support. That she could give them a chance to earn a small sum of $29.00 per month so that she could buy food for her children. I want you to please help me get work immediately. The vote I gave you should be worth that much to you. Will you let me hear directly from you, at once. And also trust that the W.P.A. headquarters will hear from you immediately.[62]

Mrs. Mollie McCarr (Auburndale) to Cone, 6 July 1937

I want to know if the dependent Children will include my crippled daughter who will soon be 18 years old but isn't in shape to do any kind of work. She has a chance of going to the Rehabilitation Vocation School for aflicted people but she isn't able to go yet and she hasn't any shoes, or clothes to wear & I can't fix lunches as I havnt any work now. I work in the Packing house & been through over a month. Went over to sign up to work in the sewing room & they aren't taking any applications for work. So what am I to do as we need food & I'm able to work for it if I can just get he work to do[.] Isn't there any chance of me getting on in the sewing room for I need to work now. If there is any chance of me getting on in the sewing room tell me what to do to get on. And tell me what to do & all about it if there is any chance for me to get aid for my crippled daughter. We need some thing and that right away. I want to work for we need it bad. Please let me hear from you at once[.] Hoping I will get a favorable reply soon.[63]

Mrs. C. A. Gibson, widow, (Tampa) to ER, 9 July 1937

I will write and ask you if you will intercede for the suffering people. Like Esther who knows but you have come to the White House for such a time as this, I believe you are sympathetic and if you see the suffering that I do you can't help speaking to the President and to Congress to have those pension bills brought out of the Ways & Means Com. for discussion, and we feel like when they are that the best one will pass. Of course I think The General Welfare Act H R 4199 is the best—it may need amending. The Pension this state offers supposed to be $30.00 per month but no one has been able to get that. And a friend said you would have to deed them your home if you had one also any money or insurance & then get eight or ten dollars per month.

Is that a pension? Then one must be in Fla. five years before they can apply. There is so much red tape. I don't think Senators & others have to go through such a questioning.

Well I appeal to you & your good husband to see that those other pension bills are brought out and use your influence to pass the best one. One that will help humanity and cure the depression. A revolving pension will help young & old.

>Poem
>Who can go on singing
>When millions are in tears

Who can live in smiling faith
With millions torn by fears.
Who can say that life is sweet
With millions robbed of bread & meat?
Yet I shall go on singing
Though foolish I may be
And I shall have hope with sturdy faith
A better world to see.
Yes we all shall go on singing
Every woman and man
Until our good President Roosevelt
Signs the Townsend Plan.

Excuse nervous writing.[64]

Mrs. L. P. Keaton (Maitland) to Cone, 9 July 1937

I am a young mother 20 years old. I have a baby that is 2 month old. We are in a terrible fix. My husband was in a car wreck near Titusville, Fla. He is out of jail on a $1,000 bond for man slaughter. We are practically on starvation. We have no money saved, but he is working hard. He was drunk at the time of the accident. It was the first time he had gotten that way since we've been married last Aug. He says he will never drink another drop of any kind of liquor. You are the one I'm appealing to. I need my husband very badly and you can help me keep him by not letting them convict him when his trial comes up Oct 12th. I'm begging you to help me, Governor. We are going to live in Winter Park now. He is making $10.80 a week. You can realize how far that goes. We pay $2 a week for rent. We have no clothes and are trying to save every penny towards his trial. He is not guilty, Governor and I need him so! Won't you please help me. Please. Please.[65]

Miss Susie Mae Sherrod (Chattahoochee) to Cone, 9 July 1937

1930 census, listed as Sharrod: Susie is 10 years old and is one of seven children of Arlin, a woodcutter for a railroad. They live in River Junction. The family is white.

I am writing and asking you to please aid me in getting work at Florida State Laundry.

I applied for work at the Florida State Hospital on the wards but have failed to secure work there yet.

I am (18) eighteen years of age, and will graduate from High School next term if I go. There is no way for me to finish unless I get work and get it quick. My parents are very poor and disable to work, I haven't any way of support, only of my own labor, and there is only nearly two months that I could work if I had it.

Please notify me wheather you can or cannot help me in getting work.[66]

Mrs. C. C. Gilbert (Pahokee) to Cone, 31 July 1937

Can you have my child [A.] Gilbert white (age 6 yrs) admitted to State hostipal for insane. If they havint got room at Gainesville hostipal yet.

As child has been pronounced feeble minded and insane by Dr. of State of Florida.

You may remember I have been trying to have this child admitted to one these hostipal for insane for the past one year.[67]

Mrs. C. C. Gilbert (Pahokee) to Cone, 5 August 1937

Please find place for my child at once. He has just hit collor [colored] child in head. Cut head open. Child may die. I dont know how bad he hurt. My little boy is getting worse every minit. My god do help me now. What will I do if negro child dies.

Pleas why cant you help me now. I dont want my child to killed some one. Its so cruled. Not to put this child in some hostipal.

Do help me now. Child is six. Its so unhuman to let this child do harm to other folks. Cant he be sent to state hospital.[68]

Mrs. H. C. Smyth (Tampa) to Cone, 23 August 1937

In the election last fall, my husband and I and thousands of other old folks voted for you and worked for your election because you made sure promises to us that you would give us a State pension. How have you fulfilled that promise?

The counties are paying a pension to a few and they never investigated a lot of the applicants. Their offices here in Tampa are filled with young girls who draw a good salary, smoke cigarettes and what do they care for the suffering of the old & needy? My husband & I made applications to the county for a pension more than 90 days ago, and have gone back repeatedly to inquire why they did not send an investigator to us.

We are both past 72 and have no means of support. The Hillsborough County Bldg & Loan Association of Tampa, Took all we had in this world & has for 12 years refused to pay us one dime. We are not the only ones that are left to starve, there are thousands who are suffering as we are, and Governor Cone we need help its not our fault that we are in this condition[.] it's the fault of the crooked bankers est.. You understand what I mean?

If all of the numbers of the legislature would come in contact with the old people who suffer want and privation & yes hunger, I think it would cause them to think seriously of the "Townsend Plan," which is the only measure directed towards improvement of our country, it would free the country of chiselers, selfish, wealthy, ghouls & make of us a happy people. I have written this letter in desperation[.] we need help & need it soon, you promised to give us a State pension, why not do it at once, now, why the delay? Why not rush the old age pension bill through? We are looking to you to do this. We have confidence that you will keep your promise.

Thanking you & asking you to patiently read this letter & consider it seriously.[69]

Mrs. David L. Parkhouse (Miami) to Cone, 9 September 1937

Am enclosing copies of two letters of recent date. Do you know of some agency that will be able to give us a little help. My husband's eyes are so much worse, he works with a continual headache, his eyes smart and pain him dreadfuly. I would get out and work but I have leakage of the heart, have had neuritis and intestinal trouble for years, the doctor has told me I need milk and fresh fruit and vegetables which we [are] unable to get on acount of the small amount of wages.

My husband has tried many times to get work else where, but very few employers will hire a man past thirty-five, my husband is a good electrition but can not get work of any kind.

Please be kind enough to do something.[70]

Mrs. W. D. Respress (Frost Proof) to Cone, 13 September 1937

1930 census: Cleola is 19 years old and white with three children. Her husband, William, is a laborer in a citrus grove.

We are just a nother poor family with nothing. no place to live only from Pillar to Post, we have five children, three in school and my husbon only makes $10.50 a week and it is hard to school our children, we owe a Dr bill and cant pay none on it. And we owe some more bills but we cant pay for a thing now[.] as low as wages is only bye us a little to eat.

My husbon and I was talking last night just wondern if you (the goverment) had any land that we could home stid so we could have a home for us and our children[.] he said he would love to get some to home stid if he could and plant him some fruit trees to try ever thing he could to make a Honest living for his little children bring them up to work and be honest and work for what thay get.

170

My husbon has been on with Gintile for going on 12 years and we get poorer all the time.

Now Mr Cone if you all have any land that we could home stid on please let us hear from you rite away. We would love to have some down here where the children could go rite on to school.

Mr Cone why has we not got a school Buss? My children lives now 4 miles from school, they have to walk over a moody clay over a mile now to catch the Buss. My boys and girl are not in real good health now way.

Pleas Mr Cone let us hear from you verry soon.

Mr Cone we are not like a lot of folks that would make out like they wonted a home[.] I do wont a home, will live in a little hut of our on and be so happy for I will feel like god Blessed me and answered our prayers.[71]

The writer refers to Gentile Brothers Packing Plant, a major citrus company in the 1930s.

Mrs. A. C. Hartley (Jacksonville) to Cone, 14 October 1937

I am writing to you in regards to The Old Soldiers & Sailor's Home, which is located on Talleyrand ave. here in our city. I feel sure you will be interested in the welfare of the old home. And I am sure you don't know how things are going there.

1. The matron who is in charge there at present is not even a regerested voter. And her foster parents were in charge of the home nine years before she became matron, and the present matron lived there those nine years with her foster parents.

Her foster parents were Mr. and Mrs C. M. Kenney and they stayed there and made themselfs independent.

2. Her father and mother (Mr & Mrs. Kenney) were strictly against you, during your campain for election. And my mother and I worked three months before the election to help elect you[.] Your promises were so great to us and we truely believe your words were true.

3. My mother and I are strict workers for the Canadates. And mother has twenty one regerested voters in her family. And they are all children and inlaws. For mother has quiet a large family. She has ten children. And has been with them twenty-one years alone.

4. The Old home is used at present for young people to have parties and dancers, suppers and other intertainment.

5. The present matron has a half crazy colard man there to help look after the old men. He slaps and pushes them around something brutely. And He even sleeps with one of those helpless old men.

6. It has been reported to the board and to Mr. Irnmonger. several times. But he is a good friend of the family and does not seem to care what becomes of the Home or the old men.

The members of the Board at present are, Mr. Riding, Mr. Butts and Mr. Edmonds.

We can't understand why our mother can not get the care of the old home. When she was raised right here in our state and has raised a large family here and has brought them up to be law abiding and to be regerested voters[.] She teaches us to allways try to put the right men in office.

She is rather old now Mr. Governor but very sweet and lively. It has always been her dream to one time have the position as matron of the old home. Won't you please help that dream to be fulfilled[.] you dont know how happy it will make us (her children) to see her happy in something she wants to do.

I am sure she will be glad to get it for less than you are paying now and will take the proper care of it and the old men.

The matron there at present is Mrs. Dollie Pack. She has a daughter who is staying at the old home, and she uses the Old Home's money to enable her daughter to make pleasure trip and expencive presents. She does such foolish things as spend the money on medium readings. I know the old home will not be there much longer. Wont you please make mother happy by giving her a chance there as matron? She has made a wonderful success as Mother and I am sure she would make a success there.

She can give the best of references too. She is well known in Jacksonville.

If I understand it right under section 21–27 compiled General Laws of 1927 the Governor is authorized to apoint five person who shall constitute the Board of Managers of such homes, One of whom shall be the President of the Daughter's of the Confederacy, another the State Commander of United Confederate Veterans, and another the Comptroller of the State of Florida[.] The fifth shall be nominated by the first four members apointed under the provisions of such sections.

I know it is in your power the help my mother get this and I hope that you will answer at an early date and let us know.[72]

Mrs. Hettie Youngblood (Tyty, Georgia) to Cone, 18 October 1937

I am writting you in regards of my condition[.] I am a Floridian and I came to Ga. for the benefit of my husband. which is disable of work[.] I came up here June 1 1937 for his health & mine thinking the change would help us but I find it hasant. and he is now down and completly disable to do a thing. And we have two children one 9 years & one 6 years and I have no way to provide for them and myself and husband. And we are stranded broke and cant get one bit of help up here. And I need help and help at once. Governor Cone we are a worthy family[.] we was both borned and raised in Fla. and [this is] the first time I was ever out of the state[.] both voted for you for our governor of Fla.[.] We voted in Hardee county Wauchula Fla. Governor Cone I am asking you to assist me. Help me provide for my family. Isnt there a mother pention I can get to help me[.] We want to come back to our home state but haven't the money to come on. Cant get any help here. But doctor told me my husband was disable from work. And the Well Fair Lady told me to go back to my home state and I could get a mothers pention to help me provide for my family. So I am writting you for your advice on this. I am not well my self[.] I had a serious oppration last Jan. 1937. and haven't [illegible] that completely. Can do light work but no hard work. Please Gov. Cone help me & advise me what to do. as I need[.] we are suffering for clothes and something to eat right this day. I think I deserve help. My father was a Tax payer of Florida 50 years[.] He died in 1928[.] His name was Luther Hancock of Brooksville Fla.

Will you please write me on return mail what you can do to help me for I need help. And need it now. Please do something for us. I have no relatives able to help me and I know no one else to call on but our Governor to help me. Hoping to hear from you soon.[73]

Eva Furgison (Jacksonville) to Cone, 27 October 1937

This is Eva Furgison i am wrighting to you a gain in the name of you and the good Lord as kin you to please help me if you be so please mister can i havent got my card to go to work on the W.P.A. so in [sewing] room as yet they has bin out hear to see me a bout three week a go and i havent see or heard nothing from the cince and i dont get nothing atal al of them apple[s] i dident get one of them[.] al of the pottoes i dident get not a one of them[.] i dont now what they ex peek me to do i cant got no shoes on my feet no close to put on my back but old rag i wash them until it al most gone and the rent man told us that he is goin up on house rent[.] what can i do if i was working i could pay for a place to stay me and my children[.] would you be so please do some thing for poor me for god nose that if it is eny one nead is Poor me[.] feal my care for your sake and god sake do some thing for for me Eva Furgison 217 park st Jacksonville Fla for i can got nothing to go on.[74]

Mrs. Lavenia Hammond (Arcadia) to FDR and ER, 30 October 1937

Now that you have called a special cession of Congress, if you both would declare for N.R.A. as sponsored by Townsen[d], it would no doubt have as much influence towards making it a law, as your influence had in helping to destroy the 18th Amendment, putting that so much on the great US.

Some of the people in the West, who cried, You have given us beer now give us water have, no doubt, realized they have had too much of both, while others in the West too much of one & not enough of the other. God moves in mysterious ways.

You certainly have realized that the Social Security (Starvation) is a perfect farce. If it was a success, I for one, would be cut out, circumstances required me to leave my old Ky. Home in 31, so could not ask for the Starvation there, have not been in Fla. the required number of years to ask for it here; now what am I to do.

You are borne, not burried, the time could come if the Townsend Plan made into a law, could be a life saver to you both.

As you helped to destroy the 18th Amendment, crowning John Barley Corn again, I'm praying you may lived to see intoxicating drinks again outlawed.[75]

The destruction of the 18th Amendment refers to Roosevelt's support for the 21st Amendment, which ended Prohibition.

Mrs. Ettie Estelle Livingston "Princess Waunita" (Jacksonville) to Cone, 3 November 1937

This is Princess Waunita writing you in regards to the law governoring Fortuneteller's in this state. I see your view point in passing the law it was inorder to clean up the state of fakers.

But Governor Cone in doing so it has placed me in a very embaresing position[.] I am not a fortuneteller or a Spirtualists. I do not contact forces or spirits of the dead. A spirtualists medium is not true unless they can.

I am a Prophetess[.] I get my messages pertaining to spiritual and the temperal in vision form just as was spoken by the prophet Joel refered to in the 2 ch of Acts and 1 cor 12 ch

I believe in God and Jesus and I am following the example Jesus established in the church when he was on earth. I give Healing treatments in the name of Jesus and by the power of God evil spirits and thir curses is cast out. See 9 ch St Luke. I have had many instant Healing just by laying on hands. I have writen testimony to prove my statement.

Governor Cone can you belive my work an evil to our state to tell the truth and heal the sick. I can't see how there could be a License code on God work do you? Just because I can't a ford to have a church[.] just because I give Spiritual messages and Healing in my Home they class me as a Fortuneteller. I believe God works can be done with out going threw a lot of rotine.

Now pertaining to my self and position. I am a Divorce. widow of a veteran of the worlds war. My physical condition makes it impossible for me to do any kind of public work. any thing that excites or disturbes me much causes my heart to fail and the doctor attending me has give repeated warning and said that I was liable to go out with these spells any time. Governor Cone all the way I have to make my living is in the work out line to you. I have so far made a get by and keep my little girl 10 years old in school with ade of the sum of $7.00 per monnth the school penshion. I also have a 62 year old mother that has fail to get any govement work[.] in fact she is not able to do the work.

Governor Cone under these conditions what would you sujest for a poor girl to do. I had rather eat my own bread than to be on the state and county but this eating has got to go on, and someone has to provide the food. I am not a rude woman and refuse to be place in a position to do this that I may have the necesety of life. For myself and child. Governor Cone if I have been properly informed, the law does not provide any eximption for a worthy one, but the law does exempt veteian and there widows. And I am a citizen of your state and I am asking you my Governor to ajust my afairs so I can go on with the only work I can do sucessfully[.] by showing mercy to me I can bless others, and you will not loose your reward.

Governor Cone I have heard lots of nice things about you and I see you as a man with a heart that responses to the need of all classes in your state, and this is why I am asking you to thash out my problem. There were more than one came to me ask me what I thought of Cone for Governor[.] I told them to vote for you that God told me you was a strait shooter and a man for the office[.] of course if I would have had money I would have did more for you. But I did all I could.

Governor I guess you think funy why I use the titel of princess[.] well I am one fourth Indian Cherokee Descent and Irish.

Pleas give this your ameadit attention as I can not quit my work untill arrangements has been made for my rent and food. They have give me the second notic to stop are get a $150.25 License and tax. I am fearfull of an areast[.] it may mean my death.[76]

Mrs. Pearl Head (Madison) to Cone, 15 November 1937

I am only asking you for help. I havent had any help from you since this work have started. I am asking you for a live horse farm and to back me up to run it next year. I have 3 boys 4 girls and 2 grand children that can work[.] and a job just for one can't support the family.

If you will please give me a one or two horse farm and help me make a living[.] write to me as quick as you get this letter. I am needing your help right now because it have took every thing I made this year to pay out of debt and Dr. bills[.] I will move to the place you fix for me and stay the balance of my days. If you are going to let me have a 2 horse farm[.] Write back to me and tell me who to see about the place and house. I am needing a home and a farm I've got 10 in family and no husband and farm work is all we know to do.

I will close for this time hoping to hear from you at once if you are going to let me have a farm and furnish the supplies to make some thing next year. Answer back at once letting me know and a letter to give your agent to see about the place.[77]

Miss Mary Ellen Blume (no address given) to Cone, 19 November 1937

Will you please send me some money to buy me some winter close and shoes. We have not got any money to buy with[.] Daddy does not make but ten dollars a week and when he buys something to eat it is all gone. Daddy can not get the old age money because he makes ten dollars a week but we all are in hopes that the townsend plan will go through. So he will get some money then. We do not get a thing from the W.P.A. I have to go to school and in the sixth grade. my Daddy and Mother voted for you. So will you please send me some money. I will thank you for all you will send.[78]

The phrase "old age money" refers to Old Age Assistance, under the Social Security Act.

Mrs. E. G. Jones (Umatilla) to Cone, 20 November 1937

I know you get many letter and have many duties to perform but I hope this letter will not be too much trouble for you. I want to make two requests of you, and I feel that you will do all you can for me since you have made us such a splendid governor, and I am sure you have the best interests of all your people at heart.

My mother, Mrs. Martha Reedy, is a widow 63 years old. She is in poor health and unable to make money in anyway. Her children are all married and have homes of their own. She has a 40 acre farm and we hope she can get tax exemption on it. She has no minor children. There is a farm mortgage on the place and it is about all we children can do to pay that, the fire insurance, and take care of mother's needs. If we could get full tax exemption it would mean a great deal. She was granted exemption last year, but as she has no minor children it was denied her this year. Anything you could do about it would be greatly appreciated.

The second matter I wish to take up with you is this: I am a teacher having taught fourteen years in Lake County—six years as principal of my present school. I have sent my daughter, Merle Keel, four years to Tallahassee, and my three sons to the University of Fla. One of them is in his Junior year there now. One is working in Washington DC and attending Benjamin Franklin University at night.

I have recently purchased a home in Umatilla and I want to procure an FHA loan to complete payment and make some needed repairs on it. I feel that if I cannot procure a loan that I may lose my home. I am not wanting charity—only a chance to borrow and pay for my home. I can pay the required amounts monthly. Payments can be made directly out of my county superintendents office if necessary.

I do not know where to go to make applications for such a loan in our county.

I will be very grateful of any interest you take in this matter.[79]

Mrs. Ella Bird (Fernandina) to Cone, 29 November 1937

1930 census, misspelled as "Birt": She is 21 years old and African American, works as a laundress, and has two children. Her husband is a mill hand at a sawmill.

I am a poor colored woman mother of Six (6) children and am asking your help[.] the rent has gone up so high since the coming of the pulp and paper mills until we cant hardly make it on whate my husband make[.] of course he cant get on at the pulp mills because he is ruptured but he picks up from $5. to six ($6) dollars a week and my rent is two and a half dollars ($2.50) a week and you know how hard it is to feed my family on the balance[.] So if you could help me secure a home of my own we could make out on what my husband make but right now we all need winter clothes[.] if you can help me I will be ever so thankful to you.

Please let me know whether or not you can do anything for me.[80]

Miss Burnie Beal (Pensacola) to Cone, 30 November 1937

1930 census: She is 43 years old, white, and unmarried and lives with her widowed mother. Neither of them works.

some time ago I wrote you asking help. I need help now more then I needed it when I wrote you first[.] I need winter clothes and my wheelchair is badly in need of repair[.]

A lady from the childrens home of Pensacola came to see me[.] she said you sent her[.] she didn't do any thing for me[.] if I didn't need help I wouldnt ask for help[.] there is some way you can help me[.] thanking you for what you have done[.] let me hear from you by return mail.

[signed] Miss Burnie Beal, invalid[81]

Mrs. Gladys J. Detrick (Orlando) to ER, 3 January 1938

1930 census: She is 31 years old, was born in Ohio, and lives in Bradenton.
Her husband is a public-school teacher; she does not work. They are white.

Prior to this letter I have prayed that it may go directly in your hands as I
so need your advise and help. I fully realize how full and busy your life is but
I am asking so little of you which would mean so much to us.

My husband for the last seventeen years has been in school work, coach-
ing, teaching & finally supervising principal. Salaries dropped so low he
applied Educational Advisor in C.C.C. which wasn't much better a living.
After serving in the Apalachicola Forest for 10 months he was sent to Ft.
Benning, Ga. as C.E.A. of supply company. No more money but on the road
to something better we had hoped. Last spring the Supply co. went out and
my husband went with the F.E. Compton Co. That was March. We have had
one month (August) to really make anything. He is still trying to sell the
books but with little success. We are clear down to rock bottom and living in
a tourist camp. My husband has an A.B. & B.S. but not an M.A. Most states
are requiring a masters degree before you can secure a principalship. Are
there any positions in an educational line you could help us get. Or any kind
of a position that pays a salary. My husband is 40 years old and can send you
the best of reference. He's past president of Bradenton, Fla. Rotary Club. Was
a 32nd degree mason but had to drop it as he was unable to pay the dues. If
you have any doubts as to our character you could write my rector Rev. F. M.
Brunton, Christ Episcopal Church, Bradenton, Fla.

I have never done a thing like this before but I'm really desperate.

I follow you day by day in the paper also "This is my Story." You seem so
understanding and human. Please do not treat this as a silly, begging letter as
I am not that kind of person. I have a ten and a half year old daughter whom
I adopted when she was a baby.

Hoping you treat this confidential and I get a reply directly from you. I am
your most humble admirer.[82]

Miss Clara Thompson (Tallahassee) to ER, 15 January 1938

First, let me beg your pardon for trespassing on you at all, but please forgive me, and another favor I ask is that you read and consider me yourself
and if you have no suggestions, don't send my letter to anyone just destroy
it and forget it.

Here is the story. I am an ex-school teacher but being the oldest of seven
children with a father, who was ill from my earliest recollection and finaly
died of cancer. I have faithfully supported and raised respectfully the
younger children, since 1904, but I never finished college therefore I can not

178

teach now, so I am at present simply just selling encyclopedias, not earning a decent living, and need something that pays much better, at the earliest possible moment.

We lost our home by fire (no insurance) A mortgage took the lot, leaving my dear seventy-two year old afflicted mother and a brother who is unable to work without a home. In fact we lost everything during the Fla real estate boom 1926. Then the depression finished us.

I have voted a straight Democratic ticket and worked some for the candidate whom I thought best for the [place?] with no thought of reward. So I have no especial friend in office, of whom I would ask for a position.

I would appreciate <u>heaven</u> <u>only</u> <u>knows</u> <u>how</u> <u>much</u>, a position that pays enough that we could live comfortably, at least, so long as mother is with us but I do not even know what there is to ask for or how to go about it.

As to my <u>ability</u>, <u>truth</u>, <u>honesty</u> and <u>integrity</u>, I can furnish the best references.

Would love a responsible federal position. Am thoroughly accustomed to responsibility.

There are no words to express to you my heartfelt thanks for any helpful suggestion, at your earliest convenience.

I am <u>not</u> unaware of the fact that every moment of your precious time is taken but there is no one, or situation more deserving than is mine right now.

I greatly admire you and your ability, that is why I am writing this.

It seemed that everything I touched up until 1925 turned to gold, since then only reverses. I reckon that is why it is so hard for us to live so poorly now. We have seen better days.

I am anxious and able to work. I need something that pays well, to live on and for mother's Dr.s fees[,] medicine & etc.

As for myself. I enjoy splendid health, for which I am truly thankful.

Thanking you most kindly in advance for <u>every</u> <u>thought</u> and favor and hoping, <u>yes</u> <u>praying</u> for a favorable reply from you real soon.[83]

Mrs. Ulric L. Dupuis (Brooksville) to ER, 29 January 1938

I am appealing to you as a last measure in my efforts to realize an ambition which started on Mar 4th 1932. On that day my little 4 yr old daughter learned her first note on the piano.

The depression continued to make lives harder and each day I used my time and efforts in instructing her. From enclosed clippings you can see what I have accomplished.

I have had two offers from men in N.Y. City who are willing to promote her for Motion Pictures but they are not fair, demanding 50 % of her earnings for the length of her contract.

We are willing to pay a reasonable commission.

Last June at Tampa, she made a smash hit, in "O say can you sing," a W.P.A. production. Her records are in Washington under the "Federal Music Project," if you should care to investigate.

If we were financially able to take her to N.Y. or Calif, I [am] positive she would prove her value, or if some person qualified for judging could see her, he would be convinced.

I'm sure you know some one whom you could prevail upon to take the time to investigate her, which would bring the result I have been trying to produce for over a year.

You are a mother therefore I feel you understand my anxiety.

Many thanks for your valued time in reading this letter and any assistance you may lend me will not go unrewarded.

I would appreciate a reply if it is not asking too much.[84]

The Federal Music Project, an agency of the Work Progress Administration, hired musicians to perform free public symphonies and band concerts.

Mrs. Gladys Ogden (Miami) to Cone, 29 January 1938

1930 census: She is 30 years old, white, and the wife of a carpenter. She does not work.

I am a mother pleading for her children. Want you please help me?

My husband has lived the life of a gambler & other major offences in Miami for seventeen years, and five weeks ago, he deserted his daughter seventeen yrs. of age and a son six years of age without any means of support, after a criminal offecnce to me, and other unlawful deeds I am ashamed to write.

The county and the city officials of Miami have failed to locate him. He hasn't any means to go far, and I am sure he's in the state and probally in Miami as he was seen here recently.

Please Mr. Cone find him, as I am sure a reward would mean an early capture, and the State of Florida could not spend a petty sum of money to a better cause, than to protect the safety of an innocent woman.

Please find enclosed photograph for description.

Please consider this and reply.[85]

Mrs. Fannie Moss (Bonifay) to Cone, 28 February 1938

I helped you when you was running for office and I trust you will help me now.

I would be glad to know if there is law for a man and woman living togather with out being married? My husbon (Jac Moss, and Leaner Avery) is living togather like man & wife. I cant get the shareff nor judge to do anything. I tried to get a piece warrent for her for breaking piece between us and the judge would not give one. They stand in with all laws at Bonifay, Fla.

I am on starvation & trying to send my little girl to school[.] she had been sick with pneumonia[.] he would not help me get a Dr[.] every dallar he gets hold of he carries it to her[.] we havent nothing to eat or ware to send her to school.

Trusting if there is any law to stop him & make him support his family you will help me at once for I sure do kneed help for I can't help my self. Trusting your advice and help.[86]

Miss Maxine Roberts (Clearwater) to ER, undated but date stamped as received 28 February 1938

I am a little girl nine years old. I study fifth grade. I have been taking dancing for two years. I have always wanted to go to Hollywood and play in the movies. Mother has had to stop me because she could not aford to send me on. Is there any way to help me get into the movies. If you would be interested in helping me, are could help me I would be so grateful to you. So many people say I favor Shirley Temple. I will send you one of my pictures if you want it. I know you are a very busy lady, but I hope you can find time to help a little girl. I have 26 A's on my report card. We think that Mr. Roosevelt is the greatest president we've ever had. I have dimples and dark eyes, and dark complexion.[87]

Mrs. Lurlee Balssell (Coconut Grove-Miami) to ER, 15 March 1938

I am writing to you because I feel that if I appeal to you, you will do all in your power to help me if the circumstances permit. I will explain everything to you about my case in order to give you the whole situation.

Before the death of my husband we were a family of four with a sufficient income to support us. Since the death of my husband the only income I have is a pension of $30 which I receive from the Government, my husband having been a Spanish-American War Veteran (in fact the youngest in the U.S. as he enlisted as a Bugler at the age of 15.) I thank God for this $30 a month but it is not enough to support me. After I pay my house rent, my light and water bills I do not have a nickel left to buy myself any food.

Over six months ago I applied to the State Welfare Board for work on the W.P.A. Sewing Project and I was turned down. I have not given up, but I have been trying ever since to get on but to no avail. I have not yet given up because I am putting my trust in God who has never failed.

I was told by the state Welfare Board I could not get W.P.A. work because I had never had a previous work record, I had not tried to get private employment and because my daughter is working on the N.Y.A. and should help support me.

I have never had a previous work record because my husband was the sole support of our family and I did not have to work while he was living. Of course I worked when I was single. The only work I can do is housekeeping and I can not do that type of work now as I am going through the change of life and it is impossible for me to stand on my feet all day. Whereas if I could get on the sewing project I would be seated most of the day. Any one who has gone through the change of life and have experienced it will know my position.

As for my daughter helping me on the $14.08 a month she makes it is impossible. After she pays for her lunch, her bus fare to and from work she has hardly enough to support herself.

I am not asking for charity when I ask for W.P.A. work. I am willing to work for what I get and I feel the work is to help the needy and I am really in need. There is many a day that my children and I have nothing to eat but bread and coffee. I am a big woman and my body can not hold out at this rate and I can feel myself slipping fast and I can't hold out like this much longer. I find it very hard to have to tell this in my letter but I must tell everything as it really is and that is why I am seeking W.P.A. work. I have not applied to the Welfare Board until I found it to be the last resort.

I have presented my case to you leaving out nothing and I have written to you asking if there is any possible way you could intercede for me in trying to secure W.P.A work. I do believe if there is any way to help me you will do so. May God bless you.[88]

Mrs. Fannie Moss (Bonifay) to Cone, 17 March 1938

Refering to the Letter I had wrote to you about my husbon Joe Moss. He came home & was awful mad about it & made his threats about what he was going to do about it if he could find out who done it & I dont wont him to know that I had it done & Please do not let him see eather one of these, Letters for he will know the hands writes & if he see them he will know I had it done but if there is any way to stop him from staying with her & supporting Lena Avery, (Caryville Fla[)] in stead of me his lawfuly wife & baby I wont it done[.] I am now trying to send her to school since she got up from Pneumonia & he wont help me[.] ever word I wrote you in the other letter is the honest truth God so help & you may be rewarded[.][89]

Note previous correspondence is dated 28 February 1938.

Mrs. Effie Burns (Panama City) to Cone, 27 March 1938

please permit me in my ignorant way to ask you a few questions & for my sake do honor please grant me this favor. we are taxed to ruin[.] I humbly pray thee & beg thee do please take Some of this Taxation off of us. I know you have a christian heart & love your God as I do. I am a poor widow no husband he is dead[.] no Dad Mother Bro or Sister all dead[.] left me to battle this cold world a lone[.] no one to help me. So I have a little dance hall & a little Beer joint[.] I run it desant & nice[.] every one treats me as I was their mother nice & kind to me. I am not phisicaity able to work have a arm that is dislocated allso Suffer with rheumatism[.] all I can do to make an honest living [&] live hard at that now they have put licen on dance & victrola one hundred & fifty dollars & 25 cts[.] how can I live if you wont cut it out[?] do cut the licens down in the bounds of reason[.] just Such tax is the cause of State & Co. haveing to take care of So many people[.] those that would cant. Taxation holds them down, please dont ignore this consider. treat me as you wish to be have kind & tender mercy on me[.] do help me I humbly beg thee. & God will Richly reward thee. May God bless you & help you in all you do. & when you die receive a Shining crown Shout & Sing praises to God in Glory.[90]

Mrs. Georgia Oliver (Daytona Beach) to Cone, 5 April 1938

1930 census: She is 36 years old and white. Neither she nor her husband works.

Friends that I mentioned that I was going to write you said you would put my letter in the waste basket. But I've a friend here who was Opal Roberts of Lake City before her marriage. and she has told me how you befriended her widowed mother and others. and if I ever needed a friend it is now.

There are two lots here in Daytona Beach having a house in poor repair but livable on them.

The owner died in '24 or '25 and there has been no taxes paid on it since then—but one of the heirs lives here has collected rent since that time. I rented the place from his son in Nov. and have my rent paid until Apr. 10th[.]

now the man refuses to rent me [the] place. I've a nice garden and have 7 dependants—one almost invalid husband—one a 2½ yr old grandson—the others are all girls. Am working in a W.P.A. sewing 12 days per mo at $24.00 per mo. I've been to tax offices in Deland and find the state owns the lots.

This garden is half my living and I can find no house to rent close to it. Now I wonder if as a Gov of the state you could or would give me an order to live in place until sold by the state.

A friend advised me to buy a tax deed but with the load I already carry I cant see how I can now.

Trusting I haven't worried you with this long narrative and if you can you will send me an order by return mail or by the 10th at least[.] I beg to remain your loyal supporter.

The lots are no's 1 and 2 in Block D Ridgewood Heights Daytona Beach Fla.[91]

Mrs. W. L. Brantley (Waukeenah) to Cone, 18 April 1938

My husband W. L. Brantley is in jail in Bartow, I am sending you the letter the Sheriff wrote me.

I am left with 3 small children, without anything & no way to support them. I am willing to work for them if I could only get work. My husband has been gone 6 months. I have tried to get work on the W.P.A. working in the sewing room (as that is the only kind of work for women in this county) in Monticello every since January and they just wont let me work at all. My babies are sick & I have no money to buy medicine for them. They are suffering for things that they really need. I can't get any work at all. Will you please see that they give me work at once or Put someone in the office that will give people work that really need it. I am capable of doing something better than working in the sewing room but need the work so badly that I will be glad to work in the sewing room until I can get something better. I wish you could send someone to investigate this county (Jefferson) & let them come to my house & then go to some of the ones houses that have W.P.A jobs. Please see that I get help.[92]

Mrs. A. C. Anderson (Jacksonville) to Cone, 19 April 1938

I am writing this for Mrs. A. C. Anderson—3840 Oak St Jacksonville, Fla. Enclosed is a stamped envelope, if you will be so kind as to reply-quote.

I am an elderly blind spiritualist medium. I am seventy five years old—a widow. I have lived in Jacksonville and other sections of Florida for the past thirty five years.

You knew my son Arthur O. Anderson about thirty-five years ago at Kingsley Lake and Starke, Florida. He died in January 1937. I now have no other means of support than the small income I receive by reading and thirteen dollars a month old age assistance.

The tax collector at Jax said unless you would be so kind as to give me a permit I would have to pay one hundred and fifty dollars license fee. This I am unable to do. In previous years all that was required of me (in view of my disability) was a permit from the mayor—This I have always had.

I dislike having to ask this favor but I have no other means—and this permit means a livliehood for an old lady who would rather be independent than dependent on the state.

I can furnish Doctors references as to my condition[.] I also have bronchial asthma—I can also give good character references.

If you will be so kind as to grant me this permit you will have my sincerest gratitude and may God bless you.[93]

"Jax" stands for Jacksonville.

Mrs. Lela Knowles (Key West) to Cone, 14 May 1938

I am writing you conserning my job. I was working in the county court and got transferred to the sewing room but don't like it there. I want to be sent back to the court yard to plant tree's. Will you give this your attention as those at the W.P.A. office dont seem to make any effort to send me back there[.] I can do better there and need the work badly.

Thanking you very kindly if you look into this for me.

P.S. Im a widow with out any support and feel that you will help me in this matter.[94]

Mrs. Willie Bell (Vernon) to Cone, 11 September 1938

I am a resident of Washington County Florida[.] I am writing you in regard to matter that the government took up four years ago in helping people to get teeth extracted and plates put in. They helped me four years ago to get mine extracted but have never helped me to get plates and I am unable to pay for them myself. If necessary I can furnish you names of people right in the community that the government have furnished money to get their plates. I have ben told it was useless to write you conserning the mater but I am determined to try you out. We have welfare workers in Chipley that is doing that kind of work and I think they should help me. Please advise me what to do.[95]

Mrs. Lecy Bass Walters (Cypress) to Cone, 13 September 1938

1930 census: Lecy and Frank live in Marianna, where he works as a truck driver for a wholesale grocery. She is 33 years old and white and has a child from a previous marriage.

I am writing you to see if you can help me out some[.] I signed up for W.P.A. work in Feb. and I have been certified for 2 or 3 months and they will not send me a work card and I know of some other ladies who signed up the same day I did that have done gone to work and I am a widow with no one to look to for any thing but myself and I have got to have some help so please try to help me.[96]

185

Mrs. J. P. Allen (Lakeland) to ER, 17 September 1938

I wrote you a few days ago about C.C.C. Check which was Due me that My Son worked for at Ferandina Fla. C.C. Camps. The C.C.C. sent the Check. and I rec. it Sept 15. 1938.

Thanks.[97]

Mrs. George Stacey (Palatka) to Cone, 7 October 1938

1930 census: Doris is 23 years old and white with two children. Her husband is 27 years old and works as a truck driver in a logging camp.

I am writting you in regard to my family's condition Mr. Cone. My husband has been sick for three yrs. with Asania and toncillitis. All four of my children are troubled also[.] we have tried to get help off and on for no. of yrs. and with out result. Mr Stacey has been to the office no. of time's to get help linens[,] matressess[,] quilts[,] clothes, comotives [commodities], and haven't been help any, I will be glad to have any body investigate our conditions.

Mr. Cone the colored people gets those nice things by the stack and its pitiful to know that my four children can't get any, I know one man personal that quit a job for work at [$]2.00 a day and they knew it at the office as they took him off the work. This man is a friend and would rather not mention his name as he is a poor man. The offices is filled with [women?] but never have time to talk is give us any satisfactory about helping us[.] I have put writting to you off on account of the State of condition of health hoping you will except this letter and give it the utmost of attention[.] Mr. Stacey is Deaff and can't get a Dr. to report card for the mill or factory and can't do all kind of work but if he could get comotives & winter supply & clothing for the children it would be greatly appreciated. My children ages ar 4–7–11–14 yrs old[.] we need covers for three beds and linens[.] we can get is Oc'd [okayed] by Dr G. M. Zeigler of Palatka and Mr. J. J. Brown Grocerman off our community. We are at the limint if people ever get there.

Please answer this letter, and please send a notice to the office at once for school clothing and winter supplies[.][98]

Mrs. Maggie Brown (Palmetto) to Cone, 18 October 1938

1930 census: She is 39 years old and a white widow with a 16-year-old son. Neither of them works.

I am writing you in an emergency, and I do hope you will read and answer this letter. I have a child a son, 24 years of age who has been afflicted and crippled since birth almost helpless, paralyzed on one side, cannot write, read, or talk. I have managed with help so far to care for him, but the help has given out and I don't know what to do. I have been working on the W.P.A. sewing room, but I cannot work and stay with him too and he cannot be left alone. He is past the age for the Home in Gainesville[.] I cannot get the County mothers pension because it is an educational fund and he does not attend school[.] The pension for dependent children is not yet being paid and if it were there[,] again he would be over age. What am I to do, Gov Cone? There must be an answer somehow[.] I want to take care of my child, but how? Can you, will you help me? I am wondering about the Confederate soldiers pension, my father received until his death, then my mother until her death nine years ago. Could that somehow now be given to my child during his lifetime?

My Fathers name D. G. Robertson Mothers name May E. Robertson of Palmetto Fla. Could you possibly make an exception of this case and let him in the Gainesville Home for a time until other arrangements can be made, and I want him back with me as soon as possible. Please let me hear from you and soon. I have never called for help until I have gone my limits.

Thanking you from my heart.[99]

Mrs. Beulah Morris Valle (Lady Lake) to Cone, 3 November 1938

1930 census: She is 40 years old and a white widow, and she does not work. She is living with her brother-in-law, a freight handler.

Friends here tell me an appeal to you is never passed by, unheard. Perhaps it is most presumptuous of me to write you, but desperate conditions sometimes bring on acts of desperation. My little ten acre orange grove is mortgaged due to the Med. fruit fly spray, the freeze of 1934 and the bank closings of '29 and later. By careful management I have been able to meet my obligations promptly—but this year, when my notes are the heaviest, and the rust mite worse than it has ever been, they are talking about condemming all third grade fruit. The shippers and buyers here all tell me to just wait ten days & keep putting me into some future time, so it seems very hopeless for those in my condition. If we don't meet our notes, we will lose all we have worked so hard to gain. If all third grade fruit is condemned, we will lose a third of our crop and then if a freeze comes again our late fruit will be gone. If we could have any faith in our shippers, even that would help some. A woman who is a widow and alone as I am, cant tell anything about anything. We dont know who to trust nor turn to for advise. We only know that if we don't meet our obligations, we face the danger of losing our homes. What can we do?[100]

Mrs. Lillian Henry (High Springs) to ER, 5 November 1938

While listing to the Pres. talk tonight, Mrs. Roosevelt I am asking you will you help me[.] I am a collord woman living in Hight Spring, Florida[.] I am a widow[.] I have 2 children[.] There married & has gone.

I am 46 years old. I have a goiter on my nick now it prevents me from working to earn my daily bread. I wont to go to John Hopkin hospital to have it remove. I haven got any money & no support, no help. I ask hear, they tells me you have children & we cant consider me.

Now Mrs. Roosevelt, won't you please make some kind resvration for me so I can go & have it remove please let me hear from you by return mail[.] I am a poor anxious woman.[101]

Mrs. Inez Gil (Tampa) to ER, 19 January 1939

I am a marrige woman of 28 years old young and health[y] with a son of 2 years old willing to work. I have try in several places but I haven't has luck. So about four month ago I sign my name for the W.P.A. for work. After five weeks waiting they sent me a card so I went in again and they told me I had to be separate a whole year or to have my divorce from my husband. He has left us since Aug.

I am an American Citizen and I don't think its fair that I have all my rights to get a job in there. And they don't want to put me in. So I want you to help me how to get in the W.P.A. Because I sure need it badly, that I don't know what else to do with my self and my baby son with out a job.

I sure appreciate what you do for me. Thanking you.[102]

Mrs. Alma Bazemore (Brandon) to ER, 28 February 1939

Some time ago, I wrote to you, asking your help in getting work in the WPA Sewing Room at Tampa, Fla.

I just want to let you know that I am now working there, and feeling that I owe it to you, I want to thank you. It is meaning so much to me, and I appreciate it more than I can express.

May God bless you for your kindness, dear First Lady.[103]

Mrs. Jennie Lazara (Tampa) to ER, 4 March 1939

1930 census: She is 26 years old, was born in Italy, and works as a cigar maker. Her husband, Santo, is 32 and was born in Florida to Italian parents, and he also works as a cigar maker. They have one child.

Am writing you once more in regard to my job in the W.P.A. I do not have any words that can thank you for your assistance me in obtaining employment. now as you know They are checking on all workers. I am a Citizen by marriage: my husban[d] is a native born American and a ex cervice man of the W.War. So please look for my job. for my children sake.[104]

Mrs. D. P Powell (Belle Glade) to Cone, 16 March 1939

1930 census: Edna is 21 years old and white, and she does not work. She is married to Durwood, a sign painter, and they live with his mother.

We are writting you about a very as we think a very important matter. We are working at the packing house when we can get a job. When you ran for governor and asked us for support we did what we could and it seemed as though you went in on an overwhelming vote. Now you promised us you would show us your appreciation by helping the poor working class. You did not get elected by the northerner[s]. So they are hireing all the northern people at packing houses, and the GA—people and the native born have to stay here and see the money go out of the state, that we are entitle to and then we go on the relief and the relief people want to know why is it you need help. I can tell you it is just as I am stating, and I wonder if you the Govrnor, the head, and our father of the state and a wide trained man will stand for that[.] when the work is over the money goes north, to help the northern people and the poor southern people with big family as you know have to live on the mercy of the public. We do not mind to work, but we cant get it to do. There are 11 votes in the family that will be for your support if you ever run again. Let me hear from you at one. We cant educate our children on account of lack of work. Let us hear from you at the veriest earliest date. What good are the security cards if 12 to 16 [year olds] are going to work.

Please advise at earliest date.[105]

Miss Sadie Vastie Grover (Altha) to Cone, 20 March 1939

I am writing you for a favor that will be highly apersaited if you can grant it. I am a little girl of Mr J. J. [and] Mrs Grover at Altha Florida and I whent against their will and let a dirty bunch pirsuaide me off and married an old cripple up boy that is not able to work for his self much less a wife. and his name is Jack Adkins and my daddy though enuugh of me when he heard about it to go to the court house at Blountstown just as judge Gaskin was finishing marrying us[.] he took me by the arm and led me out and taken me back home where i would have been already if I had of thought what I was jumping into[.] this family is a mighty low degraded family if you want to [know] any thing about my daddy and his family why write professor mccall Altha Fla and also uncle shept clark at Blountstown Fla and Judge Gaskin Blountstown Fla. I could name several more and all of them is my daddy right hand friends and I wanted to ask you if there are any way that you can anual that marriage with out it costing my dad very much[.] He is a mighty

189

poor man and has a hard time for mother and us children and the Loyals [lawyers] wants to charge him not less than forty dollars and he is realy not able to pay it. and if you can anual it why please do so with out it costing dad so much and it will be Highly aperaided by me[,] dad[,] and mother and you are every in a nother campain why me dad and mother will spend a lot of time a working for you and helping you every way in the world that we can[.] my name as it stands is Sadie Vastie Adkins[.] But here is hoping when I here from you that my name will be change back to Sadie Vastie Grover[.] It was last Sunday evening that I married him and i did not live with him one minute and don't ame to[.] here is hoping to here from you soon by return mail and hoping that answer to this letter will be to Sadie Vastie Grover.[106]

Mrs. Annie Klee Dixon (Tampa) to ER, 22 March 1939

I am writting you, asking you, can you, and will you please help me. I wants to work and needs work badly. I have seven (7) childrens, and I needs help.

I want you to help me this way. Would you please write just a few lines to the W.P.A. and tell them to give me work at the sewing room so I can make a honest living for my children. Please mam write me a few lines so I can present it to the W.P.A. office.

I am a widow with seven (7) childrens, so please help me if you can.

Expecting to here from you soon. Thanking you in advance.

P.S. I have 4 boys 3 girls all small.[107]

Mrs. Lola E. Painter (Jacksonville) to W. B. Cone, Secretary, 30 March 1939

After receiving your Letter dated Feb.16th 1938 in which you so kindly offered your assistance in my hour of dire need by writting to Mr. Codrington regarding myself and nephew James Marion, we held on as long as we could without funds then I appealed to the Local Elks in Lake City borrowed $25.00 from them, and started with my nephew in my car to Pine Bluff, Ark. to my sisters. had a Blowout near Madison Fla. Wrecked my car, Broke my R[ight] Arm, and injured the boy, this was in March 1938. I returned to my little place near Lake City in May 1938[,] broke, no car and a nervous wreck[.] while James and I were in the Hospital we Recd. notice he had been approved for the $36.00 but of course he was unable to go then, so he remained at my sisters in Ky. while I returned to Lake City. I was compelled to accept relief, and in Aug. '38 was put to work on the Federal Theatre Project here as a Senior Actress at $79.80 per mo. I imediately started paying on the Little House and 6 acres near Lake City, some furniture and another

'31 Chevrolet car, hoping to be able to pay them out, so I would at least have a roof over me, and could raise a few chickens, and not be on my Governments charity list any longer than I need help. this past Nov. my eldest son who is 21, and a fine young man, nice looking, and well educated, came to me here from New York where he lost his job on account of Business Slump. [H[e has tried hard to secure a position here but so far has been unsuccessful. in Jan. I was reduced in pay to $76.80. As I was one of the last ones taken on, I was one of the first to feel the cut, although some others had been on for 3 years, and surely should have been past the relief stage by now. then a mo. ago my nephew James Hitch-Hiked back to me from a saw mill camp in Louisiana where he was trying to work, but the fellow didnt pay him and he was near starved, and I had to buy him pants first thing. I am the only home he could come to. Now Mr. Cone I want to get him in 3 Cs if I can, without the Extra Burden I could have managed but I can not on what I make. I must keep my payments up on what I am buying otherwise I will lose what I have paid. I am trying to feed us on $2.00 a week. If there is any suggestion you can offer, or help my son secure a job anywhere in the state, he would make a fine clerk in the State Road Dept. he passed the Civil service Examination in New York State but of course it may be years before he would be placed[.] I had to make this letter lengthy in order to explain things. Thanking you, and hoping Gov. Cones Health is improving and please give both he and Mrs. Cone my best regards. We think a heap of them, and you around Lake City, and Columbia Co.

P.S. If there would be any chance for my son to get on as a Guard of prisoners he is 5ft 11[,] weighs 160[,] very atheletic[.][108]

Mrs. W. J. Ward (Miami) to Mrs. Boettiger [Anna Roosevelt], 31 March 1939

Don't laugh at this letter, but try and understand it, I'm not crazy, just a worried and tired mother, some times I think, well I'll just have to give up. but that's out of the question. I have 3 nice children, that we are trying to educate, you don't know what a job that is, my Husband being a plumber, and work not steady, you can't plan ahead. He understands building construction thourghly. I thought maybe you could intercede for him, to get him a job in the F. H. Dept. if its only for a couple years to give us a breathing spell, my girls will be out of school then, and want to go in training for nurses, my boy who is 19 years old and going to Flordia State College. he is helping, with his music. I do so want him to finish, you being a mother will understand that. We don't drink, nor gamble on the horses nor dogs, which so many people do in a town like this, but we owe, and are back in all our

191

payments on everything we have bought. we all need dental work bad. and can't see our way out. You are in a place to make 5 people the most happy in the country. I'd do anything for you. come up there and work for you for about six months while your baby is small and give you the best service in the world, my girls are eighteen years old, and could do the work for their Dad and themselves, while I was away. Plase don't make this letter public. My Husband and children would think I had lost my mind, but if I could only explain more clearly. I can't in a letter. people like you who have always been so sheltered can't really understand. because you never had such hard times. but so many like our selves want, just a chance to make our way. and would be so happy if we could do so. we owe about $3,500, home inculed in that, and if my Husband could only have steady work for about 2 years of so, we could pay the most pressing bills off, and have a few of the necessary things in life. My Husband used to be in the Plumbing Business and build & sell on the side. there's lots of places he could fill, because he has had the actual experiance in that line of work. there's no one we know who could intercede for us. I'd never tell it, not even to my Husband. If you could only help us. it would be another good deed, for you & your family I know have given a helping hand to many. there's never been a family in there that the whole country like any better. Your Mother has did what no other woman before her, ever did, with her Radio work & Charity. I hope you get this letter because it means so much to me. I don't know where to turn next. Let this be just between you & I. I'm so anxious to hear from you.

Reply from Mrs. Roosevelt's secretary dated 7 April 1939:

Mrs. Boettiger gave your letter to Mrs. Roosevelt, who asks me to acknowledge it.

Mrs. Roosevelt can imagine how difficult things are for you and she read your letter with deep understanding. She regrets, however, that she knows of no jobs. Her suggestion is that your husband apply directly to the Federal Housing Administration, the Home Owners Loan Corporation, and the United States Employment service in the Department of Labor, stating his experience.

Mrs. Roosevelt hopes that your husband will find steady work and that things will be better for you in the future.[109]

Miss Bertila Sainz (Tampa) to ER, 26 April 1939

1930 census: She is the 4-year-old daughter of Bernardo and Lucille. All three were born in Cuba. Bernardo works as a cigar maker.

After wishing you my best wish. I write you because you are the only one that can help us. I am a little girl 13 yrs. old. The oldest one that can write to tell you to please help us. I have a brother and sister smaller than I. And my mama was the only one to support us. and she was working in the W.P.A. and she was lay-off just because she was an alien. She made her application for her America paper. because she came to Tampa when she was a little girl. And we where born here. But still she had to wait 9 months for her citizenship paper. And we are starving since They lay-off my mama. I have no father. So please see what you can do to help us. My mother name is Lucille Sainz. 1915 5th Ave. Please answer and may God bless you.[110]

Mrs. Lois Byrd Godwin (Tampa) to ER, 12 May 1939

I am very sorry that I find it nessery to take my troubles to you but I cant sit still an see my children go hungry. I have been on relief for about four 4 years. but there was 75 wemen laid off on our Project April the 7th and I was one of them.

An they tell me at the office that my case is closed that I will not get another work card. because I was married again.

I did marry in Dec with iedy [idea] that I could stay at home with the children but in just a few days I found that I had married a drunkard a man that is not fit to be around children. an he drinks worse an worse all the time. so you see I did not say any thing about bing Married at the office for I could not afford to lose my job but I guess they must have found it out any way an closed my case. but wont you Please tell them to put me back to work[.] I have tried so hard to get work any kind that I could suport my family on but there is no jobs for a woman of 48 years. With many thanks for any help you may give me.[111]

Mrs. Frances Bell (Tampa) to ER, 27 May 1939

I have been working in the sewing room 11 mo. and am laid off now 2 weeks. And I am afraid I wont get back to work. As it seems a person has to have a pull which I have none.

I am asking you to see that I do go back to work. I am 50 years old no parents no husband brother or children. One sister she is a widow and dont live here.

And no one of my age can get a job other than W.P.A.

I am going to thank you in advance.[112]

Mrs. Dorothy Beneboy (Tampa) to ER, 13 June 1939

I am writing to you for help. I have been working on the W.P.A. but was laid off a month ago.

I have a child twelve years old to support. Also Mrs. Roosevelt if I could work a while long[er], and get my teeth attended to I might be able to get other employment. I had been paying the dentist so much a week but have nothing much to live on.

Tooth ach is not so hot you know.

If you could help me get my job back for a while. I would appreciate it very much. I know you are a very busy Lady. but do hope this letter reaches you.

I have a little incident to tell you. When I was a baby Mr. Teddy Roosevelt going through Solomon Kansas stopped off & made a speech at the depot & I being the only little baby picked me up, pushed my curls back, and told the public I would be a very great musician if given the chance.

I never received the chance. But feel quite honored by being held by a President of our country.

I hope you get this letter. And do hope that you & Mr. Roosevelt will still be in the white house the next four years.

With best regards to you both. From just a little potatoe in a field of [a] thousand other potatoes.[113]

Mrs. Mary V. Bond (Tampa) to ER, 16 June 1939

As I have tried every thing else possible to secure imployement and failed. I though I would write you maybe you could help me solve my problem. I am a widow with 2 small, unhealthy children and a 74 yr old mother whom is blind to support. and I was laid off the W.P.A. May 12th and have been unable to get back on. or secure imployement of any kind. and I cannot even get an investigator out to my house for the A.D.C. pension.

Now Mrs. Roosevelt my family is suffering and I do not no what to do. I have no one to turn to for help. Cant you please help me some way to get back on W.P.A. or something. if something doesnt happen & happen soon I cant stand it we are desprate.

May God bless you is you can help in some way. Thanking in advance from the bottom of my heart.[114]

ADC is Aid to Dependent Children, the federal program that replaced state mothers' pensions. It served as the foundation for today's Aid to Families with Dependent Children.

Mrs. Amada Hernandez (Tampa) to ER, 23 June 1939

Expressing my respects and sincerety I'll pass [pause] to asking you a favor.

My family has long existed only thru the means provided by the W.P.A. laborer wage that my husband had until recently received.

On May 7, 1939, my husband was taken to the hospital with a heart attack. On the 15th of the same month he was sent home and ordered by the doctor to remain in bed the greater part of the day and not to do any work.

I tried to have his work transfered to me and all the answer I can get is "We'll see what we can do for you."

My son Gustavo suffers from epileptic attacks which makes him unable to work. We need medicine for both him and my husband, but we haven't even enough to eat.

I've enclosed proof of my husband's illness. I also gave the W.P.A. office a doctor's certificate of his condition.

We can't live like this very much longer, won't you please give me a helping hand?

Thanking you in advance and praising all your benevolence deeds.[115]

Mrs. Rachel E. Bradley (Tampa) to ER, 9 July 1939

I am taking the liberty of writing to you as you were once kind enough to answer my letter and to help me out, but of course I know you do not remember me but I shall never forget your kindness. I am writing to ask you to use your influence to get me reinstated on the W.P.A. as I have been laid off and as I am a woman fifty years old it is impossible for me to get work in the commercial world at present any way, and too my eyes are in such a bad condition that I can not see to do work that requires a great deal of strain. I am a widow absolutely alone and sorely dependent upon my own efforts for a living. I was Forewoman on soft Toy Project #4156–8 which I could do very well as it did not require a lot of eye strain and so am asking you to please help me to get back my job as it really means food and shelter to me.

Thank you Mrs. Roosevelt and may God guide and protect you and Our President is the prayer of Rachel E. Bradley.[116]

Mrs. Marie Brosseau (Jacksonville) to ER, 11 June 1939

Am writing you a few lines concerning the women who have been cut off the W.P.A. This little clipping from a newspaper is one of the biggest falsehoods ever uttered or printed, for most of the women laid off here are in dire distress. Most of them are elderly women, who can not get work elsewhere on account of their age, and with the $40 a month taken away from them they are destitute. My own case is just an example of many more. The $40 a month was all I had to live on. I have not a soul on earth to go to. Am all alone with the exception of a partially dependent daughter. She has a drunken husband who cannot hold a job very long and while he would be out of work I had to look out for her; now how am I going to do it with my job taken away from me. She's unable to support herself.

Starvation & ejection are staring me in the face. Appealed to my landlord about staying on for awhile. But he said no, when my rent was up I must get out. It is up in a few days. I have no place to go: What am I to do?

When they "weeded" out the ladies on the W.P.A., they <u>did not</u> take the ones not needing the work. They cut off the ones mostly in need. There are dozens & dozens on the job who <u>do not need it.</u> Some have husbands working, some own their own homes & rent out rooms. Some own rental properties. Some keep rooming houses. Some have small places of business, with husbands tending them and many of them drive fine cars, which $40 a month could not afford.

The needy $40 a month women were cut off & their salaries went to increase the wages of the higher salaried ones. They made new supervisors, instructors, inspectors, head cutters & created a new job as designers for 2 all with big salaries, and we poor needy women were put off in order that our wages could go to the higher paid ones. Do you see anything fair about that? Was there any economy?

I do not think the President realizes the true situation here for he has said many, many times "no needy ones will be put off." But they were put off & they are in a most pitiful situation. We helped keep the President in the Whitehouse & I do not believe he will allow this situation to continue once he realizes the real situation.

Where and how we are to live is an unsolved problem. We cannot just lie down and pass out. If we could we would gladly do it and get out of an almost intolerable situation. But we are here & must stay here until God sees fit to call us Home, no matter how misserable our earthly existance may be.

If those Congressmen could go out among these destitute, elderly women, surely their hearts would fail them and they would gladly make the necessary appropriation and put us all back to work, so we could care for and support ourselves. Could you not go before the congressmen and plead our cause? Most of us are fully able to work and want to work and care for ourselves, if we could only get the work to do.

Mr. Schroder said, in making these reductions, "need and efficiency would count." But it didn't, for no one could be in need of this work any more than myself. Every supervisor and instructor I worked under said my work never needed inspecting for it was perfect.

Yet I got cut off. Why? So my $40 a month could go to increase the salary of a higher paid one.

I could cite you to a great many who do not need the W.P.A. aid but I've already taken up to much of your time.

I'm just trying to get the true situation, concerning this cut off, before the President, & I knew of no better way than thru you.

We were informed it would do no good to write to Washington, for the letters would all be returned headquarters here. But I'm taking chances with you & know you will help our cause so far as you can, because you are full of willingness to help the needy.

Pardon me for writing so much & believe me in being sincerely true in all my statements, and hope you will help our cause in every way you can, and thanking you in advance.[117]

Mrs. Cornelia Rosemond Curry (Tampa) to Florence Kerr, 20 June 1939

1930 census: She is 40 years old, was born in Michigan, and does not work. Her husband, Elmer, is 51, and is the manager of an oil company. They have two children at home. The family is white.

Yours of the 14th received. I am <u>not</u> complaining of the curtailment of W.P.A. program. My complaint is: that women with no dependents are left on relief rolls and stuff themselves until they look like barrels. While I with two dependents was dismissed by an envious and inconsiderate Supervisor and <u>now</u> have to depend upon "Family service" here to give me $2.00 a week to exist.

Then too, there are women with grown children in their homes earning from $40 to $60 a month and the mother making $40.00 more in W.P.A. Sewing Room.

This is my <u>seventh</u> week off, I who have been complimented on my needlework countless times.

I <u>have been</u> keeping in touch with U.S. Employment service. I'm supposed to be efficient in several line—but there are lines and lines now waiting in the bread lines. All because the work goes to the <u>greedy</u> and <u>not</u> the needy.

Must I actually sit by and allow these conditions to exist? My sons <u>are</u> losing weight. The roof leaks the electric current has been turned off. . . . [illegible] for my son's bicycle and it was stolen where he was at a Drug Store where he made deliveries.

He did make a few dollars there, but is NOT working now. Will graduate next February from the 12th grade at 16 years. My seven year old son is in the 3rd grade.

I am writing for an assignment to again be allowed to make $10.00 a week at least.

How much longer is this unfairness to continue? I want to know!

Will you kindly tell me? Right away! If the quota is filled, <u>why not</u> release those who have been working for 3 and 4 years and give us a chance to earn at least enough for necessary food. I had worked for 13 months and was almost caught up with paying bills—now <u>WHAT</u> <u>are</u> we to do?

I have lived here twenty years and <u>now</u> need the work—being a widow—but on relief rolls here, we find tourists even and other greedy folks.

Please pardon my writing on both sides but I have but this last sheet. Anxiously awaiting something to change this unbearable situation.[118]

Eva Furgison (Jacksonville) to Cone, 5 July 1939

This is Eva Furgison 217 Park St Jacksonville fla[.] governor i Havent get eny thing yet no one bin out hear to see me not yet and i haven't got enny thing in my home to eat i haven't had a strait meal in two week[.] me and my children nothing to Pay my rent with and the rent man tell me that I hafter move and i cant got no wear to go an nothing to go with and my child is sick on my hand for about little over a munth the back step broke in with her with a bucket off water and hert her side and allmost nock out two off her teath and she is still sick sum time up and some time down it ceam like sum thing ortor be done with these rent man putting people out door when they eant got no work to do and in come at oll For you no that i havent got no one to help me at all and i nead a little help now and would you Please help me to get my card back so i can go to work and help my self for i due a mounth rent i owe for June 12 Dollar would you please help me for i eant got no mother no father and no husband to care for poor me[.] would you help poor me iff you please for you no that i am cripple in the hipp and cripple in one off my hand by that you no that i nead some ade from you.[119]

Mrs. Mae Gaddis (South Jacksonville) to ER, 17 July 1939

I am writing to you regarding my trouble in getting a work card from the W.P.A. here.

My husband is gone, he walked off five weeks ago and left me with a baby boy four years old who is crippled and has been since birth. My husband was working on the W.P.A. before he left but he had a check made, he drew that check and walked of with it leaving me and my baby without anything at all to eat and no way to get anything[.] I am staying with my mother who is a widow woman with four small children to take care of and she is only getting twenty dollars a month from the mother's aid.

They have refused me the mother's aid because they say I am able to work and that I should get a work card but the officials at the W.P.A. won't even talk to me about it.

I have started divorce proceedings to gain my freedom through the Legal Aid society and my Lawyer has filed my papers. He gave me a letter to take to the W.P.A. office but they even refused to read it.

I am very much in need of relief and I am willing to work if I can just get a work card.

If you can and will help me to get a work card I will appreciate it very much.[120]

Miss Donnie Cline (Tampa) to ER, 20 July 1939

A few lines just to tell you the conditions in Tampa are deplorable since the W.P.A. reduction. I am 56 yrs old[,] no home. It took me from May 18th 1938 until Oct 24th 1938 to get on then put off again July 7th 1939[.] I just had a sewing room job $40.20 a mo. but was thankfull for it. I am qualified for a better job. You know Mrs. Col. Raymond Robins she is a sister to your friend Miss Mary Drier[.] I have a recomendation from her for work I did in the Y.W.C.A. workshop in Brooksville[.] I classified and varnished the books for her. I did not intend to make a career of W.P.A. but would like to have worked until spring. There is lots of folks on that dont need to be there but that is politics not you folks for I know the President didnt mean it that way. This W.P.A. puts me in mind of the big Plantation owners in Ga. The negro does the work after the crops are all gathered he sits down with pencil and paper and says

Ought an Ought,
Figure is a figure
All for the white man,
Nothing for the nigger.

I would like to work a while longer until I get me some false teeth and glasses. I hope you can do something for me I want to work[.] I know I cant help you any way for you dont need it. only my vote[.] I hope to hear from you if I had a line from you I can get on again for a while. Thanking you in return. Good luck for the Pres. if he runs again.[121]

Mrs. Lola Hughes (Tampa) to ER, 1 August 1939

Knowing that a great deal of your time, and that of your secretaries, has been used in correspondence such as this letter solicits, I have hesitated to write you. But being urged by friends, I have decided as a last resort to lay my condition before you.

I am a widow 57 years of age; I have a sister several years older than I who is my dependent; my sister is in failing health; my job, as a $40.00 worker in one of the local sewing rooms was terminated by a 403 slip three months ago today.

My suffering through these three months has been more painful than I can convey to you through the medium of a letter.

At the present time, I owe $42.00 rent to the "Max Law Realty Co." The water in my home has been cut off for several weeks, and I have had three notices to vacate the property in three days. Except for the refusal of Judge Cornelius, Co. judge, to sign the ejectment papers[,] I would have been put upon the street.

I have tried in every conceivable way to get back to work without avail. My dismissal had nothing to do with inefficiency, or the breaking of any rules. The only answer I could get when trying to be reinstated was: "Its the law" or "Our orders from Washington."

I wrote Senator Pepper who sent my letter to Roy Schroder the Florida W.P.A. administrator. Mr. Schroder answered the Senator's letter which was re-mailed to me. In the letter to the Senator Mr. Schroder said: "The main object of relief work was to give work to those who had worked prior to the beginning of such work."

I wrote then to Mr. Schroder, explaining how for over 25 years I had worked for box factories and cigar factories in Tampa, finally losing out on account of age. His answer was sympathetic, but final, saying he could do nothing for me.

I have weekly been receiving an order from the local welfare association for $2.00 in groceries but was notified it was to be discontinued on account of low funds.

This latest shock has come near to breaking my spirit.

It is only those, especially women, who struggling, have gone down to the very depths of despair, and yet no hope, who can realize the panic in my heart today.

What I have said in this letter can be verified by Max Law, the Co. judge, and the Welfare Association.

I am wondering, waiting, and hoping.[122]

"403" was the form used to terminate relief and was referred to much like the term "pink slip" is today.

Mrs. E. M. Hanks (Jacksonville) to ER, 8 August 1939

I want to write you and see if you will help me. Dear Mrs. Roosevelt, I have been working in the sewing room ten months and there came a cut so the supervisor cut me off. Dear why do they cut off women that need work so bad and hold on ladys that have their own homes and a living. I can't see how I am going to live. I have an invalid husband and he is a railroad man and is trying to get his pension, and I asked the supervisor to please let me work that when my husband got his pension I would be glad to give my place to someone else.

It seems that the railroad Co. is very slow about things. Now Mrs. Roosevelt, if you could see the way the sewing room is handled you would know more about it. People that don't need this relief is the ones that gets it. Of course, I believe if the President knew how things was with the relief would not like it. I go to the old Post Office and they will grumble because you come, they won't tell you any thing, put you off, well you know that doesn't fill our stomachs.

I have a boy ready for high school and if I don't get work I can't even send him to school. There is five or 6 women on the sewing room floor drawing pay for standing around, this many to one room drawing big pay, when 2 is enough. Mrs. Roosevelt, there is too much partiality. Will you please help me get a card? I can't get along with my sick husband without work. They cut me off because I have a son that gives me 3 dollars a week, and 5 in family and rent and water to pay out of this. Please help me do something at once. Please write the old Post Office to give me work. They won't give me clothes or anything. . . .[123]

Mrs. Bertha Ludlam (St. Petersburg) to ER, 9 August 1939

I am writing this letter to you, with a heart full of trouble and sorrow.

I am a widow 63 years of age without children or any living relative[.] I have been on the W.P.A. sewing project for the last 3 years, and have been so happy. for I have had enough to eat and a place to lay my head, now I am told that the 31 of this month I will be laid off the W.P.A. for good because I have been on 18 months. I have tried to get other work but am told that I am to[o] old[.] no one wants me.

The Welfare Society can not do anything for me they have more now than they can care for, and I am not old enough for the pension. Mrs. Roosevelt what am I going to do. Trusting you will not be offended with me for writing this letter.[124]

Mrs. Bessie C. Woodland (Jacksonville) to ER, 12 August 1939

I do trust that you will accept this personal letter from me in the faith that it is written.

My present condition is almost destitute. A readjustment is positively necessary. I am married; a college graduate with teaching experience; from one of the pioneer Negro families of Western North Carolina. My father was a Captain in the Spanish American War.

My problem is unemployment. I have tried every possible method and have failed.

I am anxious to enter Columbia University in New York City in the fall to secure a masters degree in Institutional Management. I can borrow money for my tuition, but not for my board and lodging. Do you have a friend or an acquaintance in New York with whom I might live and work for my board and lodging, with the understanding that I am to study at the University. Someone who will give me a chance. Will you please advise me?[125]

Mrs. G. W. Frohock (N. Miami Beach) to Cone, 23 August 1939

1930 census: George is a 56-year-old farmer. Alice is 50, does not work, and is living in Fulford. They have are three children, ages 10 to 18. The family is white.

I am enclosing a petition from our little farming town. Asking for help so we might make a crop like we use to, before the Canal was cut. Each year it seems to get dryer and glade fires were never, till the last three years.

Salt water from the ocean comes up the canal till vegetation all along the banks is dead and a good crop is almost imposable to make, and groves are in a bad shape.

Now if you can do any thing for us it will be greatly apriciated as this canal is not used for any thing. Most all of the signatures are old timers ours for 38 years and others just as long. The farmers and dairy men here certainly need something done to hold the water up. All they ask is a flood gate or box of dinamite.

And unless something is done they will be compelled to sit down and fold there hands.

Anything you can do will be greatly appretiated.[126]

The Cross-Florida Barge Canal was a controversial project to connect the Atlantic and Gulf coasts via an inland waterway. The project received initial funding from the PWA and was funded again during the 1960s. The potential environmental impact of the project was tremendous, and the dig was halted in 1971.

Mrs. J.M. Roberts (Lake Butler) to Cone, 6 September 1939

1930 census: James and Bessie are 56 and 44, respectively. He works as a farm laborer; she does not work. The family is white.

I am writing you concerning a widows pension for dependent children. I am supposed to be getting it as I am a widow of two years, but for some reason am not. I have three girls in school, two in high school, to feed and cloth and I don't have any man to help me make a living. There are some around my home that is getting it now and I cannot understand why I am not. I went to Mrs. Nanny Grahams' office in Lake Butler, Fla. last February and signed up and she told me I would get it by June 1st.

I would appreciate any help you could give me, because it looks as if I am going to have to stop my girls from school, something I do not want to do. Let me know by Oct. 1 what you can do.

I certainly will appreciate it.[127]

Mrs. Bessie Barnes (Hialeah) to ER, 19 October 1939

1930 census: She is 49 years old and white, and she was born in Pennsylvania. She is living in the "rural section" of Hialeah. Her husband, John, is 51 years old, and is unemployed.

I have been working on a sewing project of the W.P.A. a small project at Hialeah Fla. I have been layed off for two months now and it looks like I am not able to get back [on]. I have walked and walked all over this place to find work but I havent found any thing[.] the ones they have put back so far is the women that have no school children[.] I have a boy going to school and I will have to take him out of school if I can not get back to work as we cannot get any relief here and we have nothing to eat and I feel my boy cant hardly go to school with nothing to eat and I cant find out just who to go to get back on[.] I wonder if you could informe me who to write to to get back to work as soon as possible.[128]

Mrs. Bessie Bussard (Tampa) to ER, 25 October 1939

1930 census: She is 45 years old and white and was born in Indiana. Her husband, Don, is 49 and is a grocer.

I am writing in regards to myself. I am a widow woman 55 years old and I have a son of school age. I am one of the many who had to go on W.P.A. I had about 11 months work in one period and got laid off for 4 months and then put back to work for 6 weeks and now I'm off again and you know a widow with a son of school age has to have work and a woman of my age could not get work here and I had to take my boy out of school and I have no other means of support and I know you are sympathetic to the working class of people of this country. I am asking you to please write Mr Harkness the Area Supervisor of Tampa District or to Mrs Letha Dell Supervisor of Women's Work to please give my case consideration my case no. is 0929–27323.

I will appreciate anything you can do for me.[129]

Mrs. Dominga Alvarez (Tampa) to ER, 4 October 1939

I'm writing these few lines wishing they fine you well. I'm making these few lines asking you, to please do all what is in your power to help me get in the W.P.A. Sewing Room. I'm a girl of 24 years old, married and been separeded 1 year. I been trying to get on the W.P.A. for 10 months, and they always tell me the same thing, because they ain't taking new aplication. We are 6 in family. We got 2 babyes. and their father left them[.] we don't know where he is at. I don't have any brothers to help us. My father was working in the W.P.A. and they left him out on account of the law of the 18 month. He is been out more then a month, and he never had more help then what he made on the W.P.A. he use to make $40.10 a month. Mrs. Roosevelt: I'm asking you for a favor, that I'll never forget. We haven't anything to give our babyes only what my mother begs for on the street. We haven't got any money to pay our rent, nor any shoe to wear. My mother and father are American born. My sister[,] the babyes[,] and I are American born too.

Mrs. Roosevelt: don't you think we should have work in the W.P.A. like every body has? I have never work in the W.P.A. I think they should give me a chance. Please write to me as soon as you can. I'm in need very bad. I'm obliged to you. Thank you.[130]

Mrs. Irene Schoentag (Tampa) to ER, 18 October 1939

I am sure you are a buisy woman, but I am taking the liberty to write you to see if I can get help concerning a dress I have.

This dress was Lady Churchill's wedding dress. It is made of a very heavy beautiful piece of tafeta silk, with a shoulder shawl to match. I also have the designs croched for the underskirt, in shapes of different kinds of fruit.

My mother was English and the dress was given to the oldest daughter in each family. I have no children and am very much in need of money and sure would apreciate any thing you could do for me.

The only name I know was "Cridge," which was my grandmother's name.

The dress is now in Pennsylvania and I sure would like to get some money for it.

The dress my dear mother told me before her death was over 300 years old.

Please at your earliest convenience let me hear from you.[131]

Mrs. R. Clyde Hall (Miami) to ER, 15 November 1939

I haven't spent Christmas with my mother and family in eight years, financially unable and I haven't been home in five years. I want so much to go and think each year maybe I can. It takes all my husband makes to meet expenses and then we don't meet them all.

It will take $125.00 for train fare for my two children and myself and buy the extra clothing we will need to go.

I am crocheting a bed spread and have it 1/3 done, it would be impossible for me to finish it by Christmas for you, but will try to have it done by your next birthday.[132]

Mrs. W. E. Raddatz (Port Tampa City) to Cone, 20 November 1939

I wrote you several months ago about our condition here. We are so anxious to get off W.P.A. also to get a foot hold. Even tho my husband who is a skilled man in several trades, also he has a diploma from Cook's electrical school in Chicago, he could get no work, as the man of 50 has no chance. He could not even get common laborer work on W.P.A. until we came here and Mr. Rollins, the mayor of the city, got him on. We are on Mr. Rollins' mother-in-law's place. There are 7 acres in this place. 5 could easily be cultivated. It is late to put in strawberries but 1 acre of them would help me wonderfully[.] We need plows and a work animal to cultivate it. If we could at once get this plants and fertilizer we could get it in at once. My husband has time off from the W.P.A. to do the plowing. The children and I could do the rest. Also we need about $28.50 to fix up our truck and buy license to operate it. Then one of our girls could drive it and when berries come in we are close enough to Plant City to ship our crop through their market there. After writing you were were referred to Plant City, to Mr. Hull, and just 2 days ago a man come from there to see me, but tells us we must have 100 or more acres of land in order to get a Gov. loan. We wonder why that is, when Cubans, with 3 acres can get Federal loans. We being citizens of U.S.A. born and reared here, I, myself having lived in and around Tampa, for 37 years, all my children born here. My people live here, my first husband (deceased) was a fruit and vegetable dealer, one brother and a farmer, my father a farmer, 3 brothers fruit and vegetable dealers. My present husband a farmer from New Jersey and has been here long enough to learn quite a bit about Fla. farming. My children and I have 120 acres in Glades county, and 160 acres we could use, 40 of it being my sister-in-laws, yet we cannot get a small amount to help us here. My first husband and I lived on the property in Glades county had a nice start, but in 1918 he had to leave because Uncle Sam needed his service. We never got back to it. We owned property here, paid taxes here also in Glades but since his death I have been forced to sell the property here, also timber from the Glades county property in order to feed my babies. If my present husband could have gotten work, we would not be on relief. Now it takes every penny he makes to feed us. We are thankful for it, yet it does seem strange we can get no help. Young men are filling all the places[.] some one has to return to mother earth and till the soil. We are able to work, willing to work, taxes to pay, yet we cannot get a chance. Are we to lose our property and barely exist while the foreigner can get help and live? $1/3$ of the property (120 acres) in Glades I could give security on. It is located at what once was Adrian, 6 miles of Tasmania near good roads and Tampania trail. All kinds of truck and sugar cane does well there, also live stock. If we could line up with the sugar corporition, fence our land, build a house, get a good milk cow, tractor or animal to till the soil and a big truck, by next fall we could pay off a good size loan. We would need chicken & pigs and something to live on until we could get an income. It would take money, and I have no idea the amount but there are Gov. men who have this all figured out. It would require work, but who minds work, when we can eat and have a goal to work to. We are pilgrims and sojourners here, traveling to a better land, yet we would like to be useful here and leave this world a better place by us having lived here. If we cannot get help here on this place can there not be something done about helping us on the Glades property. Without a pull we can get nothing but if our Governor pulls for us, we can get somewhere. We have a son-in-law who is working in fruit [and] vegetables who would take care of the selling of our products, thus keeping every expense possible down. Can you and will you help us live.[133]

Mrs. Gladys Pyke (Jacksonville) to Cone, 21 November 1939

I don't suppose this is an unusual case with you, but I have tried everything and every body that anyone would suggest to me and now it's you.

My Husband William Abner Pyke has been in the Navy one year to-day and we have been married nine months and both of us has been trying since we were married to find a way to get him out and all has failed so far. Some one if you could and would write a letter to the Bureau for us.

He is third fireman and he isn't making enough to support me[,] and my father is making barely fourteen dollars a week for four besides me and anyone knows that isn't enough for one family of three, here in Jacksonville. I can honestly say that is all my father is making, and I am not able to hold a job and if I was they are scarce except waitress work and I can't hold that kind of job. I am not able. I wish if you are even in Jacksonville you would come to our house and see how we live.

W. A.'s mother's health is failing fast and it seems that is has been worse since he has been in the Navy. I do hope you will believe my story because every word of it is true. Please try and write a letter for me.

P.S. W.A. has a sister living in Tallahassee if you would like an interview[.] I will get their address.[134]

Miss Dora Erickson (Miami) to ER, 11 February 1940

Noticed in the Miami paper tonight that you will be here by Febr. 18. You are a friend of the working people, that is why I dare to write you. Came here from Cambridge, Minnesota (not far from St. Paul & Minneapolis) in November.

Being employed since the first wk. (doing general housework) but not what I want.

My parents were both born in Sweden, & my mother was a first class cook, there.

My age 32—5'8" in height. Brown hair, Blue eyes.

Honest, willing to work & learn, have good reference.

But I want to be placed in a beautiful home (an estate) as second cook.

Employment places have not these jobs listed.

I need to earn more money and I want to be a first class cook some day. And I know if you <u>can</u> you <u>will</u> help me.[135]

Mrs. Grace Cutler Evans, secretary Townsend Club No 4 (Tampa), to ER, 12 February 1940

We notice in the morning papers of February 10th where you broke a precedent by appearing before a congressional committee and made a plea for better treatment for the aged in Washington, D.C.

Of course you are accustomed to having your every move watched for criticism, but instead of criticizing, we wish to commend and then ask why Washington is any more dear to your heart than any other part of the country.

It was your honorable husband who said a certain number of people were "Ill fed, clothed and housed." Especially does this apply to the aged. We have been fighting for five years for these people, more perhaps, than any other class, and some help from you would be Oh, so welcome. True we sail under the Townsend National Recovery Plan, but a rose by any other name would be just as sweet, and we would just as soon sail under a Roosevelt plan, if a plan is adopted that would do the work. We feel that our plan is the best yet offered for both the aged and the youth.

Come join us, and lets work for America.[136]

Mrs. James Bronson (Tampa) to ER, 20 March 1940

We read your mention of Dr Townsend's visit to you, and all Townsendites over the land are watching results.

Not all of us are old and decrepit and destitute, but we, in greater numbers than ever are facing this sort of future, and we pray that thru you the President may study the Townsend Plan, and the new bill.[137]

Mrs. Harriette Emma Stoddard (Miami) to ER, 20 March 1940

We have just learned of your kind gesture—your interview with Dr. Frances E. Townsend. Also that you had invited he and his wife to the White House to be feted there by you and our dear good President. Thank you! Thank you. Our hearts are overflowing with joy and gratitude.

I wrote to Sen. Claude Pepper and the Hon. Pat. Cannon, both of whom we are very proud (last of Jan. year ago) in regard to the inequalities in the W.P.A., in that letter, I made this statement, Our great and good President will go down in history, as the greatest President we have ever had, the greatest humanitarian. He took this country over when it was in bankruptcy, being a great humanitarian with a wonderful mind, guided by our Heavenly Father['s] wisdom. He thought out a great Plan. The N.R.A. which saved millions from starvation and organized projects that have developed talents, yes helped in so many ways (cannot mention all). So much wickedness, graft crept in, no fault of his. Then I said, but now, he has the opportunity to make himself more illustrious of all the outstanding things he has done (I am a Democrat) will be to help us to have The Townsend Plan enacted into law now, while he is our President thereby the Democratic Administration, will have the (in history) everlasting credit, honor and glory of this outstanding masterpiece of legislation. This will be the biggest feather in his cap. . . . Just about everything is Townsend in Florida.[138]

Claude Pepper (1900–1989), U.S. senator (1936–51); U.S. representative (1963–89). Arthur Patrick Cannon (1904–1966), Miami, U.S. representative (1939–47).

Mrs. Sue Fench (Ft. Lauderdale) to ER, 2 April 1940

Quite by chance—I have just read the article in The Cleveland (Ohio) Press for Mar. 27–1940, about your visit from Dr. Townsend.

I havnt the least idea in the world why I'm presuming, to write to you about it—but having read the article I saw in a flash—what a wonderful thing it would be, if you, our beloved First Lady would "put your shoulder to this wheel" and start it rolling to success.

Cant you see what it would do for countless numbers? You—who have always had every thing—would scarcely realize how much misery there is in the world—

We came to Florida to live, five years ago—because it was much easier to be poor—where it is warm—than where it is cold.

At last—I seem to have regained my health, and I have plans for the coming "Season." I will be Sixty years young—in July—and I am not afraid of work—but it would be wonderful to just have a chance to rest.

Please give Dr. Townsend's Plan your un-biased thought. Picture what it would really do—if you were in need—and not the "First Lady," or what it would do for your mother, were "you all" poor. And please forgive me for my presumption.

You are my idea of a wonderful person.[139]

Mrs. C. L. Mattox (Port St. Joe) to Cone, 9 October 1940

The thirthy day of August My husband Coley L. Mattox was put in jail at Wewahitchka Florida & there was no reason for it[.] I see he had ben drinking some but he wasnt drunk. & now I want to tell you just how it came to hapen as he came in from town he had bought some shoes & ask me how did I like them & I told him I didnt like them my self & he got mad & he got almost craze.When any thing makis him mad he has always ben like that & he slap me on the face & broke my glasses & some way they cut my face just above my eye about an inch and he never had hurt me like that befor & it scared me and I went out to a neighbor house & ask her to get me a cab to go to the Doc are get one at her house & she went & ask the man we was renting frome to go & instead of the Doctor he he called the law & then we didnt no what to do so they took him to jail that nite & I didnt no what to do about it so I went to my sister the next day & stayed a week. & they had a trial while I was away & gave him 6 month in jail are $100. 25 cash & he worked at the St Joe Paper Co & he had a good job we thought & now I'm Left to do the Best I can & I have three Children & I am expecting another baby in four weeks & my baby is just 17 month old & my oldest 6 years & I have one 4 year old and the 9th of Last December he took Infantell paralysis & the thirty of December was carred to Warm Spring Foundation Warm Spring Ga For treat ment & it cost us lot to visit him & furnish his clothen & the 19 of September I got a letter from the doctor that he could be brought home & I went to the Judge & told him about every thing & he sent me to the Red Cross & the Well Fair & that has Ben four weeks & they gave me five dollars one time & last week I went and told him again we was suffer & to please let my husband out where he could get us something & he wouldnt & sent me back to the Red Cross & they gave me 3 dollars worth of grociers & said they would be out the next day to see me & they havent ben yet & the paper mill union would of paid my husband out but he didnt stand the examation they took about a year & half ago & they was just working him because he was working in the mill when it first started & hated to Descharge him & since he has had to be off the Job over ten days[.] They have Descharge him & said the company couldnt work him any more till he has an operation & the union cant get him out now. And I'm living in the cheapest place here & cant pay any rent and the man just talks to me any way Because he knowes I dont Have any one here to help me just me & the oldest chill & my baby & we are sure suffring for something to eat & we cant have any heat for the winter & they just wont help me it dont look like & now please see that I get some help till I get able to help my self. I dont have any clothes for the unborned neather my self & no doctor & nothing & now we are sure suffer for nothing[.] I'm a lady & always got along with enny body & I cant see why we are suffering like this for I ask them to Pleas keep my little crippled boy till I could get him a home to come to & they said thy keep him & few week longer & now please help us any way you can & I am sure will think you for ever. I really dont have any people to go to[.] I have a sister at Bonifay, Fla. She wrote me she was gona put the children in the children home but now they have a dady & mother is as good a Provider as hers & I stayed with her the week I was away & she told me she wasnt gona take care of us[.] I would have to beg are go stay at the jail with him[.] it isnt our well fair she warred about she just scard she will have to do something for us is why she wants us away & she is just the tipe to want to run other people Business she is my sister & I'm sorry to say thing about her[.] she is Mrs Guss Adkison Bonifay Fla. so please dont notice any thing she writes & please if you can get me some help some way for I have never forced any thing this hard befor & me like I am & no body to help me & seeing the children go hungry & my self & cold to & I have prayed to god to help us & we dont get some help soon I just cant stand it much longer I not able to go but I have to do all I can & you probably my not think much about this but if you can help me please dont pass it up for this is the only thing I no to do & I have really got to get some help soone. So please see that I get some help soone & I will never forget your kindness.[140]

Miss Dolly Loyd (South Jacksonville) to FDR and ER, 20 November 1940

I am a little girl age 11 yr. I have been wanting a wheel for three yr. But my father not making so much but we are thankful for a steady job.

So this year mother & I are selling Xmas. cards hoping we can earn enough for a wheel but if we dont I'll have to wait but I do want a wheel so bad.

I thought maby our friends would help a lots so I am working real hard. You two are real friends of ours. Can you please take about 10 or 20 boxes of our cards at $1.00 per box[?] they are beautiful cards you will like them I am sure.

Please ans. me at once with a good order please.

Your little girl.[141]

Mrs. C. K. Joyner (Warrington) to ER, 11 December 1940

I am an old lady with great-grandchildren. I've listed to your talks over the radio. I was so pleased that I've come to the conclusion that with you assistance that we, The Crochet Women of America, by crocheting and knitting beautiful work and turning it over to you, to dispose of at bazaars or at raffles, will help the cotton growers and the thread weavers in the mills.

The money which comes from this sale to be used for the fight against tuberculosis or Infantile Paralysis. Just as you and a committee, appointed by you, will decide.

Each lady will attach to her contribution her name and address. In this way, any person desiring additional pieces will know to whom to write.

I hope you like this suggestion. And if in your talks on the radio you would appeal to the people and explain the reason behind it, I am sure you will receive thousands of donations. I am sending you a sample of my own work.

Now, it is up to you, I hope that you will act on my suggestion.[142]

EPILOGUE

A Funeral for Mr. Depression

The following is an account of a "funeral" for the Depression, conducted at an African American church in Orlando in 1933. It is included here because it represented the optimism that people felt about the New Deal, even before it was really underway. The "funeral" was held, after all, when the New Deal was in its infancy. Placing it at the end of the volume, rather than in the section covering 1933, highlights the bittersweet nature of the funeral. It was an expression of unrestrained enthusiasm by the public, but it was also an expression of some of the naiveté of the public. Their expectations of FDR may have been unreasonably high. By 1940 one could easily surmise that the public expected miracles that no one, not even "St. Roosevelt," could deliver.

Morris B. Ives, of Dickson-Ives Co. (Orlando) to FDR, 2 December 1933

I am enclosing a most unique obituary written by one of Orlando's Colored women, which was read at the funeral of MR. DEPRESSION at one of our local Colored Churches.

This was in the form of a play and I felt that you would be interested in reading just how this Race felt towards you. The reason they dated it November 25th was on account of the Federal Civil Works program starting in Orlando on that day.

As a Democrat and admirer of the fine work that you are doing, I would like to add my commendations to your policies—not only GOLD but also the NRA.

If at any time we can be of service to you in any way, please command us.
[enclosure]
FUNERAL OF DEPRESSION at Shiloh Baptist Church (Colored) T. C. Collier, Pastor.

OBITUARY OF MR. DEPRESSION:
Written and read at the funeral of MR. DEPRESSION held at Shiloh Baptist Church, Monday Night, November 27th, 1933, by Ethel Robinson

212

Epilogue

Mr. Depression was born in the year of 1927 on the banks of the Western Hemisphere, he was nursed by results of the War and raised on the echoes of Big Bertha, the War Gun. Mrs. Boom was his mother. He found this world in prosperity so he began his job not in a hurry, taking it slow, these are some of his works.

Poor Old Georgia, he took her first from large plantations to small farms[,] from fertile fields to gardens, boll weavils he did spread. Mr. Depression was in his youth—he looked above the clay hills of Georgia and spied the East coast of Florida—Hollywood that beautiful Beach, buildings of marble and chalk; streets where negroes wasn't allowed, but they couldn't keep Mr. Depression out. He mounted the East Coast Flyer and when he landed in Miami, Ft. Lauderdale, Sebring and West Palm Beach, he didn't ask for a job but he went to work, uprooted trees and blew fish on land, swept men into the ocean and started the Red Cross to work—Happy was he. Orlando thought she had missed him, but he made an invisible fly who lit in the mind of President Hoover; that Mediterranean Fruit Fly to ruin Florida, the Land of Flowers. He hung out signs: "No Help Wanted." He reached up and pulled the real estate down. Caused Parks to become fields and Mansions to become tramps' and insects' hiding places. Caused the Insane Asylum to be over-packed; Caused hundreds of suicides in the U.S.,—has torn up thousands of homes. He has seen to it that marriages have become complete failures. He sifted his net and started Christians to praying. The weak Christians fell entirely out. He had a job for them. He established the Bolita in Orange County and Florida and started them going from house to house. Mr. Depression sat the men down and put women in power. He stretched forth his hand and closed the Banks Doors. Caused thousands of Men, Women and Children to be in the bread lines. Where "Miss Ann" used to have help she is doing the work herself—where we used to have two meals we are having one and calling it keeping thin.

When Pres. Roosevelt took his seat, Mr. Depression took the bed. The doctors announced that he was run down from over work. President Roosevelt sent out a gas known as the N.R.A. It found its way into poor old Mr. Depression's weak system—he died after a great struggle from a disease known as the N.R.A. He departed this life November 25th, 1933. He leaves rejoicing over his body, many of the rich, all of the poor and the whole U.S. at Large.

We hated you and glad you are gone. Sleep on Mr. Depression, we know you are tired. We thought we hated you but President Roosevelt hated you worst. Therefore he has seen fit to call you out of this world, and we gladly commit your body to the ground—earth to earth, ashes to ashes, dust to dust, hoping that you will never rise to come back to us.[1]

213

APPENDIX

Alphabetical Listing of Correspondents

Adams, Mrs. W. G.	25 January 1935
Adams, Mrs. W. R.	25 April 1935
Adkison, Mrs. Marandia	4 May 1933
Allen, Mrs. J. P.	17 September 1938
Altman, Mrs. Ruth	19 February 1935
Alvarez, Mrs. Dominga	4 October 1939
Alvis, Mrs. Elsie	17 August 1939
Anderson, Mrs. A. C.	19 April 1938
Anderson, Mrs. A. L.	29 June 1937
Anderson, Mrs. G. L.	4 December 1933
Anderson, Miss Theo E.	4 April 1935
Armengol, Mrs. M. L.	2 February 1937
Bacon, Mrs. Elizabeth Lucas	1 March 1934
Bailey, Mrs. J. L.	30 December 1934
Balssell, Mrs. Lurlee	15 March 1938
Barber, Mrs. Edgar	7 May 1934
Barnes, Mrs. Bessie	19 October 1939
Barnett, Miss Eliza	28 August 1934
Bartenfels, Mrs. Annie Esser	21 April 1931
Bartlett, Mrs. Sarah L.	10 September 1935; 14 November 1935
Baxter, Mrs. Louise	26 September 1934
Bazemore, Mrs. Alma	28 February 1939
Beal, Miss Burnie	10 November 1937
Beaty, Miss Bessie	16 September 1935
Bell, Mrs. Frances	27 May 1939
Bell, Mrs. Norma	5 March 1937
Bell, Mrs. Willie	11 September 1938
Bender, Mrs. Bessie T.	18 January 1935
Beneboy, Mrs. Dorothy	13 June 1939
Bennett, Mrs. Carl C.	26 January 1934
Bennett, Mrs. Stella G.	1 June 1935

Bird, Mrs. Ella	29 November 1937
Blackwelder, Miss Reba	5 July 1932
Blume, Miss Mary Ellen	19 November 1937
Bond, Mrs. Mary V.	16 June 1939
Bradley, Mrs. Rachel E.	9 July 1939
Brantley, Mrs. W. L.	18 April 1938
Brast, Mrs. Gustav	14 December 1935
Braswell, Mrs. Mabel G.	17 May 1937
Brice, Mrs. J. M.	2 May 1935
Bridges, Miss Euvah	26 June 1935
Briggs, Rena M. (Mrs. G. W.)	13 June 1934; 18 January 1935
Brightwell, Mrs. Gertrude M.	24 November 1934
Bronson, Mrs. James	20 March 1940
Brosseau, Mrs. Marie	11 June 1939
Brown, Mrs. Maggie	18 October 1938
Brown, Miss Mary A.	8 September 1935
Bullard, Mrs. P. E.	28 June 1930
Burns, Miss Christina	1 December 1936
Bussard, Mrs. Bessie	25 October 1939
Burns, Mrs. Effie	27 March 1938
Bye, Mrs. Frances M.	17 April 1935
Cadman, Mrs. Annie V.	13 August 1935
Cain, Mrs. Joanna	26 February 1937
Capes, Mrs. Carol	19 July 1934
Caster, Mrs. Bessie Lee	25 April 1929
Cauthen, Mrs. Victoria	30 August 1933
Chavis, Mrs. Vivian G.	22 January 1935
Chestnut, Miss Martha	29 November 1935
Clements, Mrs. Virginia	7 January 1934
Cline, Miss Donnie	20 July 1939
Cobb, Lizzie	10 January 1930
Cogswell, Mrs. W. D.	23 April 1937
Coker, Mrs.	12 July 1929
Coleman, Mrs. E. R.	7 June 1937
Collier, Mrs. Beulah	7 August 1927
Collins, Mrs. Alice G.	2 August 1935
Collins, Mrs. Ethel	9 July 1929
Collins, Mary Wolcott (Mrs. J. Purser)	27 August 1934, 5 October 1934
Combs, Mrs. Thelma	13 April 1937
Comer, Mrs. Mary E.	29 May 1935

Conley, Mrs. Fannie	21 December 1934
Connor, Mrs. Essie Mae	4 July 1937
Cook, Mrs. Mary	27 January 1937
Coon, Mrs. Etta	10 July 1930
Cortino, Mrs. Mary I.	7 August 1934
Cortis, Mrs. Ella S.	18 December 1930
Craig, Mrs. F. M.	11 September 1935
Crews, Mrs. Ava	30 December 1933
Croft, Mrs. Bette	11 May 1937
Cropper, Mrs. Bessie	9 September 1932
Curry, Mrs. Cornelia Rosemond	20 June 1939
Curry, Mrs. Nelia	14 October 1935
Daniels, Mrs. Alma	11 May 1934
Davis, Mrs. Dinah	8 July 1929
Deaux, Mrs. F. L.	29 June 1937
Dees, Miss Ethel	14 September 1929
Delegal, Miss Philo.	17 September 1935
Detrick, Mrs. Gladys	3 January 1938
Dixon, Mrs. Annie Klee	22 March 1939
Douglass, Mrs. M.	3 February 1936
Doyle, Mrs. Margaretha	20 December 1933
Dozier, Mrs. C. I.	20 August 1935
DuBose, Mrs. W. H.	29 January 1938; 14 December 1934
Duncan, Mrs. Maude V.	4 June 1935
Dupont, Mrs. Johnnie M.	7 August 1934
Dupuis, Mrs. Ulric L.	29 January 1938
Eddy, Mrs. Doris Isabel	24 March 1934
Ensey, Maude (Mrs. E. R.)	22 November 1934
Ergle, Mrs. Missouri	24 June 1937
Erickson, Miss Dora	11 February 1940
Evans, Mrs. Grace Cutler	8 January 1936; 12 February 1940
Evans, Mrs. Izola	22 October 1936
Evans, Mrs. Lora	16 November 1936
Faudel, Mrs. Iola E.	22 October 1934
Fench, Mrs. Sue	2 April 1940
Ferrero, Miss Annie	28 June 1935
Fielder, Mrs. Rosabel	6 July 1937
Fields, Mrs. Rufus	26 June 1937
Fleeschman, Mrs. Joseph (Alma)	24 January 1934

Foard, Mrs. Wallace (Jimmie C.)	22 April 1929
Ford, Miss Olive S.	17 March 1937
Fort, Mrs. Frances Schley	22 February 1935
Fowler, Mrs. W. H.	28 February 1937
Frazier, Edith H.	4 December 1934
Frohock, Mrs. G. W.	23 August 1939
Funk, Mrs. Edna	12 June 1934
Fuqua, Mrs. Millie	26 August 1935
Furgison, Eva	July 1936; 27 October 1937; 5 July 1939
Gaddis, Mrs. Mae	17 July 1939
Galvins, Mrs. Bertha	24 June 1935
Gardner, Miss June	23 March 1935
Garritt, Mrs. Massie	10 March 1937
Gay, Miss Mary	21 July 1935
Gay, Mrs. Minnie	26 May 1933
Gibson, Mrs. C. A.	24 April 1937, 9 July 1937
Gil, Mrs. Inez	19 January 1939
Gilbert, Mrs. C. C.	31 July 1937, 5 August 1937
Glenn, Mrs. L. D.	5 June 1934
Godwin, Mrs. Lois Byrd	12 May 1939
Godwin, Mrs. W. V.	9 April 1937
Gran, Mrs. Gerda	5 September 1936
Goodman, Mrs. William W.	9 October 1933
Grant, Mrs. Daisy	5 September 1934
Gray, Miss Nellie	20 May 1935
Green, Mrs. Catherine	27 July 1936
Green, Mrs. Maggie A.	26 April 1937
Grover, Sadie Vastie	20 March 1939
Hagin, Mrs. Nellie D.	24 May 1937
Hagler, Mrs. Elibeth	12 November 1936
Hamilton, Miss Marion	12 August 1933
Hall, Mrs. R. Clyde	15 November 1939
Hall, Mrs. Vassie Lee	12 March 1937
Hammond, Mrs. Lavenia	30 October 1937
Hanks, Mrs. E. M.	8 August 1939
Harper, Mrs. Della	31 December 1934
Harris, Mrs. Alice Barton	28 September 1936
Harris, Mrs. Sarah	21 June 1933
Hartley, Mrs. A. C.	14 October 1937
Haudenschild, Mrs. J. W.	12 March 1934

Haye, Mrs. Lelia	8 April 1937
Head, Mrs. Pearl	15 November 1937
Heap, Mrs. Cecil R.	17 December 1935
Helfrick, Miss Mildred	14 December 1935
Henderson, Mrs. Ruth	13 June 1935
Henry, Mrs. Lillian	5 November 1938
Hernandez, Mrs. Amada	23 June 1939
Hernandez, Miss Wilhelmena	11 November 1934
Herrington, Miss Evelyn	17 May 1937
Hicks, Mrs. J. W.	14 January 1934
Hirst, Edith M.	6 October 1934
Holtman, Betty Bryan	22 November 1934
Hood, Mrs. Milton Yancey "Mary"	16 September 1935
Hopkins, Mrs. B. T.	23 May 1934
Horn, Mrs. Miriam	9 February 1937
Hosmer, Mrs. Marie	7 April 1935
Howell, Mrs. Z. Pearl	12 January 1933
Howland, Mrs. J. P.	15 September 1934
Huggins, Miss Margaret	1 February 1934
Hughes, Callie	23 June 1937
Hughes, Mrs. Lola	1 August 1939
Humphrey, Mrs. Gertrude	1 July 1935
Ingraham, Mrs. Millie	7 May 1936
James, Miss Ethel	29 March 1929
Jennings, Mrs. Bertie	21 January 1936
Jernigan, Mrs. Mollie	8 March 1930
Johnson, Mrs. J. E.	12 May 1937
Johnson, Mrs. M. A.	11 May 1934
Jones, Mrs. E. G.	20 November 1937
Jones, Mrs. Rosa	23 May 1929
Jones, Mrs. Rosa J.	10 November 1934
Joyner, Mrs. C. K.	11 December 1940
Keaton, Mrs. L. P.	9 July 1937
Keen, Mrs. Essie	23 July 1935
Kennedy, Mrs. Lillie	13 August 1933
Kimbrough, Mrs. J. R.	5 August 1929
Knowles, Mrs. Lela	14 May 1938
Kraft, Mrs. Aline M.	21 January 1934
Kunze, Mrs. Ida M.	19 December 1934
Lamb, Mrs. N. S.	16 August 1933

Lanzl, Mrs. Peter	23 September 1933
Lazara, Mrs. Jennie	4 March 1939
Leonard, Miss Rebecca	18 December 1929
Lewis, Mrs. H. N.	22 February 1935
Lewis, Mrs. Maude	9 February 1934
Lightfoot, Mrs. Nettie	12 July 1933
Livingston, Mrs. Ettie Estelle	3 November 1937
Lockard, Mrs. Mary J.	14 June 1935
Longley, Mrs. Louise	9 July 1934
Longo, Miss Josephine	21 April 1934
Loyd, Miss Dolly	20 November 1940
Ludlam, Mrs. Bertha	9 August 1939
Lynch, Miss Rose Elizabeth	1 May 1935
Mallett, Mrs. Bessie	4 August 1933
Marlowe, Mrs. J. R.	26 February 1935
Mattox, Mrs. Coley L.	9 October 1940
Mayenhoff, Mrs. Fritz D.	23 March 1937
Mayers, Mrs. Juanita	27 August 1936
McCarley, Mrs. C. S.	6 April 1933
McCarr, Mrs. Mollie	6 July 1937
McCullars, Mrs. M. N.	11 December 1935
McDaniel, Mrs. W. A.	8 March 1937
McIntyre, Mrs. E. L.	7 April 1935
McKay, Mrs. J. G.	1 December 1935
Meridith, Mrs. C. M.	10 April 1935
Meriwether, Miss Helene	22 October 1934
Messina, Mrs. Etta	23 March 1937
Minor, Mrs. Emma	27 September 1934
Mixon, Mrs. R. L. (Mabel)	27 June 1930
Moore, Mrs. C.	21 June 1937
Moss, Mrs. Fannie	28 February 1938; 17 March 1938
Murphey, Miss Oretha	9 November 1933
Musy, Miss Toots	16 October 1935
Nicholson, Mrs. J. S.	17 February 1937
Nodin, Mrs. Mary E.	2 April 1934
Nowling, Miss Lola	28 January 1933
Nutt, Mrs. M. A. Nutt	15 June 1934
Ogden, Mrs. Gladys	29 January 1938
Ogden, Mrs. John (Lena)	20 August 1934; 29 October 1934
Oliver, Mrs. Georgia	5 April 1938
O'Brien, Mrs. C.	9 May 1929

O'Quinn, Mrs. A. B.	26 May 1937
Page, Mrs. Barton	9 February 1935
Painter, Mrs. Lola E.	30 March 1939
Parker, Ruth	29 October 1934
Parker, Mrs. Annie	15 July 1934
Parker, Mrs. Mattie	8 February 1929
Parkhouse, Mrs. David L.	9 September 1937
Parrish, Mrs. L. E. (Ida)	22 January 1934
Peacock, Mrs. Catherine	21 October 1929
Peden, Mrs. M. A.	6 July 1934
Peters, Mrs. Lizzie	17 April 1934
Porter, Mrs. Mary	5 November 1933
Powell, Mrs. D. P.	16 March 1939
Preiss, Mrs. Theo	23 November 1931
Prescott, Mrs. Wealtha	21 June 1933
Pyke, Mrs. Gladys	21 November 1939
Raddatz, Mrs. W. E.	20 November 1939
Ramsey, Mrs. B. O.	24 January 1934
Ray, Mrs. A. N.	11 January 1933
Ray, Mrs. Lonnie R.	6 November 1934
Read, Mrs. Thelma Faust	20 February 1937
Reddick, Mrs. Susie H.	21 February 1935
Reed, Mrs. Laura	30 December 1932
Reeves, Mary	4 June 1935
Respress, Mrs. W. D. (Cleola)	13 September 1937
Richardson, Mrs. Rosa	2 January 1930
Roberts, Mrs. J. M.	6 September 1939
Roberts, Miss Maxine	28 February 1938
Robinson, Mrs. Lila	14 September 1935
Rosemond, Mrs. Ida B.	26 November 1934
Salter, Mrs. Emma	5 March 1936
Sainz, Miss Bertila	26 April 1939
Sapp, Mrs. M. J. (Marion C.)	5 September 1935
Schoentag, Mrs. Irene	18 October 1939
Scott, Mrs. J. C.	15 April 1935
Scranton, Mrs. S. P.	26 August 1934
Sears, Mrs. Mozell	9 February 1934
Sellers, Mrs. N. J.	9 June 1937
Sheffield, Mrs. W. L.	18 May 1929
Scott, Mrs. D. L.	27 August 1932
Scott, Mrs. E. C.	28 November 1933

Sherrod, Susie Mae (Miss)	9 July 1937
Sikes, Mrs. F. E.	3 June 1929
Silcox, Mrs. Tilla	3 November 1934
Simmons, Mrs. Phoeby	6 August 1929
Sims, Mrs. Alice G.	7 June 1937
Sloan, Miss Nettie	12 August 1935
Smith, Mrs. L. A. N.	18 August 1932
Smyre, Mrs. Emily	7 February 1934
Smyth, Mrs. H. C.	23 August 1937
Sorenson, Mrs. Ada	17 February 1930
Spence, Mrs. J. W.	7 March 1929
Spencer, Mrs. Louise K.	22 October 1934
Stacey, Mrs. George	7 October 1938
Stephens, Mrs. Charles A. (Minnie)	18 December 1934
Stephens, Mrs. H. T.	22 August 1935
Stephenson, Mrs. L.	19 February 1930
Stewart, Mrs. Alice B.	15 September 1934
Stewart, Mrs. E.	14 August 1934
Still, Mrs. Pearl	13 June 1935
Stoddard, Mrs. Harriette Emma	20 March 1940
Story, Mrs. Mattie J	6 June 1935
Suggs, Mrs. J. A.	29 January 1934
Sutton, Mrs. Josephine	1 June 1934
Thomas, Mrs. M. B.	13 March 1933
Thomas, Mrs. Nancy	11 February 1934
Thomas, Mrs. Odia	21 June 1937
Thompson, Miss Clara	15 January 1938
Tillman, Mrs. Ida E.	22 May 1933
Timmons, Julia B.	12 November 1929
Tounsell, Mrs. Alice	10 July 1929
Townsend, Mrs. Victoria	27 June 1933
Trimmings, Mrs. M. L. D.	25 June 1934
Tucker, Mrs. E. A.	4 June 1934
Tullis, Mrs. Jesse	17 March 1937
Tyson, Mrs. Adam	1 February 1937
Valle, Mrs. Beulah Morris	3 November 1938
Varn, Mrs. John	12 December 1929
Vaughan, Mrs. B. D. (Rose)	2 December 1934
Ventry, Mrs. M. A.	24 June 1937

Walker, Gula (Mrs. David E.)	5 July 1929; 7 March 1937
Walters, Mrs. Lecy Bass	13 September 1938
Ward, Mrs. W. J.	31 March 1939
Warner, Mrs. Frank B. (Emma)	22 October 1934
Weissinger, Mrs. A. J.	10 January 1929
Wesley, Mrs. Lucile C. F.	15 December 1935
Whidden, Mrs. O. C.	10 June 1930
Whitaker, Miss Clifford C.	11 July 1934
White, Mrs. Flora A.	8 May 1934
William, Mrs. Dorothy	19 September 1935
Williams, Mrs. Holl	21 November 1931
Wilson, Mrs. H. E.	18 February 1937
Wilson, Mrs. Virginia	18 October 1934
Witter, Miss Martha	26 June 1937
Wolf, Mrs. Sam J.	9 May 1934
Wollam, Mrs. M. P.	11 March 1937
Wood, Mrs. Eleanor	25 May 1932
Wood, Mrs. Kate	13 November 1934
Woodland, Mrs. Bessie	12 August 1939
Youngblood, Mrs. Hettie	18 October 1937

NOTES

Introduction

1. Michael Gannon, *Florida: A Short History* (Gainesville: University Press of Florida, 1993), 82–85; William W. Rogers, "Fortune and Misfortune: The Paradoxical Twenties," in *The New History of Florida,* ed. Michael Gannon (Gainesville: University Press of Florida, 1996), 294–97.

2. Gannon, *Florida,* 86–88; Maxine D. Jones, "The African-American Experience in Twentieth-Century Florida," in *The New History of Florida,* ed. Michael Gannon (Gainesville: University Press of Florida, 1996), 379–84.

3. William W. Rogers, "The Great Depression," in *The New History of Florida,* ed. Michael Gannon (Gainesville: University Press of Florida, 1996), 304–5; James William Dunn, "The New Deal and Florida Politics" (Ph.D. diss., Florida State University, 1971), 13.

4. Helen C. Mawer, *Organization and Activities of the State Board of Public Welfare, January 1, 1931 to January 1, 1933* (Tallahassee: State Board, 1933), 6–7.

5. Rogers, "The Great Depression," 305. In July 1931 only fifteen of the sixty-seven counties had social welfare offices with a full-time paid caseworker. Mawer, *Organization and Activities of the State Board of Public Welfare,* 27.

6. Mawer, *Organization and Activities of the State Board of Public Welfare,* 33.

7. State Board of Social Welfare, *Biennial Report of the Florida State Board of Social Welfare, Covering the Period August 1935 to March 1937* ([Jacksonville]: State Board, 1937), 9.

8. Dunn, "The New Deal and Florida Politics," 12.

9. *Ninth Annual Report of the Duval County Welfare Board, Jacksonville, Florida for the Year Ending December 31, 1931* (Jacksonville: State Board, 1932?), 3. Copy available in the Florida State Library, Tallahassee.

10. According to the 1930 federal census.

11. *Tallahassee Democrat,* 11 August 1932.

12. Mawer, *Organization and Activities of the State Board of Public Welfare,* 12, 44.

13. The literature on the New Deal and on Franklin Roosevelt is vast and still growing. Useful recent works include Patrick J. Maney, *The Roosevelt Presence: A Biography of Franklin Delano Roosevelt* (New York: Twayne, 1992); Frank Freidel, *Franklin D. Roosevelt: A Rendezvous with Destiny* (Boston: Little Brown, 1990); Michael E. Parrish, *Anxious Decades: America in Prosperity and Depression, 1920–1941* (New York: W. W. Norton, 1992); David M. Kennedy, *Freedom from Fear: The American People in Depression*

and War (New York: Oxford University Press, 1999); James R. McGovern, *And a Time for Hope: Americans in the Great Depression* (Westport, Conn.: Praeger, 2000).

14. Jerrell Shoffner, "Roosevelt's 'Tree Army': The Civilian Conservation Corps in Florida," *Florida Historical Quarterly* 65 (April 1987): 433–56.

15. Rogers, "The Great Depression," 310–18.

16. David Nelson, "Camp Roosevelt: A Case Study of the NYA in Florida," 10 (unpublished paper in author's possession).

17. Important specialized studies on these programs include Anthony J. Badger, *Prosperity Road: The New Deal, Tobacco, and North Carolina* (Chapel Hill: University of North Carolina Press, 1980); James A. Hodges, *New Deal Labor Policy and the Southern Cotton Textile Industry, 1933–1941* (Knoxville: University of Tennessee Press, 1986); Theodore Saloutos, *The American Farmer and the New Deal* (Ames: Iowa State University Press, 1982); Olen Cole Jr., *The African-American Experience in the Civilian Conservation Corps* (Gainesville: University Press of Florida, 1999).

18. On Eleanor Roosevelt, see especially Blanche Wiesen Cook, *Eleanor Roosevelt,* vol. 1, 1884–1933, vol. 2, 1933–1938 (New York: Viking, 1992, 1999).

19. Reprinted in *The Public Papers and Addresses of Franklin D. Roosevelt* (New York: Random House, 1938), 1: 624.

20. Linda Gordon, *Pitied but Not Entitled: Single Mothers and the History of Welfare, 1890–1935* (New York: Free Press, 1994), 248.

21. This example is taken from secretary to Mrs. Maude Ensey (Walton), 28 November 1934, Eleanor Roosevelt (ER) papers, series 140 "Merchandise for Sale," box 991.

22. There are literally thousands of such responses in the ER papers. This one comes from secretary to Mrs. C. T. Walker (Laurelhill), 5 November 1934, ER papers, series 70 "Correspondence with Government Departments," box 276.

Chapter 1: Before the New Deal

1. William W. Rogers, "The Great Depression," in *The New History of Florida,* ed. Michael Gannon (Gainesville: University Press of Florida, 1996), 304–5.

2. Helen C. Mawer, *Organization and Activities of the State Board of Public Welfare, January 1, 1931 to January 1, 1933* (Tallahassee: State Board, 1933), 34.

3. The 1930 census listed poor houses or poor farms in Alachua, Brevard, Dade (2), Escambia, Hillsborough, Monroe, Palm Beach, Pinellas, Putnam, Santa Rosa, Seminole, Sumter, and Volusia counties.

4. See especially Theda Skocpol, Marjorie Abend-Wein, Christopher Howard, and Susan Goodrich Lehmann, "Women's Associations and the Enactment of Mothers' Pensions in the United States," *American Political Science Review* 87, no. 3 (1993): 686–701; and Mark H. Leff, "Consensus for Reform: The Mothers' Pension Movement in the Progressive Era," *Social Service Review* 47, no. 3 (1973): 397–429.

5. Wilson Doyle et al. *The Government and Administration of Florida* (New York: Thomas Y. Crowell, 1954), 238.

6. Those counties were Bay, Citrus, Clay, Collier, Flagler, Franklin, Glades, Gilchrist, Hamilton, Jackson, Lake, Leon, Liberty, Marion, Monroe, Nassau, Pasco,

Okaloosa, Sumter, Suwannee, Union, and Wakulla. Emma O. Lundberg, *Mothers' Pensions in Florida, 1933* (Tallahassee: State Board of Public Welfare, 1934), 5.

7. Lundberg, *Mothers' Pensions in Florida,* 6.

8. Winifred Bell, *Aid to dependent Children* (New York: Columbia University Press, 1965), 10.

9. Lundberg, *Mothers' Pensions in Florida,* 24.

10. For further details, see my article "Protecting Confederate Soldiers and Mothers: Pensions, Gender, and the Welfare State in the U.S. South, a Case Study from Florida," *Journal of Social History,* 39 (June 2006).

11. Lundberg, *Mothers' Aid in Florida,* 6. It should also be noted that several thousand Floridians were receiving federal pensions for their service in the Union armies. In 1910 there were 4,244 federal pensioners in the state, getting an average annual grant of $172. Theda Skocpol, *Protecting Soldiers and Mothers: The Political Origins of Social Policy in the United States* (Cambridge: Harvard University Press, 1992), 134, 541. I cannot calculate how many federal pensioners there were in the 1930s since the Pension Bureau no longer reported the numbers by state.

12. See especially Ann Shola Orloff, *The Politics of Pensions: A Comparative Analysis of Britain, Canada, and the United States, 1880–1940* (Madison: University of Wisconsin Press, 1993); and Jill Quadagno, *The Transformation of Old Age Security: Class and Politics in the American Welfare State* (Chicago: University of Chicago Press, 1988).

13. Josephine C. Brown, *Public Relief, 1929–1939* (New York: Henry Holt, 1940), 27. Much like mothers' pensions, however, the state old age pension programs were entirely inadequate to the needs of the population. Walter I. Trattner, *From Poor Law to Welfare State: A History of Social Welfare in America,* 5th ed. (New York: Free Press, 1994), 230.

14. The 1933 report stated, "The most advanced method of caring for the aged is a system of old age pensions . . . Eighteen states have such laws." Mawer, *Organization and Activities of the State Board of Public Welfare* (1933), 39. The 1935 report went a little further: "Either they [the elderly] will be cared for inadequately on the old county pauper basis and in county homes—or the state will get abreast of other progressive states with some form of Old Age pension suited to social and financial conditions of the individuals involved." Ruth W. Atkinson, *Organization and Activities of the State Board of Public Welfare, January 1, 1933, to January 1, 1935* (Tallahassee: State Board, 1935), 24.

15. Richard Lowitt and Maurine Beasley, eds., *One Third of a Nation: Lorena Hickok Reports on the Great Depression* (Urbana: University of Illinois Press, 1981), 169.

16. Florida State Archives (FSA) series 204, box 15, folder 15.

17. FSA series 204, box 7, folder 17.

18. FSA series 204, box 66, folder 3.

19. FSA series 204, box 83, folder 1.

20. FSA series 204, box 46, folder 1.

21. FSA series 204, box 2, folder 12.

22. FSA series 204, box 30, folder 20.

23. FSA series 204, box 68, folder 1.
24. FSA series 204, box 81, folder 1.
25. FSA series 204, box 47, folder 5.
26. FSA series 204, box 84, folder 7.
27. FSA series 204, box 93, folder 10.
28. FSA series 204, box 21, folder 7.
29. FSA series 204, box 15, folder 15.
30. FSA series 204, box 85, folder 1.
31. FSA series 204, box 15, folder 15.
32. FSA series 204, box 82, folder 1.
33. FSA series 204, box 48, folder 5.
34. FSA series 204, box 73, folder 13.
35. FSA series 204, box 22, folder 1.
36. FSA series 204, box 67, folder 8.
37. FSA series 204, box 7, folder 12.
38. FSA series 204, box 87, folder 6.
39. FSA series 204, box 92, folder 4.
40. FSA series 204, box 17, folder 4.
41. FSA series 204, box 50, folder 1.
42. FSA series 204, box 67, folder 8.
43. FSA series 204, box 75, folder 1.
44. FSA series 204, box 15, folder 15.
45. FSA series 204, box 82, folder 13.
46. FSA series 204, box 83, folder 3.
47. FSA series 204, box 46, folder 47.
48. FSA series 204, box 95, folder 11.
49. FSA series 204, box 59, folder 9.
50. FSA series 204, box 10, folder 17.
51. FSA series 204, box 14, folder 2.
52. FSA series 204, box 96, folder 3.
53. FSA series 204, box 6, folder 9.
54. FSA series 204, box 71, folder 6.
55. FSA series 204, box 96, folder 6.
56. FSA series 204, box 7, folder 18.
57. FSA series 204, box 82, folder 7.
58. FSA series 204, box 80, folder 9.
59. FSA series 204, box 17, folder 14.
60. FSA series 278, box 95, folder 17.

Chapter 2: 1933–1934

1. William W. Rogers, "The Great Depression," in *The New History of Florida,* ed. Michael Gannon (Gainesville: University Press of Florida, 1996), 309.

2. See: Merlin G. Cox, "David Sholtz: New Deal Governor of Florida," *Florida Historical Quarterly* 46 (October 1964): 142–52.

3. Francis E. Townsend, *Old Age Revolving Pensions: A Proposed National Plan* (Long Beach, Calif.: Old Age Revolving Pensions Inc., 1934). See also Richard L. Neuberger and Kelley Loe, *An Army of the Aged: A History and Analysis of the Townsend Old Age Pension Plan* (1936; reprint, New York: Da Capo Press, 1973); Joseph E. Harvey, *Get behind the Townsend Plan* (Portland, Ore.: the author, 1935); Sheridan Downey, *Why I Believe in the Townsend Plan* (Sacramento, Calif.: Sheridan Downey Pub. Co., 1936).

4. David M. Kennedy, *Freedom from Fear: The American People in Depression and War, 1929–1945* (New York: Oxford University Press, 1999), 224–25.

5. Walter I. Trattner, *From Poor Law to Welfare State: A History of Social Welfare in America,* 5th ed. (New York: Free Press, 1994), 227–31.

6. Kennedy, *Freedom from Fear,* 225.

7. FSA series 278, box 94, folder 1.

8. FSA series 278, box 90, folder 9.

9. FSA series 278, box 84, folder 11.

10. FSA series 278, box 110, folder 11.

11. FSA series 278, box 77, folder 1.

12. FSA series 278, box 80, folder 10.

13. FSA series 278, box 6, folder 5.

14. FSA series 278, box 110, folder 11.

15. FSA series 278, box 48, folder 1.

16. FSA series 278, box 53, folder 2.

17. FSA series 278, box 91, folder 12.

18. FSA series 278, box 111, folder 4.

19. FSA series 278, box 71, folder 10.

20. FSA series 278, box 74, folder 8.

21. FSA series 278, box 52, folder 10.

22. FSA series 278, box 66, folder 2.

23. FSA series 278, box 67, folder 2.

24. FSA series 278, box 3, folder 1.

25. FSA series 278, box 17, folder 1.

26. FSA series 278, box 67, folder 2.

27. FSA series 278, box 50, folder 1.

28. FSA series 278, box 90, folder 9.

29. FSA series 278, box 83, folder 3.

30. FSA series 278, box 101, folder 10.

31. FSA series 278, box 4, folder 8.

32. Eleanor Roosevelt (ER) Papers, series 150.1: Material Assistance Requested, boxes unnumbered, 1933

33. ER Papers, series 150.1: Material Assistance Requested, boxes unnumbered, 1933.

34. ER Papers, series 150.1: Material Assistance Requested, boxes unnumbered, 1934.

35. ER Papers, series 70: Correspondence with Government Departments, box 267.

36. ER Papers, series 150.3: Positions sought through Mrs. Roosevelt, box 2381.

37. ER Papers, series 150.1: Material Assistance Requested, boxes unnumbered, 1934.

38. ER Papers, series 140: Merchandise for Sale, box 992.

39. ER Papers, series 150.1: Material Assistance Requested, boxes unnumbered, 1934.

40. ER Papers, series 150.3: Positions sought through Mrs. Roosevelt, box 2383.

41. FSA series 278, box 9, folder 6.

42. FSA series 278, box 107, folder 6.

43. ER Papers, series 150.3: Positions sought through Mrs. Roosevelt, box 2381.

44. ER Papers, series 70: Correspondence with Government Departments, box 274.

45. FSA series 278, box 68, folder 8.

46. ER Papers, series 70: Correspondence with Government Departments, box 274. A response from ER's secretary, dated 20 February 1934, says she regrets that she can do nothing personally "as it seems to be one which would come under the jurisdiction of local authorities."

47. FSA series 368, box 91, folder 1.

48. ER Papers, series 150.9: Miscellaneous Requests, box 2431.

49. ER Papers, series 140: Merchandise for Sale, box 991.

50. ER Papers, series 150.3: Positions Sought through Mrs. Roosevelt, box 2381.

51. ER Papers, series 140: Merchandise for Sale, box 992.

52. FSA series 278, box 88, folder 10.

53. ER Papers, series 140: Merchandise for Sale, box 992.

54. ER Papers, series 70: Correspondence with Government Departments, box 261.

55. FSA series 278, box 19, folder 11.

56. ER Papers, series 140: Merchandise for Sale, box 993.

57. FSA series 278, box 28, folder 1.

58. FSA series 278, box 65, folder 6.

59. FSA series 278, box 59, folder 6.

60. FSA series 278, box 107, folder 6.

61. ER Papers, series 70: Correspondence with Government Departments, box 276.

62. ER Papers, series 150.1: Material Assistance Requested, boxes unnumbered, 1934.

63. FSA series 278, box 46, folder 12.

64. ER Papers, series 150.9: Miscellaneous Requests, box marked "2431, 2432, 2433, 2434."

65. ER Papers, series 140: Merchandise for Sale, box 992.

66. ER Papers, series 150.1: Material Assistance Requested, boxes unnumbered, 1934.

67. FSA series 278, box 111, folder10.

68. FSA series 278, box 72, folder 7.

69. FSA series 278, box 88, folder 10

70. FSA series 278, box 119, folder 11.

71. FSA series 278, box 87, folder 2.

72. FSA series 278, box 16, folder 2.

73. ER Papers, series 150.1: Material Assistance Requested, boxes unnumbered, 1934.
74. FSA series 278, box 33, folder 1.
75. ER Papers, series 140: Merchandise for Sale, box 993.
76. ER Papers, series 100.1: Children Named for Eleanor Roosevelt, box 827.
77. FSA series 278, box 101, folder 11.
78. ER Papers, series 140: Merchandise for Sale, box 991.
79. ER Papers, series 70: Correspondence with Government Departments, box 261.
80. FSA series 278, box 51, folder 11.
81. ER Papers, series 150.9: Miscellaneous Requests, box marked "2439, 2440, 2441."
82. ER Papers, series 70: Correspondence with Government Departments, box 267. [Original letter not included, only this response. Staff note at bottom says letter was referred to Reconstruction Finance Corporation.]
83. ER Papers, series 150.3: Positions Sought through Mrs. Roosevelt, box 2381.
84. ER Papers, series 140: Merchandise for Sale, box 992.
85. ER Papers, series 140: Merchandise for Sale, box 991.
86. ER Papers, series 70: Correspondence with Government Departments, box 267.
87. FSA series 278, box 120, folder 3.
88. ER Papers, series 150.1: Material Assistance Requested, boxes unnumbered, 1934.
89. ER Papers, series 150.9: Miscellaneous Requests, box marked "2434, 2435, 2436."
90. ER Papers, series 70: Correspondence with Government Departments, box 274.
91. ER Papers, series 70: Correspondence with Government Departments, box 276.
92. ER Papers, series 100.1: Children Named for Eleanor Roosevelt, box 827.
93. FSA series 278, box 87, folder 2.
94. FSA series 278, box 103, folder 4.
95. ER Papers, series 140: Merchandise for Sale, box 992.
96. FSA series 278, box 65, folder 8.
97. FSA series 278, box 55, folder 4
98. Franklin D. Roosevelt (FDR) Papers, Official Files, series 494a : Old Age Pensions, box 1.
99. ER Papers, series 140: Merchandise for Sale, box 991.
100. FSA series 278, box 59, folder 6.
101. ER Papers, series 150.9: Miscellaneous Requests, box marked "2431, 2432, 2433, 2434."
102. FSA series 278, box 99, folder 5.
103. ER Papers, series 70: Correspondence with Government Departments, box 276.
104. FSA series 278, box 46, folder 12.
105. ER Papers, series 75: Old Age Pensions, box 433.
106. FSA series 278, box 84, folder 13.
107. ER Papers, series 75: Old Age Pensions, box 434.
108. ER Papers, series 75: Old Age Pensions, box 433.
109. FSA series 278, box 23, folder 3.
110. FSA series 278, box 7, folder 1.
111. ER Papers, series 75: Old Age Pensions, box 433.

Chapter 3: 1935–1936

1. There is no single comprehensive history of the WPA. Specialized accounts include Barry B. Witham, *The Federal Theatre Project: A Case Study* (Cambridge and New York: Cambridge University Press, 2003); Kenneth J. Bindas, *All of This Music Belongs to the Nation: The WPA's Federal Music Project and American Society* (Knoxville: University of Tennessee Press, 1995); Marlene Park and Gerald E. Markowitz, *Democratic Vistas: Post Offices and Public Art in the New Deal* (Philadelphia: Temple University Press, 1984).

2. "State Welfare Statistics," *Florida Social Welfare Review* 1 (May 1936): 11.

3. Susan Ware, "Women and the New Deal," in *Fifty Years Later: The New Deal Evaluated,* ed. Harvard Sitkoff (New York: Knopf, 1985), 130.

4. Linda Gordon, *Pitied but Not Entitled: Single Mothers and the History of Welfare, 1890–1935* (New York: Free Press, 1994), 194–95. In some states, the percentage of women in the sewing rooms was as high as 84 percent of all women on relief.

5. Narrative Report, May 1937, p. 13. WPA, Records of the Division of Professional and service Projects, 1935–1941. Narrative Reports, box 5, folder "Florida Jan–June 1937."

6. *Biennial Report of the Florida State Board of Social Welfare, Covering the Period August 1935 to March 1937* ([Jacksonville]: State Board of Social Welfare, 1937), 21–22.

7. On Social Security, see especially Jill S. Quadagno, *The Transformation of Old Age Security: Class and Politics in the American Welfare State* (Chicago: University of Chicago Press, 1988); W. Andrew Achenbaum, *Social Security: Visions and Revisions* (Cambridge and New York: Cambridge University Press, 1986); and Roy Lubove, *The Struggle for Social Security, 1900–1935* (Cambridge: Harvard University Press, 1968).

8. ER Papers, series 75: Old Age Pensions, box 433.

9. ER Papers, series 75: Old Age Pensions, box 433.

10. FSA series 278, box 1, folder 2.

11. FSA series 278, box 87, folder 3.

12. FSA series 278, box 3, folder 2.

13. ER Papers, series 140: Merchandise for Sale, box 994.

14. ER Papers, series 150.9: Miscellaneous Requests, box marked "2447, 2448, 2449." Some names here and throughout have been abbreviated by the editor.

15. FSA series 278, box 68, folder 10.

16. ER Papers, series 150.9: Miscellaneous Requests, box marked "2447, 2448, 2449."

17. ER Papers, series 140: Merchandise for Sale, box 994.

18. ER Papers, series 150.3: Positions Sought through Mrs. Roosevelt, box 2383.

19. ER Papers, series 140: Merchandise for Sale, box 995.

20. ER Papers, series 70: Correspondence with Government Departments, box 286.

21. FSA series 278, box 78, folder 12.

22. ER Papers, series 140: Merchandise for Sale, box 996.

23. ER Papers, series 150.3: Positions Sought through Mrs. Roosevelt, box 2383.

24. FSA series 278, box 1, folder 2.

25. FSA series 278, box 73, folder 1.

26. ER Papers, series 150.9: Miscellaneous Requests, box marked "2442, 2443, 2444."

27. FSA series 278, box 71, folder 12.

28. ER Papers, series 150.9: Miscellaneous Requests, box marked "2450, 2451, 2452."

29. FSA series 278, box 51, folder 13.

30. FSA series 278, box 21, folder 2.

31. ER Papers, series 140: Merchandise for Sale, box 994.

32. FSA series 278, box 32, folder 15.

33. ER Papers, series 140: Merchandise for Sale, box 996.

34. FSA series 278, box 107, folder 2.

35. ER Papers, series 140: Merchandise for Sale, box 995.

36. FSA series 278, box 105, folder 6.

37. ER Papers, series 140: Merchandise for Sale, box 995.

38. FSA series 278, box 48, folder 4.

39. FSA series 278, box 12, folder 9.

40. FSA series 278, box 43, folder 1.

41. FSA series 278, box 60, folder 4.

42. FSA series 278, box 48, folder 1.

43. ER Papers, series 150.9: Miscellaneous Requests, box marked "2444, 2445, 2446, 2447."

44. FSA series 278, box 21, folder 2.

45. FSA series 278, box 16, folder 4.

46. FSA series 278, box 32, folder 13.

47. FSA series 278, box 10, folder 6.

48. FSA series 278, box 47, folder 2.

49. FSA series 278, box 100, folder 3.

50. FSA series 278, box 13, folder 9.

51. FSA series 278, box 7, folder 12.

52. FSA series 278, box 26, folder 8.

53. FSA series 278, box 97, folder 6.

54. FSA series 278, box 8, folder 11.

55. FSA series 278, box 31, folder 3.

56. ER Papers, series 70: Correspondence with Government Departments, box 284.

57. FSA series 278, box 120, folder 1.

58. FSA series 278, box 27, folder 11.

59. FSA series 278, box 83, folder 5.

60. FSA series 278, box 7, folder 12.

61. FSA series 278, box 17, folder 7.

62. ER Papers, series 140: Merchandise for Sale, box 995.

63. ER Papers, series 150.9: Miscellaneous Requests, box marked "2447, 2448, 2449."

64. FSA series 278, box 53, folder 14.

65. ER Papers, series 150.9: Miscellaneous Requests, box marked "2450, 2451, 2452."

66. FSA series 278, box 33, folder 14.

67. FSA series 278, box 12, folder 9.

68. ER Papers, series 75: Old Age Pensions, box 435.

69. FSA series 278, box 64, folder 3.

70. FSA series 278, box 32, folder 11

71. FSA series 368, box 81, folder 1.

72. FSA series 278, box 61, folder 2.

73. FSA series 368, box 34, folder 14.

74. FSA series 278, box 23, folder 4.

75. FSA series 278, box 51, folder 12.

76. FSA series 278, box 76, folder 9.

77. ER Papers, series 75: Old Age Pensions, box 435.

78. ER Papers, series 150.3: Positions sought through Mrs. Roosevelt, box 2383, folder 1936 A-K (C).

79. FSA series 278, box 39, folder 3.

80. FSA series 278, box 52, folder 1.

81. FSA series 278, box 39, folder 3.

82. FSA series 278, box 14, folder 8.

Chapter 4: 1937–1940

1. The best analysis of the late New Deal and the Roosevelt recession remains Alan Brinkley's *The End of Reform: New Deal Liberalism in Recession and War* (New York: Knopf, 1995).

2. William W. Rogers, "The Great Depression," in *The New History of Florida,* ed. Michael Gannon (Gainesville: University Press of Florida, 1996), 307.

3. Carlton W. Tebeau, *A History of Florida,* 2nd ed. (Coral Gables: University of Miami Press, 1980), 408–9.

4. Douglas L. Smith, *The New Deal in the Urban South* (Baton Rouge: Louisiana State University Press, 1988), 129.

5. Narrative Report, November 1938, p. 19. WPA Women's Division, Narrative Reports, box 4. WPA Papers, National Archives II, College Park, Md.

6. Narrative Report, July 1937, pp. 1, 3. WPA Women's Division. Narrative Reports, box 4A.

7. The sit-down tactic was very new in 1937, and American labor leaders considered it too radical for women workers. In other cities, such as Flint, Michigan, women workers were sent home by strike leaders and not permitted to join the sit-down. See Sharon Harman Strom, "Challenging 'Woman's Place': Feminism, the Left, and Industrial Unionism in the 1930's," *Feminist Studies* 9 (Summer 1983): 364.

8. There is only one article published to date on the sit-down strike. James Tidd, "Stitching and Striking: WPA Sewing Rooms and the 1937 Relief Strike in Hillsborough County," *Tampa Bay History* 11, no. 1 (1989): 5–21. I have an essay in progress on the sit-down.

9. Brinkley, *The End of Reform,* 100.

10. George B. Tindall, *The Emergence of the New South, 1913–1945* (Baton Rouge: Louisiana State University Press, 1967), 484.

11. Pepper had been chosen to fill the remainder of the term when Senator Duncan Fletcher died in office in 1936. Pepper then had to face a regular election in 1938.

12. Tindall, *Emergence of the New South,* 535; Brinkley, *The End of Reform,* 102–3.

13. Bruce J. Schulman, *From Cotton Belt to Sunbelt: Federal Policy, Economic Development, and the Transformation of the South, 1938–1980* (New York: Oxford University Press, 1991), 45.

14. Tindall, *The Emergence of the New South,* 544.

15. Tindall, *The Emergence of the New South,* 551–53.

16. See especially Christopher E. Linsin, "Something More Than a Creed: Mary Mcleod Bethune's Aim of Integrated Autonomy as Director of Negro Affairs," *Florida Historical Quarterly* 76, no. 1 (1997): 20–41; Henry B. Sirgo, "Women, Blacks and the New Deal," *Women and Politics* 14, no. 3 (1994): 57–76; Joyce Bickerstaff and Wilber C. Rich, "Mrs. Roosevelt and Mrs. Bethune: Collaborators for Racial Justice," *Social Education* 48, no. 7 (1984): 532–35.

17. FSA series 363, box 18, folder 14.

18. FSA series 368, box 92, folder 4.

19. FSA series 368, box 4, folder 1.

20. FSA series 368, box 41, folder 1.

21. FSA series 368, box 63, folder 7.

22. FSA series 361, box 103, folder 4.

23. ER Papers, series 150.3: Positions sought through Mrs. Roosevelt, box 2391.

24. FSA series 368, box 13, folder 1.

25. FSA series 368, box 33, folder 21.

26. FSA series 368, box 7, folder 6.

27. FSA series 368, box 100, folder 1.

28. FSA series 368, box 58, folder 4.

29. FSA series 368, box 38, folder 1.

30. FSA series 368, box 103, folder 7.

31. FSA series 368, box 41, folder 1.

32. ER Papers, series 75: Old Age Pensions, box 435.

33. FSA series 368, box 92, folder 4.

34. FSA series 368, box 37, folder 8.

35. FDR Papers, Official Files, series 312: Confederate Matters, folder 1933–1944.

36. FSA series 368, box 42, folder 1.

37. FSA series 368, box 37, folder 19.

38. FSA series 363, box 17, folder 19.

39. ER Papers, series 75: Old Age Pensions, box 435.

40. ER Papers, series 75: Old Age Pensions, box 435.

41. ER Papers, series 75: Old Age Pensions, box 435.

42. FSA series 368, box 39, folder 1.

43. FSA series 368, box 20, folder 8.

44. FSA series 368, box 50, folder 18.

45. FSA series 368, box 10, folder 3.

46. FSA series 368, box 43, folder 5.

47. FSA series 368, box 41, folder 1.

48. FSA series 368, box 66, folder 3.

49. FSA series 368, box 17, folder 19.

50. FSA series 368, box 83, folder 22.

51. FSA series 368, box 82, folder 10.

52. FSA series 368, box 60, folder 10.

53. FSA series 368, box 91, folder 1.

54. FSA series 368, box 46, folder 8.

55. FSA series 368, box 28, folder 1.

56. FSA series 368, box 99, folder 1.

57. FSA series 368, box 32, folder 6.

58. ER Papers, series 150.3: Positions sought through Mrs. Roosevelt, box 2391.

59. FSA series 368, box 3, folder 10.

60. FSA series 368, box 23, folder 10.

61. FSA series 368, box 18, folder 14.

62. FSA series 368, box 32, folder 6.

63. FSA series 368, box 58, folder 4.

64. ER Papers, series 75: Old Age Pensions, box 435.

65. FSA series 368, box 52, folder 8.

66. FSA series 368, box 83, folder 18.

67. FSA series 368, box 37, folder 7.

68. FSA series 368, box 37, folder 7.

69. FSA series 368, box 84, folder 6.

70. FSA series 368, box 68, folder 1.

71. FSA series 368, box 74, folder ?.

72. FSA series 368, box 65, folder 2.

73. FSA series 368, box 104, folder 1.

74. FSA series 368, box 34, folder 14.

75. ER Papers, series 75: Old Age Pensions, box 435.

76. FSA series 368, box 55, folder 14.

77. FSA series 368, box 42, folder 5.

78. FSA series 368, box 9, folder 1.

79. FSA series 368, box 51, folder 3.

80. FSA series 368, box 9, folder 9.

81. FSA series 368, box 6, folder 6.

82. ER Papers, series 150.3: Positions sought through Mrs. Roosevelt, box 2392.

83. ER Papers, series 150.3: Positions sought through Mrs. Roosevelt, box 2392.

84. ER Papers, series 150.3: Positions sought through Mrs. Roosevelt, box 2392.

85. FSA series 368, box 65, folder 1.

86. FSA series 368, box 61, folder 1.

87. ER Papers, series 150.3: Positions sought through Mrs. Roosevelt, box 2394.

88. WPA Central Files: State, 1935–1944. Florida series 661–62, box 1118, folder 662 A-J. Standardized reply from Florence Kerr—she is forwarding the letter to the Florida WPA.

89. FSA series 368, box 61, folder 1.

90. FSA series 368, box 11, folder 10.

91. FSA series 308, box 65, folder 1.

92. FSA series 368, box 10, folder 4.

93. FSA series 368, box 3, folder 11.

94. FSA series 368, box 52, folder 15.

95. FSA series 368, box 7, folder 7.

96. FSA series 368, box 100, folder 2.

97. ER Papers series 70: Correspondence with Governmental Departments, box 317.

98. FSA series 368, box 86, folder 8.

99. FSA series 368, box 11, folder 1.

100. FSA series 368, box 99, folder 2.

101. WPA Central Files: State, 1935–1944. Florida series 661–62, box 1118, folder 662 A–J.

102. WPA Central Files: State, 1935–1944. Florida series 661–62, box 1118, folder 662 A–J.

103. WPA Central Files: State, 1935–1944. Florida series 661–62, box 1118, folder 662 A–J.

104. WPA Central Files: State, 1935–1944. Florida series 661–62, box 1118, folder 662 K–Q.

105. FSA series 362, box 77, folder 12.

106. FSA series 368, box 40, folder 3.

107. WPA Central Files: State, 1935–1944. Florida series 661–62, box 1118, folder 662 A–J.

108. FSA series 368, box 68, folder 3.

109. ER Papers, series 150.3: Positions sought through Mrs. Roosevelt, box 2394.

110. WPA Central Files: State 1935–1944. Florida series 662–663, box 1119, folder 662 SA–XYZ.

111. WPA Central Files: State, 1935–1944. Florida series 661–62, box 1118, folder 662 A–J.

112. WPA Central Files: State, 1935–1944. Florida series 661–62, box 1118, folder 662 A–J.

113. WPA Central Files: State, 1935–1944. Florida series 661–62, box 1118, folder 662 A–J.

114. WPA Central Files: State, 1935–1944. Florida series 661–62, box 1118, folder 662 A–J.

115. WPA Central Files: State, 1935–1944. Florida series 661–62, box 1118, folder 662 A–J.

116. WPA Central Files: State, 1935–1944. Florida series 661–62, box 1118, folder 662 A–J.

117. WPA Central Files: State, 1935–1944. Florida series 661–62, box 1118, folder 662 A–J. [She received a standardized reply from Florence Kerr, and her letter was indeed referred to the state office.]

118. WPA Central Files: State, 1935–1944. Florida series 661–62, box 1118, folder 662 A–J.

119. FSA series 368, box 35, folder 1.

120. WPA Central Files: State, 1935–1944. Florida series 661–62, box 1118, folder 662 A–J.

121. WPA Central Files: State, 1935–1944. Florida series 661–62, box 1118, folder 662 A–J.

122. WPA Central Files: State, 1935–1944. Florida series 661–62, box 1118, folder 662 A–J.

123. WPA Central Files: State, 1935–1944. Florida series 661–62, box 1118, folder 662 A–J.

124. WPA Central Files: State, 1935–1944. Florida series 661–62, box 1118, folder 662 K–Q.

125. WPA Central Files: State 1935–1944. Florida series 662–63, box 1119, folder 662 SA–XYZ. [Florence Kerr's reply: "This office is not in a position to assist persons in securing work outside the WPA program. Our activities are limited to providing work on public projects for employable persons certified as in need of relief."]

126. FSA series 368, box 35, folder 1.

127. FSA series 368 box 76, folder 11.

128. WPA Central Files: State, 1935–1944. Florida series 661–62, box 1118, folder 662 A–J. [Standardized rely from Florence Kerr—she is forwarding to Florida WPA.]

129. WPA Central Files: State, 1935–1944. Florida series 661–62, box 1118, folder 662 A–J.

130. WPA Central Files: State, 1935–1944. Florida series 661–62, box 1118, folder 662 A–J.

131. ER Papers, series 140: Merchandise for Sale, box 1006.

132. ER Papers, series 140: Merchandise for Sale, box 1005.

133. FSA series 368, box 75, folder 3.

134. FSA series 368, box 72, folder 3.

135. ER Papers, series 150.3: Positions sought through Mrs. Roosevelt, box 2395.

136. ER Papers, series 75: Old Age Pensions, box 436.

137. ER Papers, series 75: Old Age Pensions, box 436.

138. ER Papers, series 75: Old Age Pensions, box 436.

139. ER Papers, series 75: Old Age Pensions, box 436.

140. FSA series 368, box 57, folder 4.

141. ER Papers, series 140: Merchandise for Sale, box 1008.

142. ER Papers, series 140: Merchandise for Sale, box 1007.

Epilogue

1. FDR Papers, Official Files, series 93: Colored Matters (Negroes), folder 1933.

BIBLIOGRAPHY

Articles and Sections of Books

"The WPA in Tampa: A Photographic Essay." *Tampa Bay History* 16, no. 2 (1994): 68–78.

Cofer, Richard. "Bootleggers in the Backwoods: Prohibition and the Depression in Hernando County." *Tampa Bay History* 1 (Spring–Summer 1979): 17–23.

Cox, Merlin G. "David Sholtz: New Deal Governor of Florida." *Florida Historical Quarterly* 46 (October 1964): 142–52.

Findlay, James A., and Margaret Bing. "Touring Florida through the Federal Writers Project." *Journal of Decorative and Propaganda Arts* 23 (1998): 288–305.

George, Paul S., and Thomas K Petersen. "Liberty Square: 1933–1987: The Origins and Evolution of a Public Housing Project." *Teciuesta* 48 (1988): 53–68.

Henderson, Ann, and Stetson Kennedy. "The WPA Guide to Florida: A Conversation between Ann Henderson and Stetson Kennedy." *Florida Forum* 9 (Fall 1986): 10–13.

Long, Durward. "Key West and the New Deal, 1934–1936." *Florida Historical Quarterly* 46 (January 1968): 209–18.

Lowry, Charles B. "The PWA in Tampa: A Case Study." *Florida Historical Quarterly* 52 (April 1974): 363–80.

McIver, Stuart. "She [Lorena Hickok] Did Not Mince Words." *South Florida History* 27, no. 4 (1999): 18–25.

Mohl, Raymond A. "Trouble in Paradise: Race and Housing in Miami during the New Deal Era." *Prologue* 19, no. 1 (1987): 7–21.

Rainard, R. Lyn. "Ready Cash on Easy Terms: Local Responses to the Depression in Lee County." *Florida Historical Quarterly* 64 (January 1986): 284–300.

Rogers, William W. "The Great Depression." In *The New History of Florida,* edited by Michael Gannon, 294–97. Gainesville: University Press of Florida, 1996.

Shoffner, Jerrell. "Roosevelt's 'Tree Army': The Civilian Conservation Corps in Florida." *Florida Historical Quarterly* no. 4 (1987): 433–56.

Snyder, Robert E. "Marion Post and the Farm Security Administration in Florida." *Florida Historical Quarterly* 65, no. 4 (1987): 457–79.

Stoesen, Alexander R. "Claude Pepper and the Florida Canal Controversy, 1939–1943." *Florida Historical Quarterly* 50 (January 1972): 235–51.

Bibliography

Sullivan, John J. "The Civilian Conservation Corps and the Creation of Myakka River State Park." *Tampa Bay History* 9 (Fall 1987): 4–16.

Sweets, John F. "The Civilian Conservation Corps in Florida." *Apalachee* 6 (1963–67): 77–86.

Books

Best, Gary Dean. *FDR and the Bonus Marchers, 1933–1935.* Westport, Conn.: Praeger, 1992.

Carlebach, Michael L., and Eugene F. Provenzo Jr. *Farm Security Administration Photographs of Florida.* Gainesville: University Press of Florida, 1993.

Kersey, Harry A. *The Florida Seminoles and the New Deal, 1933–1942.* London: Florida Atlantic University Press, 1989.

McDonogh, Gary W., ed. *The Florida Negro: A Federal Writer's Project Legacy.* Jackson: University Press of Mississippi, 1993.

Powell-Brant, Evanell K. *WPA Federal Writer's Project: With Emphasis on the Florida Writers and Carita Doggett Corse.* Lake Panasoffkee, Fla.: E. K. Powell-Brant, 1990.

Dissertations and Theses

Bordelon, Pamela G. "Mirror to America: The Federal Writers' Project's Florida Reflection." Ph.D. diss., Louisiana State University, 1991.

Brunson, Jeana. "Patterns of Community: Quiltmaking in Florida during the Depression Era." Ph.D. diss., Florida State University, 1996.

Bulger, Peggy A. "Stetson Kennedy: Applied Folklore and Cultural Advocacy." Ph.D. diss., University of Pennsylvania, 1992.

Dunn, William James. "The New Deal and Florida Politics." Ph.D. diss., Florida State University, 1971.

Evans, J. S. "Florida Politics in the Shade of War: The 1940 Governor's Race." M.A. thesis, Florida State University, 2000.

Helmick, Evelyn Thomas. "The New Deal in Florida." M.A. thesis, University of Miami, 1966.

Kabat, Ric A. "From New Deal to Red Scare: The Political Odyssey of Senator Claude D. Pepper." Ph.D. diss., Florida State University, 1995.

Leslie, Vernon M. "The Great Depression in Miami Beach." M.A. thesis, Florida Atlantic University, 1980.

Tidd, James Francis. "The Works Progress Administration in Hillsborough and Pinellas Counties, Florida, 1935 to 1943." M.A. thesis, University of South Florida, 1989.

INDEX